Brighton Crime
and Vice
1800–2000

By the same author:

The Saltdean Story
The Church in a Garden
Foul Deeds and Suspicious Deaths around Brighton

Brighton Crime and Vice

1800–2000

DOUGLAS d'ENNO

Wharncliffe Books

For Peter, Juliet and Sophia

First published in Great Britain in 2007 by
Wharncliffe Books
an imprint of
Pen & Sword Books Ltd
47 Church Street
Barnsley
South Yorkshire
S70 2AS

Copyright © Douglas d'Enno, 2007

ISBN 978-1845630300

The right of Douglas d'Enno to be identified as author of this work has been asserted by him in accordance with the Copyright, Designs and Patents Act 1988.

A CIP catalogue record for this book is available from the British Library.

All rights reserved. No part of this book may be reproduced or transmitted in any form or by any means, electronic or mechanical including photocopying, recording or by any information storage and retrieval system, without permission from the publisher in writing.

Typeset in 10/11.5 Plantin by
Concept, Huddersfield, West Yorkshire

Printed and bound in England by
CPI UK

Pen & Sword Books Ltd incorporates the imprints of Pen & Sword Aviation, Pen & Sword Maritime, Pen & Sword Military, Wharncliffe Local History, Pen & Sword Select, Pen & Sword Military Classics and Leo Cooper.

For a complete list of Pen & Sword titles please contact
PEN & SWORD BOOKS LIMITED
47 Church Street, Barnsley, South Yorkshire, S70 2AS, England
E-mail: enquiries@pen-and-sword.co.uk
Website: www.pen-and-sword.co.uk

Contents

Preface

This kaleidoscope of crime, interspersed with the occasional vice, is a portrayal of Brighton's dark side over two centuries, a side necessarily only touched upon in the conventional histories of the town. It is a review not only of the changing face of crime but also of society's response to it; hence there are references to, and sometimes dedicated entries on, key legislation, the judiciary and its workings and the origin, development and work of the local police. A mere catalogue of crime would give only part of the picture. No claim is made to exhaustiveness in respect of different kinds of misdeed or vice and there are inevitable overlaps, indicated by cross-references to offences, cases, individuals and concepts.

It has occasionally been necessary to stray somewhat from the stated 1800–2000 time frame of the book – prior to 1800 in order to record a significant event of relevance to a particular entry (e.g. the pursuit and shooting of Daniel Skayles, the notorious smuggler, in 1796) and after the year 2000 to follow through on certain cases (such as the – ultimately disappointing – breakthrough in 2006 in the Keith Lyon murder enquiry and, on a literary note, to accommodate notable Brighton-based crime fiction in the shape of two books by Glenn Chandler featuring the detective Steve Madden).

Geographically, too, the boundaries of the town have sometimes been crossed. The criterion adopted throughout has been the strength of the victim's or perpetrator's link with Brighton. Hence, as in my *Foul Deeds and Suspicious Deaths around Brighton*, attention is given to Lefroy's killing of Frederick Gold. This victim died on the London–Brighton railway line but lived near Preston Park Station. Similarly, the Wiltshire/Somerset border area was the scene of the murder to which Constance Kent confessed.

My sources have largely been contemporary press reports and local and/or specialist books and publications. Without online resources such as the *Argus* archive (1998–) or the *Times Digital Archive* (1785–1985), compilation of this collection would have been immeasurably more laborious. Having said that, the internet has disappointed on more than one occasion (as in the case of Barbara Gaul, a victim whose killing was big news in its day).

A number of the cases will be familiar to readers of the 'PastPresent' feature in the *Argus*'s Weekend Supplement. It is pleasing to think that a number of my contributions have been made permanently available in one accessible volume.

A new departure from the traditional crime casebook is the recording, cheek by jowl with factual entries, of Brighton crime as depicted in film and fiction. After all, *Brighton Rock* and *Quadrophenia* have become as much a part of the town's history and image as its true crimes, vices and unrest.

Guidance notes for readers

For more details on authors named as sources by surname in the text, reference will need to be made to the Bibliography.

Capitalised names, subjects, etc within entries cross-refer to a dedicated entry for the person or subject in question.

Pre-decimal currency references have not been converted to decimal. A 'shilling' (symbol 's') is today 5p and would have been made up of 12 old pennies (symbol 'd'). There were 20 shillings to the pound. A half-crown was 2s 6d, while a 'guinea' was 21s (21 shillings).

Crimes are listed by perpetrator, where known. Entries by victim are clearly designated as such. Of course, many crimes and vices are listed by category or type rather than by person. A generic heading such as 'HOTELS AND BOARDING-HOUSES' will encompass a number of offences.

Unless otherwise indicated, the illustrations in this volume are from the author's own collection.

Acknowledgements

I should like to thank fellow-author and local historian, Peter Mercer, for so readily making available to me his 2001 MA Dissertation in English Local and Regional History entitled *Brighton: Crime in a Fashionable Town c1800-1850*, which proved an invaluable resource in the preparation of parts of this volume.

Local historian Chris Horlock provided telephone help on 1960s Brighton and, as in the case of my last book, very willingly loaned a number of rare images from his unique collection.

I am also grateful to JJ ('Jim') Marshall, ex-Brighton CID, for the long telephone conversations we had concerning a number of cases in which he was involved, and also for the biographical details on which the entry devoted to him in this book is based.

As in the case of *Foul Deeds and Suspicious Deaths around Brighton*, I am indebted to Rupert Harding, the publisher's commissioning editor, for guidance and advice throughout the production of this volume. The book was his idea. I am also grateful to my editor, Brian Elliott, for his input and suggestions.

Author, distinguished journalist and friend, Michael Thornton, made a number of helpful comments and suggestions.

I am indirectly grateful to the writer Fergus Linnane, whose comprehensive *Encyclopedia of London Crime and Vice* (2003) was a forerunner of, and model for, this work.

Thanks, finally, to my wife, Caroline, for her patience and occasional feedback.

Others I wish to acknowledge are listed below. To anyone inadvertently omitted, I offer sincere apologies.

Assistance with the text and research
Michael Abatan, Kevin Bacon, David Beevers, Sally Blann, Nina Bouch, Abigail Brooke, Tim Carder, Jill Chambers, Glenn Chandler, Margaret Daly, Jean Drew-Bear, Andy Freeman MCIPR, Jay Glanville, Stephanie Green, Valerie Hart, Ian and Nigel Heffron, Geoff Hellman, Peter Hines, Paul Jordan, Loretta Lay, Jo Makepeace, Phil Mills, the late John Montgomery, Christine Morris, Paul Robb, David Rowland, Keith Sherwood, Donna Steele, Oliver Stempt, Adam Trimingham, Christopher Whittick, Brenda Whyman, Richard Witts, Helena Wojtczak and Gibby Zobel.

Assistance with images
Glenn Chandler, Brigid Chapman, Kate Elliott, Neal d'Enno, Colin Finlay, Laura Hitchcock, Juliet McConnell, Judy Middleton, Cara Minns, Dick Richardson and Henry Smith.

A–Z Listing

A

ABATAN, JAY (victim)

On 14 June 2000, Michael Abatan, supported by his family, lit a candle outside Brighton police station to mark the 500th day since his elder brother, Jay, a black father of two, was murdered. The gesture was also intended to reinforce his appeal to the public for help in bringing his killers to justice. 42-year-old Jay, from Eastbourne, died in hospital five days after sustaining severe head injuries when he was attacked by a gang outside the *Ocean Rooms* nightclub in Morley Street, Brighton, following an argument about a taxi on 24 January 1999. When the attack was over the men simply drove away in the disputed taxi.

His brother Michael and a friend, who had been out celebrating Jay's promotion, were also attacked. Michael was beaten and kicked and sustained a cut and black eye in the assault. Although two men were arrested after Jay's death, they were eventually only charged with affray and actual bodily harm to Michael by the time of the trial due to a lack of witnesses. In 2000, they were cleared of assaulting him – and laughed at him as they left court. The jury had not been allowed to hear of Jay's death as the judge ruled that this would prejudice the trial.

The 'Justice for Jay' campaign was subsequently launched by Michael, Jay's partner Tanya Haynes and MP Peter Bottomley.

Despite new witnesses coming forward following an appeal on the BBC's *Crimewatch* programme in May 2000 and the £75,000 reward put up by Sussex Police and Jay's family, the investigation has been dogged by problems and setbacks. Crucial information lost in the first hours and days after the assault was irretrievable, while Sussex Police's investigation was mishandled. A report on that aspect of the case has been carried out by Avon and Somerset Constabulary but it has taken the Abatan family three years of fighting to get a copy – only to find some parts omitted. The last straw is being told by Sussex's Chief Constable that there will not be an inquest for Jay. The family therefore now have another fight on their hands for a jury inquest. This they find unbelievable.

No one has yet been tried for Jay's murder and Michael and his supporters continue to campaign for justice for his brother.

ABDUCTION

Abduction is so often the prelude to murder. The victim may escape, only to die later as a direct or indirect result of his/her ordeal (see TAYLOR, WEAVER AND DONOVAN).

Russell Bishop, a father of three, was handed down a life term for the abduction and attempted murder in 1990 of a 7-year-old Whitehawk schoolgirl at the beauty spot north of Brighton called Devil's Dyke. He grabbed the child, who had been roller-skating near her home, and forced her into the boot of his car. She was choked, sexually assaulted and left for dead in dense undergrowth. (For a previous charge against Bishop, for murder, see the BABES IN THE WOOD case).

In another case, Katie Archer, 18, a former heroin addict of Birdham Road, Brighton, snatched six-month-old George Tipping from a café in Brighton in October 1999 and

Russell Bishop: Guilty of abduction and attempted murder. The Argus

took him to her boyfriend's mother, Sue Appleby, in Hampshire pretending the child was hers. Mrs Appleby grew suspicious and called the police. Archer was arrested and baby George was returned to his mother, having been missing for 11 hours. The teenager was jailed for 18 months after pleading guilty to abduction.

Also in October 1999, a 2-year-old girl underwent a three-hour abduction ordeal at the hands of two 12-year-old girls. The pair, one from Brighton and one from Hove, were arrested at the Marina on suspicion of child abduction after little Lois Grenham was snatched from outside her home in Hove where she had been playing. She was taken by bus to Brighton seafront and was discovered in Marine Drive following a massive search by police and neighbours.

ABORTION
Legal background
No statutes relating to abortion existed before the nineteenth century. As long as a foetus had not reached the stage of 'quickening' (the point in pregnancy when the movement of the foetus was felt), killing it was not considered a crime. Although killing a child in the womb after that point during pregnancy was considered an offence, very few prosecutions were brought.

The first abortion statute, enacted in 1803, provided for the death penalty for a person performing an abortion after quickening and a sentence of up to 14 years' deportation or lashing with a whip for a person performing an abortion before quickening. In 1837 the law was amended, but it was not until the Offences Against the Person Act of 1861 that statutory abortion law took the form that it would keep for over a century. Under the Act, anyone intending to procure the miscarriage of a woman and unlawfully administering any noxious thing or using any means was liable to 14 years' imprisonment. The same penalty applied to a pregnant woman who undertook the same act or consented to its performance.

The Infant Life (Preservation) Act of 1929 introduced the offence of 'child destruction', the killing of a child capable of being born alive (gestation age of 28 weeks or more) unless the act that caused the death of the child was done in good faith for the sole purpose of preserving the life of the mother.

In 1967, the Abortion Act legalised abortion in Britain in extremely limited cases. A 24-week legal time limit for terminations, other than in cases of severe abnormalities or where the mother's life was in danger, was introduced in 1990. A Bill to reduce this period to 21 weeks was voted against by MPs on 31 October 2006.

The tragedy of Emily Hockley, 1878
A case heard at the Summer Assizes of the South-Eastern Circuit on 10 July 1878 before Lord Justice Thesiger revealed a sordid trade in back-street abortion being conducted in Brighton by a trio of perpetrators. Before the judge were Robert Charles Moon, surgeon, Henry Charles Darley, chemist, and a woman named Julia Brown, 46, described as a 'herbalist'.

They had been indicted for the murder of Emily Hockley at Brighton on 9 April. Moon had also been indicted for using an instrument with intent to procure her miscarriage and Darley for administering a noxious thing for the same purpose. The charge against Julia Brown was the same as that against Darley, she having caused the miscarriages of Eliza Hollands in January 1878 and Emma Jones in November 1877.

Hockley, who had been in service, had found herself pregnant. Fearing exposure and having heard of Darley, she had gone to him for assistance. In return for a considerable sum, he gave her some liquid but it failed to work. He then sent her to a friend 'who never failed'. This was Moon. What he did was not known, for the woman would not say. She afterwards became unwell and, supposedly suffering from typhoid fever, was admitted to hospital. There she had a miscarriage, which she somehow managed

to conceal from the staff with the assistance of her friends. Ten days later, however, she died, and a post-mortem revealed the truth. Bottles were then found in her box, the contents of which were analysed. The cause was found to be inflammation, but it was uncertain, on the medical evidence, whether this inflammation was caused by the drugs or by an instrument, or by both.

Nevertheless, the coroner's jury found Moon and Darley guilty of murder and they were tried. The difficulty facing the Assize court was as to proof, a difficulty increased by Hockley's reticence up to the time of her death. On the two respective defence counsels declaring they could not offer a defence on the charge of administering a noxious drug with the intent charged, his lordship directed the jury to acquit both the accused of the charge of murder.

Moon and Darley did, however, plead guilty to the charge of administering noxious drugs with intent to procure abortion. The case against Julia Brown in regard to Emma Jones was on the same charges that the professional men had faced. Jones was married and had had four children. Finding herself pregnant, she had gone to Brown but the drug she was given failed to work and the child was delivered at full term. However, the case broke down for lack of evidence. Indeed, Jones was criminally liable on the charge of using the drug with the intent to procure abortion.

As there was no evidence to corroborate Jones' case and as she was in law an accomplice, Brown had to be acquitted. She was also acquitted on the other charge in relation to Eliza Hollands, who was too ill to attend and there was not sufficient evidence without her.

The Lord Justice, in passing sentence on Moon and Darley, spoke severely about the nature of their crime. From the wretched women who resorted to them, they wrung every shilling they could by the promise of remedies which were either delusive or injurious. Such crimes were, he declared, far too common and were of the utmost mischief to society. As there was often difficulty as to proof, any sentences had to be exemplary. The conduct of Moon, who was a surgeon and a member of an honourable profession, was therefore all the more criminal and the sentence was 15 years' penal servitude. In Darley's case, it was ten.

An unreferenced printed document in Brighton Local History Centre relates to the Hockley case. Among its badly-written verses are these lines lamenting what the prosecution described as 'a detestable traffic':

> *A sad tale, I'll tell if you'll pay attention*
> *The Brighton disclosure I now will relate,*
> *Of poor Emily Hockley her death I will mention,*
> *At Pelham Street, Brighton, she there met her fate,*
> *Committed for trial, that inhuman surgeon,*
> *And Darley the chemist as you may all read*
> *For causing the death of that wretched female,*
> *If guilty they'll suffer for that cruel deed.*
>
> *No thought of her fate crossed the mind of their victim,*
> *As she straight to Dr Morris's house did repair*
> *To take his advice never dreaming of danger*
> *Or that she poor creature would die in despair,*
>
> *[...]*
>
> *So young girls give heed to these words I have penned,*
> *or perhaps when too late you may think of this caution*
> *And repent when at last you are meeting your end.*

ABSCONDING – see also THEFT (1837)

On the east side of Church Hill (now Dyke Road), on a site roughly opposite the Royal Alexandra Hospital for Sick Children, a new workhouse, replacing Brighton's establishment in Bartholomews, was erected in 1821.

On 16 November 1836, John Hedgecock, a boy of about 14, was charged with absconding. Samuel Thorncroft, the Overseer, said he did not wish to press charges against him as he was not so sharp as he might be and had a greater propensity to evil than to good. The following exchange took place between the notorious David Scott (see MAGISTRATES) and the escapee:

The main frontage of Brighton Workhouse, facing what is now Dyke Road. Author's collection

Scott: 'Why did you leave the Workhouse?'

JH: 'Cos, I don't like it. I want to go to sea. That would do me good.'

Scott: 'Well, I dare say Mr Thorncroft would be very glad if he could find you a berth.'

JH: 'Aye, that Workhouse won't do me any good.'

Scott: 'And you won't do it much good.'

JH: 'If I go to sea, I could do a good deal of good. I'm sharp enough to get over anybody' (laughter).

Scott: 'Aye, you're not such a fool as you're taken for.'

JH: 'No, that I b'aint.'

Scott: 'You're sharp enough to get over walls.'

JH: 'Yes' (laughter).

Scott: 'You wouldn't be sharp enough to get over the House of Correction walls.'

JH: 'I don't know.'

Scott: '21 days' House of Correction and there you'll learn to pump water against you go to sea' (laughter).

The editor of the *Brighton Guardian* commented:

> *The constant straining of witticisms at the expense of unfortunate persons manifests a very common-place understanding and great want of feeling in those who so indulge.*

Just over a century later, a 15-year-old boy who had escaped three weeks earlier from an approved school in Ware, Herts, broke into Brighton bedrooms at night and on one occasion searched a man's trouser pockets while he was asleep. At the town's Juvenile Court on 13 July 1938, he was charged with breaking and entering a house and stealing a purse, keys and £2 10s and also with stealing biscuits and cigarettes.

On one occasion, he hid beneath a bed while the woman lay terrorised all night. He had been in the house when he heard someone coming upstairs. He got under a bed and an elderly lady came in, undressed and got into bed. She knew there was someone under the bed but was too terrified to move or scream. The boy meanwhile, calmly went to sleep. She saw him when he woke up in the morning and when the police interviewed her later she was in 'a very distressed condition'.

The boy had escaped seven times from approved schools and had stolen on nearly every occasion. He was unsettled, unstable and a source of trouble. He pleaded guilty to seven additional charges of stealing. He was ordered back to the school, the other charges against him being adjourned *sine die*. He was anxious not to go back, no doubt fearing ridicule from those who had helped him abscond.

ABUSE OF POSITION

It was not long before Brighton's new Workhouse was beset by scandal. The first was in 1824, when the Directors and Guardians were severely criticised and a committee of the Vestry was appointed to examine their conduct. This body reported that about 13% of the poor-rate assessed remained uncollected, although the Assistant Overseer considered this inevitable. Due economy had not been observed, however, concerning the prices of some articles supplied to the institution but, worst of all, officers of the parish had in some cases themselves supplied articles to the workhouse (no names were mentioned), had benefited from such transactions and had themselves subsequently passed the accounts.

Towards the end of 1836 considerable irregularities were discovered in the accounts of the Directors and Guardians of the Poor. Their Clerk, Frederick Cooper, was being paid at the rate of £500 a year as against the £300 voted him by the Vestry. In addition, the two

Surgeons of the workhouse were receiving £125 a year instead of £100. Moreover, in the two preceding quarters the sums of £34 3s. and £22 7s. respectively had been spent on brandy, gin, port and sherry. The Vestry concluded this had been 'consumed otherwise than for the sustenance of the Poor to which alone it appears to them that it should be applied'. Local historian Antony Dale records that two years later, a worse case occurred:

> In February another committee of the Vestry was appointed to investigate affairs at the workhouse and reported that some of the Directors and Guardians of the Poor were accustomed to dine twice a week at the workhouse at the expense of the parish, and ordered expensive dishes of fish and other articles for the purpose, as well as dish-covers for their table. A summerhouse in the garden had been fitted up for these repasts. Wines were sent in from outside at the expense of the Directors and Guardians, but in addition 'a considerable quantity of brandy', as well as tea and coffee 'in which brandy was infused', and cigars, were consumed at the expense of the parish. 'Some of the members of the body became affected by the Spirituous liquors consumed by them.' The expenditure involved amounted to £139 3s 1d. Bartlett, the Governor of the workhouse, only gave evidence to the committee reluctantly for fear of victimisation, but what he said was confirmed by other employees. The committee roundly condemned the whole practice but did not try to enforce restitution of the money spent as they admitted that the practice did not originate with the existing body of Directors and Guardians. They were of the opinion that the evils resulted from the removal of the relief of the poor from the Town Hall to the workhouse, which was far away up Church Hill.

As late as 1862, these scandals were remembered by Erredge. In his *History*, he provides even more details than the Vestry books, noting that the Guardians

> pampered their appetites with john-dorees, salmon, lobsters, Norfolk squab pie and joints in profusion; red and white wines by the dozen and spirits by the gallon; cigars by the box, and snuff by the pound; with a handsome snuff-box too.

Blacking was also ordered and a Guardian whom he named as Paul Hewitt – presumably by then dead – sent his boots to the workhouse to be cleaned. Another named Storrer sent his dog to be kept there when it was inconvenient to have it at home.

ADULTERY

Today, adultery is well established as a ground for divorce. However, the principle was only established for women in 1923 under the Matrimonial Causes Act, when the ground became the same for both sexes. Formerly, a husband's adultery was a sin but it did not affect the validity of the marriage, while a wife's adultery was both a sin and an offence against the husband's property rights. It was the latter fact which justified the divorce.

The Matrimonial Causes Act of 1937 took matters to a new level by allowing divorce without requiring proof of adultery.

In *The Brighton Metropole*, local historian Judy Middleton mentions the hotel's role as a place to provide evidence of adultery in divorce cases. Nothing was advertised and everything was done discreetly (the other large hotels at Brighton were also familiar with the routine). She notes:

> If the couple wanted their marriage to end, and if the husband had not in fact committed adultery, the practice was for him to hire a woman and take her for a weekend on a trip to an expensive hotel at the seaside. All that was required of the woman was to be seen in the same bed as the man when the maid brought in the early morning tea. This was then known

The resplendent Metropole Hotel, *from a poster marking its opening in 1890. A 'weekend at the Metropole', with all its connotations, was referred to in TS Eliot's modernist poem* The Waste Land *(1922).* Author's collection

as a 'hotel bill case' because the hotel bill or the evidence of a chambermaid could be cited as evidence in court.

Farcically, nothing improper, as a rule, occurred between the two parties. They might have spent the night playing cards, drinking or sleeping in separate beds. This nonsensical state of affairs was pilloried in more than one novel. *Holy Deadlock* (1934), AP Herbert's satire exploring the inconsistencies, injustices and hardships of English law, involves a couple who wish to divorce to marry others and encounter problems in doing so. The book starts off with the hero sitting in a first-class carriage with a strange young woman travelling down to Brighton.

The very term 'Holy Deadlock' describes a feature of English law whereby neither husband nor wife can obtain a divorce if each has committed adultery.

In Evelyn Waugh's *A Handful of Dust*, published in the same year as Herbert's novel, the situation is made hilarious when the hired lady has a frightful cold and insists on her 8-year-old daughter accompanying her.

AFFILIATION – see also CHILD SUPPORT

The procedure whereby an illegitimate child's paternity is determined and the obligation of contributing to its support is enforced.

Under the Bastardy Act of 1845 and its amending acts of 1872 and 1873, the mother of a bastard could summon the putative father to petty sessions within twelve months of the birth (or at any later time if he was proved to have contributed to the child's support within twelve months after the birth). After hearing evidence on both sides, the justices could, if the mother's evidence was corroborated in some material respect, adjudge the man to be the putative father of the child and order him to pay a sum not exceeding 5s a week for its maintenance, together with a sum for expenses incidental to the birth (or the funeral expenses, if it died before the date of order) plus the costs of the proceedings. An order ceased to be valid after the child reached the age of 13. When a bastard child whose mother had not obtained an order became chargeable to the parish, the guardians could proceed against the putative father for a contribution.

In Brighton, in 1858, a case was fought between Colonel d'Aguilar and a widow by the name of Mrs Thatcher whom he had promised to marry. When a child had been born, out of wedlock, he had given her a £30 allowance for two years but had then stopped paying. In the resulting proceedings, he was ordered to continue the payments. Mrs Thatcher was not so successful in a later action against the colonel for Breach of Promise of Marriage. When her 14-year-old daughter testified that her mother often had gentlemen friends to stay the night, the case was immediately dismissed.

AFFRAY

The fighting of two or more persons in a public place (a fight in private is assault and battery, not an affray).

A fracas took place at Brighton's *New Inn* on the morning of 30 October 1806 between three gentlemen and the waiters and other staff of the house. So violently and improperly did the guests behave, that a constable was summoned. He was unable to restore order on his own and had to call to his aid a detachment of the picket guard of the South Gloucester MILITIA. Before they arrived, he sustained a black eye and the brawlers smashed the window panes and broke glasses, decanters, etc. The guard apprehended the miscreants and secured them for the night. When they were brought before the magistrates at Lewes the next morning, they acknowledged their misconduct and agreed to pay all expenses and give the proceeds to the poor of the parish. The constable was accordingly induced to pardon the insult he had suffered and they were consequently discharged.

The New Inn *in 1818. It is today the* Royal Pavilion Tavern, *7 Castle Square.* Author's collection

ALIMONY

Non-support with assault, 1835

Towards the end of April, Harriet Boyes complained before the magistrates of the conduct of her husband, James Boyes, a tailor living at 8 Crown Gardens. They had quarrelled and agreed to part seven months earlier when he had promised to allow her 10s towards the support of their five children. However, over the whole period he had only paid her 5s 6d. When she sent for him the previous week to tell him her landlady had put a distress for rent into her house in Market Street, her husband struck her and used violent language, saying he would not be happy till he had murdered her. He was bound over to keep the peace for 12 months in the sum of £20 and to find two sureties of £10 each, or one in £20, and to give 24 hours' notice of bail.

AMBUSH

In early June 1963, an ambush in Madeira Place yielded £11,000 for bandits. A hire car used to transfer money from the National Provincial Bank to the Westminster Bank suddenly found itself sandwiched between a grey Jaguar and a lime green Mini-van, which pulled out from the kerb behind it to block the bank car's retreat. Masked men leaped from the Jaguar and the van, smashed in the windows of the bank car and began a battle with the driver and bank officials who were acting as guards. The car driver, Charles King, 66, of Queen's Park Road, was struck over the head. Public-spirited Alan James, 23, was kicked in the mouth when he hit one of the bandits on the jaw, knocking him down, but some of the raiders picked up their mate and dragged him into

Madeira Place, east side. Mrs Dorgan was murdered on the opposite side of this street of violence.
Chris Horlock collection

their car. James remembered three of the men being coloured. Two men were knocked unconscious in the raid: 21-year-old bank clerk, Michael Griffiths and PC Keith Collins. The officer had to have 12 stitches put in his head wounds. He had dragged the stocking mask off one man, whom he was sure was coloured. Both Collins and Griffiths made a satisfactory recovery.

Scores of people saw the four men, with black stockings pulled over their faces and wielding 2-inch thick sticks painted red and white, make their getaway in the stolen Jaguar after scooping up banknotes scattered all over the road. They were halted for a few seconds, however, at the junction of Madeira Place and the sea front by 40-year-old Mr Ernest Ellett, who drove his giant petrol tanker across their path. Shoppers and people from nearby offices chased after the car, pelting it with dustbin lids and any other missile they could find. The Jaguar reversed, mounted the pavement, and roared away past the tanker. It turned up Broad Street, down St James's Street and jumped the red traffic signals at the Old Steine. It then tore up Church Street – risking a blockage by going against the traffic stream in the one-way street. A few hours later it was found abandoned in Brunswick Street East, Hove, by a patrolling policeman. It is believed the raiders transferred to another car which they had waiting there. Police later discovered that the Jaguar had been stolen in Chelsea on 23 March and had presumably been kept hidden for more than two months in readiness for just such a raid as this. The Mini-van had been stolen in Greenwich earlier in the week.

ANDERSON, PERCY CHARLES

On 25 November 1934, Percy Charles Anderson, a motor mechanic of Lennox Street, Brighton, was arrested for killing his girlfriend, Edith Constance Drew-Bear, of 8 Ship Street, on East Brighton Golf Course. The crime was apparently the result of a sudden argument.

The couple, both aged 21, had been together for five months and seemed happy, going out on most free afternoons and evenings. On the fateful day, they went to Rottingdean for a walk. At 5 pm, two brothers named Crane heard shots and screams on the golf course. Shortly afterwards, they found Edith's body floating face upwards in one of two concrete tanks, each of them 5 ft square and some 2 ft deep, used for watering the greens. She had been strangled by a scarf, later identified as Anderson's, which was wound twice around her neck; it had been so tightly knotted around her throat that it had to be cut off. There were no less than five bullet wounds in her body. Signs of drowning were absent and the cause of death subsequently ascertained was asphyxia due to strangulation. The brothers looked for a policeman and in due course returned with Constable Hayes to the water tanks. Edith was identified from the contents of her handbag, found nearby.

At 7 pm, Anderson boarded a westbound No. 4 bus at Ovingdean Gap in an agitated state, wet through and without a jacket, waistcoat or shoes. At his home that evening, he told officers: 'We went for a walk by Roedean College and came to where there are two wells. We sat down and had a row and after that I had a pain in my head. The next thing I remember was when I was in the sea. I don't know where I left her.' When told that a young woman had been found dead at the one of the wells, he replied: 'I took my pistol out to shoot rats. Murdered! Oh, my God!'

At the police station, he told Detective Inspector Pelling that when Edith accused him of smiling at another girl, he became annoyed. Heated words followed and both lost their tempers. 'Then I got a pain through my head. I started swimming for my life after that . . . I was in the sea between Ovingdean and Rottingdean.' This was probably a ploy for a defence of insanity.

After a whole series of appearances before the magistrates at Brighton Town Hall, Anderson's trial opened on 7 March 1935 at Lewes before the Lord Chief Justice, Lord Hewart. Mr Eric Neve, defending, pleaded insanity on the part of his client (an attack of masked epilepsy at the time Anderson attacked Edith meant he was not responsible for his actions) but the Crown produced strong medical evidence to refute this. Anderson testified that he had suffered from blackouts and headaches ever since he was 12 and that when he and Edith had sat down on the edge of the water tank on the golf course he seemed to get a pain across his head and a blackness came over him.

Neve fought for a 'guilty but insane' verdict. The prosecution, however, drew attention to Anderson's rational removal of his mackintosh before he went into the sea. Also, he had made no inquiries of a woman he professed to love yet last recalled leaving on a cold and dark golf course.

It took the jury just 40 minutes to find Anderson guilty of murder. Anderson's calm response was: 'If I did it, I did not know what I was doing.' An appeal, heard on 29 March, was dismissed and the execution went ahead, despite the presentation of two petitions, the first bearing more than 10,000 signatures and the second 90,000.

The execution of Percy Charles Anderson took place at Wandsworth Prison at 9.00 am on 16 April 1935. Several hundred people gathered outside the gates. At precisely 8.00 am, Mrs Van Der Elst, the spirited campaigner against capital punishment (who, interestingly, owned Woodingdean House, near Ovingdean, at the time) arrived and the police rushed to prevent her car getting any closer. Leaflets were distributed, signatures were collected and the campaigner spoke, declaring that the authorities were hanging an innocent and insane man. Within six months, she forecast, capital punishment would be abolished.

ARSON

Also known as 'firesetting', especially in the US, and 'incendiarism'. It was once a capital offence. Damage to property in pre-Victorian times was viewed seriously by magistrates and the punishment of offenders reflected this.

Around 40% of all fires deliberately started in the UK are thought to be caused by juveniles. In 2000, 5,300 fires were started by children under the age of 10. These fires led to 13 deaths and 5,300 injuries and were estimated to have cost £40 million.

The Marine Hotel *tragedy, 1968*

Perhaps the worst peacetime blaze in the history of Brighton in terms of lives lost was caused by 18-year-old night porter James Casey at the *Marine Hotel*, Marine Parade, early on the morning of 17 November 1968. No fewer than seven people died when fire swept through the building; two other guests, both women, were detained in hospital. Five of the guests who died had been attending a birthday celebration party before the fire broke out at about 2.45 am. These people had, Casey said,

annoyed me about the drinks. They were getting aggressive. They told me I didn't have to serve them if I didn't want to. I was so annoyed with them that when they went to bed, I set light to the curtains. I thought the fire wouldn't come to much and that by getting them out of bed this would annoy them. I didn't intend to harm them or kill anybody, but unfortunately it did. I thought they would be disturbed and that the fire brigade would come and put it out. But it had gone beyond their control by the time they arrived. I am terribly sorry for what happened and I will regret it as long as I live.

Jailing Casey for five years at the Sussex Assizes, Mr Justice Shaw said: 'I wish at some stage during this trial you had shown some pity for those whose lives you brought to an untimely and terrible end.' Casey, of County Kerry, Eire, had pleaded not guilty to arson and not guilty to manslaughter.

The Marine Hotel, a Grade 3 listed building, after the fire. Today, Marine House, a block of flats with an exterior resembling the hotel's, occupies the site. Chris Horlock collection

Fire at the Royal Pavilion, 1975

On the night of Saturday, 1 November 1975, 22-year-old art student Leonard Kirzynowski, 23, of Waverley Crescent, Brighton, deliberately kicked in a window of the famous Music Room, poured in petrol and set fire to the curtains, 'because it was the sort of place people looked up to'. The flames blew back on Kirzynowski, setting his clothes alight. He was chased across the Pavilion Lawns and detained by Ossama Fahd, a 17-year-old Arab medical student.

The damage caused by the disastrous blaze was later assessed at £250,000. In his report to East Sussex Public Protection Committee, Chief Fire Officer Eric Whitaker stated:

> This fire provided yet another example of the benefit to be obtained from the installation of automatic fire-detection equipment at premises linked to a fire service control room, for soon after the fire started the alarm bells were ringing in the control room and appliances were on their way.

The end result was that the Royal Pavilion opened as usual to visitors on the following day.

The damage caused could have been far worse. All but one of the original wall paintings survived and the furniture (which included some original pieces returned by the Queen) had been taken out of the room only the day before so that a reception could be held there. Another stroke of luck was that the room had been insured for a quarter of a million – the assessed cost of the damage. The pay-out enabled conservationists to work for more than a decade to restore the room to its original splendour.

Kirzynowski, who had bought a gallon can of petrol from Caffyns' self-service station in Lewes Road, suffered second-degree burns to his arms and legs. He had, he stated, acted as he did because he was 'feeling anti-social'. He was later sentenced to six years in prison.

A misguided shop manager, 1975

> Suddenly flames were leaping towards me. I did not think it would ever go like that.
>
> (Stuart Simpson)

What the radio department manager of a Brighton music shop heard when his managing director's office was 'bugged' may have led him to start a £75,000 fire, Brighton Crown Court was told in January 1976.

The manager, Stuart David Fraser Simpson, 24, overheard that his department was going through financial difficulties. He misguidedly and bizarrely believed that by setting fire to the Lyon and Hall shop in Western Road, Brighton, it would help the company out of its troubles. Simpson, of Vere Road, Brighton, married with one child, was jailed for four years after pleading guilty to setting fire to the shop in August 1975. The prosecution told the court that the fire caused £35,000 worth of damage to the shop and £40,000 worth of damage to an adjoining shoe shop. He was sentenced to concurrent terms of nine months' imprisonment after pleading guilty to stealing a £178 TV set and a £140 tuner amplifier from the shop on dates before the fire. The business subsequently went into voluntary liquidation with debts to creditors totalling £36,771.

ASSASSINATION, ATTEMPTED
James Ings and the Cato Street Conspiracy, 1820

James Ings reputedly lived, and for a time worked as a butcher, in Brighton's West Street, roughly opposite Cranbourne Street.

On 23 February 1820, Ings, on the information of a confederate, was apprehended with eight others in a hay-loft in Cato Street, Paddington for his involvement in a plot to assassinate the King's Ministers while they were at a cabinet dinner that evening at the residence of the Earl of Harrowby, the President of the Council, in Grosvenor Square, London.

The plot is known as the Cato Street Conspiracy. It was arranged that when Arthur Thistlewood, the group's leader, presented a parcel at the door of Lord Harrowby's house, Ings should head the rest of the conspirators, rush in where the company were assembled and massacre the whole of them indiscriminately.

Ings armed himself fully for the desperate enterprise and also put on two bags like haversacks, into which he resolved to place two heads and one of Lord Castlereagh's hands, which he would preserve in brine.

All the conspirators were found guilty of High Treason. On the morning of 1 May, Thistlewood, Ings and three others were hanged and decapitated at Newgate. The other traitors were transported. To efface recollection of the conspiracy, Cato Street was renamed Homer Street.

Ings' executioner – JAMES BOTTING – also lived in Brighton.

The **Grand Hotel** *Bombing, 1984*

> *The air was full of thick cement dust: it was in my mouth and covered my clothes as I clambered over discarded belongings and broken furniture towards the back entrance of the hotel. It still never occurred to me that anyone would have died.*   (Margaret Thatcher)

Not since the Gunpowder Plot of 1605 had there been so deadly an attack on the British Government as that which took place at 2.54 am on Friday, 12 October 1984 at the *Grand Hotel* on Brighton's seafront. The target was that year's Conservative Party conference. Five people were killed and over 30 were injured by the Provisional IRA's Semtex bomb, which had been planted in Room 629 the previous month and set on a long-delay timer.

Sir Donald Maclean was staying in the room with his wife, Muriel, when the device exploded. She died later and Sir Donald was seriously injured. The other fatalities were those of Conservative MP Sir Anthony Berry, Chief Whip John Wakeham's first wife Roberta, Eric Taylor and Jeanne Shattock. Thirty-four people were hospitalised but recovered from their injuries. Several were left permanently disabled, including Margaret Tebbit, the wife of Norman Tebbit, then President of the Board of Trade. The chief target, Prime Minister Margaret Thatcher, and her government ministers were unharmed. 'Those who had sought to kill me,' she later wrote, 'had placed the bomb in the wrong place.' The IRA claimed responsibility the next day.

When the bomb went off, Mrs Thatcher was still awake, working on her conference speech. It ripped through her bathroom barely two minutes after she had left it, but neither she nor her husband, Denis, was hurt. The first rescuer to reach her was Leading Fireman Dave Norris, whom she greeted with the words: 'Good morning, pleased to see you.' He couldn't believe it, saying later: 'She looked like she had just come out of the hairdresser's.' She changed her clothes and was led out of the building. She and Denis

The severely damaged Grand Hotel *after the bombing in the early hours of 12 October 1984.*
Chris Horlock collection

were then escorted by the security guards to Brighton police station; after some time there, they were taken to Lewes Police College, then unoccupied, for the rest of the night.

The following morning, undeterred, the Prime Minister began the next session of the conference at 9.30 am as scheduled. The body of the hall was only about half full, she recollected, because the rigorous security checks held up the crowds trying to get in. But the ovation was colossal.

> *All of us were relieved to be alive, saddened by the tragedy and determined to show the terrorists that they could not break our spirit . . . I did not dwell long in the speech on what had happened. But I tried to sum up the feelings of all of us.*

Claiming the bombing was 'an attempt to cripple Her Majesty's democratically elected Government,' she declared '. . . this attack has failed . . . [and] all attempts to destroy democracy by terrorism will fail.'

The hunt for the bombers began. Police in Northampton discovered an IRA arms cache which had one timer missing. Because the timer could be set a month in advance, the date the bomber had stayed at the hotel could be pinpointed. When detectives checked all the staff, guests and friends of guests at around that time, there was only one name unaccounted for – that of Roy Walsh. This was the name used by Belfast IRA member, Patrick Magee.

In September 1986, then aged 35, he was found guilty of planting and exploding the bomb and of five counts of murder. Of the eight life sentences he received, seven were for offences relating to the Brighton bombing, and the eighth for a separate bombing conspiracy. The judge's recommendation was that he serve a minimum term of 35 years. This was later increased by Home Secretary Michael Howard to 'whole life'. However, after serving only 14 years in prison (including the time before his sentencing), he was released in 1999 under the terms of the Good Friday agreement. An appeal by the then Home Secretary, Jack Straw, to prevent it was turned down by the Northern Ireland High Court.

Police always maintained another person was with Magee in *The Grand* but no one was ever charged. Ex-Detective Chief Superintendent Jack Reece, who led the Sussex investigation, said (in 1990): 'We know who that man was but there was never enough evidence to bring him to court.'

Following his release, Magee reportedly said: 'I stand by what I did' and admitted only partial responsibility for planning the attack, maintaining that the fingerprint evidence found on a registration card recovered from the hotel was faked. He told *The Argus* in 2004: 'I will never say I was guilty of Brighton – I was responsible for Brighton ... I've never been back. I think that would be wrong. There is more to lose than to gain from it.' He declared that in the same circumstances he did not feel he would have acted differently had he been asked to do it again.

Yet that same year, on the 20th anniversary of the atrocity, 12 October, Magee did return for the first time since the bombing – and received a standing ovation. At a historic meeting at St Nicholas' Church in Dyke Road, he met Jo Berry, the daughter of one of his victims, Enfield Southgate MP Sir Anthony Berry. Magee and Ms Berry had been in regular contact following a process of reconciliation through the victim support programme LIVE (Let's Involve The Victim's Experience). The gathering, attended by an invited-only audience of 60, was chaired by broadcaster and journalist Simon Fanshawe, who declared it a success. *Argus* columnist Jean Calder said 'there was a real sense something has been achieved'.

However, in a letter to *The Argus* published on 18 October, a Mr DA Coles of Peacehaven no doubt expressed the view of many when he deplored 'a once great city like Brighton and Hove' paying homage to a murderer such as Patrick Magee. In any decent society, he claimed, the meeting would have been met with mass demonstrations against it. Criticism must also go, he felt, to the *Grand Hotel*, which was refusing to place a memorial in the building to commemorate those who died there in 1984.

At the time of the bombing, the owners of the building, Greenall Whitley, considered demolishing it but decided it was too important and should be restored. The hotel reopened in 1986 after an £11 million rebuild.

In *The Brighton Bomb*, a documentary shown on the UKTV History Channel on 28 October 2005, Magee's name was not mentioned once.

ASSAULT – see also INDECENT ASSAULT
Clifftop violence, 1810
Suspended from the cliffs at West Street Gap was Brighton's fire-cage, made of iron hoops within which, at night, a fire of material gathered from the seashore and common coal was lit to serve as a guide to fishermen returning to shore. On New Year's Day, 1810, the two men employed to attend to the fire, named Rolfe and Barton, had some words in the course of the evening. Rolfe therefore decided to arrange the beacon by himself, obtaining a new iron frame and suspending it. No sooner had he done this than Barton tried to cut the fastenings and let it fall over the cliff; as Rolfe attempted to prevent this happening, Barton thrust a knife into his abdomen so deeply as to let out some

of his bowels. Barton escaped but following a £20 reward being offered through the Town Crier for his apprehension, he was captured. His term of imprisonment was, however, only brief, since Rolfe, although enduring great pain, eventually recovered.

Assorted early cases

Assaults on the POLICE were not dealt with any more harshly than assaults on others, as John Rowland found out when he was fined only £5 in 1830. Altogether there were 23 common assaults on Brighton policemen between 1810–30, the worst case being in 1825 when six men assaulted a nightwatchman. In 1831 Frederick Trussler was imprisoned by the magistrate for one month for a violent assault on a constable, but in 1834 Peter Kippy was bound over only after pleading guilty to assaulting a policeman and rioting. William Sheppard was not so lucky when he and two others were sent to prison for 14 days in 1841 for also assaulting a policeman.

Men assaulting women were treated no differently by the magistrates; in 1824, for example, John Carrol was only fined 1s for assaulting Hannah Fry, a well-known miscreant of the town. Six years later Daniel Bishop was fined 4s for a similar offence. The harshest sentence served on a man for assaulting a woman was given by Sir David Scott on James Sayer for assaulting Harriet Savage in 1824. Sayer received a three month jail sentence. By contrast, when Ann King assaulted Albert Tull in 1822 she was acquitted.

Men assaulting men was a common crime. The most lenient sentence possible – acquittal – was handed down in 1816 to bookseller William Kirby. Four years later, William Burchall was fined only 1s for a similar offence. In 1823 James Freeman was up before the bench (not for the first time) and was given six weeks' hard labour and bound over for £50 for an assault on William Wymark. In 1847 Richard Sawyer and two others assaulted a Mr Winchester and were sentenced to six months' hard labour.

Cases of **women assaulting women** sometimes came up at the Petty Sessions. In 1825 a woman was charged for striking a young girl and pulling her hair. The watchman threw her into the BLACK HOLE to cool off. In April of the same year, a young female oyster seller had her basket of oysters thrown at her and was struck in the face by a woman. Both were bound over. Another two women in court in 1825 had argued, one saying that 'she would slap her in the face every time she saw her'.

Other inter-personal crimes occasionally occurred and may be found in the *Sessional Offenders' Lists*. They include an acid attack in 1839 by Sarah Helmsley, child abandonment in 1835 by Caroline Ford, disposing of children's bodies in 1835 and 1836 by Emma Chapman and Frances Cornwall, duel challenging in 1816 by William Fleet, four assaults on Poor Law Union Officers in 1838 and 1839, four cases of attempted RAPE between 1822 and 1835, and four cases of wife beating in 1829 (twenty cases were reported in East Sussex between 1825 and 1838). The *Brighton Borough Petty Sessional*

Divisional Minute Book for petty larceny and other more minor crimes also lists some interesting assault cases.

Assault by beggars was dealt with at the Petty Sessions and a dozen or so cases were recorded in 1816. Most were dismissed and the offenders bound over to keep the peace.

In **cases involving soldiers** (see also MILITIA), one John Wallis was committed in 1816 for stabbing or cutting unlawfully Patrick Reynolds, a private in the 51st Regiment. A case in 1817 involved Thomas Smith, a Waterloo soldier, striking a constable after refusing to leave a house. He was fined £10 and told to keep the peace (the size of this fine indicates that soldiers received a harsher sentence than civilians for similar offences). *The Patriot* reported on a case in 1835 in which a soldier received 300 lashes for THEFT, a punishment they described as 'degrading and disgusting' – especially since, six years earlier *The Herald* had reported that two officers of the 10th Hussars had defended a poor woman against being robbed.

Family assaults were occasionally heard at the Petty Sessions. Sarah Walkley told the magistrates that her husband, James, was drinking and gambling at the *White Lion* and in the last six weeks she and her three children had only received 8s 9d. Sworn witness Harriet Neal confirmed this, saying Walkley was 'often very drunk'; after offering the Governor of the Workhouse 10s a week during the summer and 'always if he can' for his wife, Walkley was discharged. Assault cases against wives were more often heard at the Quarter Sessions, although in the first of two cases against husbands dealt with at the Petty Sessions, a husband had allegedly abused his wife and kicked her out of doors, and in the second, heard in 1829, James Barnard was bound over after his wife claimed 'he would do her some bodily harm'.

A blot on his copybook, 1877

'Captain' Fred Collins was the jovial face of Brighton. His striking, genial looks, his powerful build, his black shiny waterproof hat, slightly tilted, the stout dark stock tied round his neck and his white jacket marked this pleasure-boat operator out as a true son of the sea, nowhere happier than on Brighton beach. In a letter dated 8 June 1867, Charles Dickens wrote a letter referring to having enjoyed 'a trip in the famous Skylark and it was a lark'.

Collins was also a publican, who kept a beer-house in the King's Road Arches called the *Welcome Brothers*. It was there on 25 July 1877 that an incident occurred with potentially dire consequences. A scuffle took place between Frederick Collins Jnr and a boat builder named George Winder over alleged wrong change at the bar. The Captain intervened to help his son, throwing Winder over the counter. The man died four days later from inflammation of the brain and father and son were charged with manslaughter.

'Captain' Fred Collins (1832–1912). Author's collection

At the Lewes Spring Assizes of 1878, before Lord Chief Justice Cockburn, the defence drew attention to Collins' otherwise blameless character and his well-known kindness. The jury did not even retire, immediately returning a Not Guilty verdict, although Collins left the court with the judge's stern admonition to restraint ringing in his ears.

Hurting the one you love, 1977

A man stabbed a woman 58 times in Forte's Restaurant in Western Road on 20 August 1976. Polish-born Charles Juchimiec, 46, of Wilbury Villas, Hove, was jailed for seven years at Lewes Crown Court for the attack. Mr Justice Purchas said it was a brutal attack for which there was no excuse.

Incredibly, his victim, 22-year-old Miss Michelle Sopher, of Sackville Road, Hove, not only survived but went on to marry her fiancé.

Juchimiec, who was described as a 'lonely middle-aged man', was befriended by the couple, who felt sorry for him. He claimed the relationship with Michelle had been an intimate one, but this was denied by her. When she told him their friendship would have to cease as she was about to be married, he pulled out a knife and repeatedly stabbed her. Had she not played dead, she would certainly have been killed. She spent 11 days in hospital. Dr Michael Bailey said the victim would have died within half an hour of admission but for immediate surgery. The nerve of her left arm was damaged, making that limb and hand almost useless.

Juchimiec had come to this country in 1948 after his family had suffered badly at the hands of the Nazis. He had never married and his weaknesses were gambling and drink.

Brighton's Western Road, looking east in the 1970s. Royal Pavilion, Libraries and Museums, Brighton and Hove

He had known Michelle for about six months and believed he was very close to her. He had been drinking but was not drunk. Asked why he stabbed her, he replied:

> *I don't know, it happened suddenly. In my eyes I saw someone coming out of the mist then I saw a person standing in front of me. A person came out of the mist and something was coming my way. Something hit me; it must have been a chair, I have no knowledge of stabbing her. I never intended hurting her.*

After the attack, Juchimiec went up onto the roof of the building and stayed there for three hours, threatening to throw himself off or stab himself. Eventually, a friend and a senior police officer arrived and he came down quietly, surrendering the knife.

B

'BABES IN THE WOOD' MURDERS

Nicola Fellows, aged nine, and Karen Hadaway, 10, from Newick Road on Brighton's Moulsecoomb estate, were found murdered in nearby Wild Park within 24 hours of going missing at around tea-time on Thursday, 9 October 1986. They had nipped to a local shop to get a bag of chips and vanished in the thickening mist.

Dressed in her green Coldean School sweatshirt and pink trainers, Karen had told her mother, Michelle, that she was going out to play. Her best friend Nicola, in tartan skirt and red shoes, told her own mother, Susan, that she was just going across the road and wouldn't be long.

After calling at the chip shop, the pair crossed the busy Lewes Road to the Park. When the friends had still not turned up in time for their TV favourites *Top of the Pops* and *EastEnders*, something bordering on panic set in and both mothers called at the houses of friends and scoured every garden nearby. They even ventured into the Park, which was now dark, joined by family, neighbours and police, in a frantic search for the girls. When their vision became shrouded by a heavy mist, however, they let the police take over.

Nicola Fellows. Mirrorpix   *Karen Hadaway.* Mirrorpix

Just after 4 pm the following day, the bodies of the two young girls were found in a leafy den-like clearing in a thickly-wooded area in the Park. Karen's head was resting on Nicola's lap. They had been indecently assaulted and strangled. Nicola had been hit in the face.

When Susan Fellows was told, the awful truth was too much to bear and she passed out. She then had to be heavily sedated.

It appeared that the young victims had gone willingly to the spot where they died, leading to the belief that they had known their killer. In a massive operation, the first of many, detectives traced more than 120 people who had been in Wild Park on Thursday evening. The park keeper remembered seeing the girls there playing in a tree and at around the same time had also spoken to a 21-year-old man by the name of Russell Bishop, an unemployed roofer from nearby Hollingdean. Bishop had known the girls and he and his girlfriend had actually been at Nicola's home on the previous afternoon when he called to see if his friend, the Fellows' lodger, was in. He was one of the first on the scene after the bodies were discovered and it was he who confirmed to Michelle Hadaway that her daughter was dead.

Three weeks later, Bishop was arrested and charged with murder. He went on trial at Lewes Crown Court in November 1987 in a case which the press dubbed the 'Babes in the Wood' murders.

A Pinto sweatshirt which the prosecution alleged was worn by Bishop on the night of the killings was found near Moulsecoomb Station. Fibres on it linked to clothes worn by the victims and those worn by Bishop's then girlfriend. He categorically denied it was his. Following four weeks of evidence, the trial collapsed when the forensic evidence was called into question. To the fury of the families and the misgivings of many, Russell Bishop was found Not Guilty.

Yet three years later, Bishop was again in court (see ABDUCTION). This time he was jailed for life.

While in prison, Bishop spent a great deal of time preparing a case against Sussex Police, alleging they tried to frame him over the 1986 murders. When, however, he faced them in court in 1994, he dropped his lawsuit after just one full day under cross-examination. Repeated attempts since then by the girls' families to bring Bishop back before the courts have all failed.

Both families moved away from Brighton after the tragedy and both girls' parents eventually divorced. Karen's father suffered a fatal heart attack in 1998, brought on, his family believes, by the stress of losing his daughter. Nicola's mother, Susan, remarried and became Mrs Eismann. She is now living and working in Brighton again. In August 2002, she broke her silence of nearly 16 years to tell of her ongoing nightmare and her family's fight for justice.

Sussex Police have re-opened the investigation, along with a number of others. With the repeal in April 2005 of the 800-year-old 'double jeopardy' laws, under which there could be no second trial for a case already heard, there were hopes that Bishop could be tried again if new evidence pointing to his guilt were to emerge.

On 28 July 2006, the family of Nicola Fellowes relaunched a civil action they hoped could lead to a retrial. Susan Eismann, Nicola's uncles Nigel and Ian Heffron, and aunt Ivy Streeter, issued a summons at Brighton County Court to reinstate a civil action against him originally commenced in 1991. They had at that time been forced to launch an action which had to be limited to the ground of damaging Nicola's clothing. Nigel Heffron said: 'If we can prove he damaged the girl's clothing, we can go on to say he did this in the act of murder.' The family said they had new evidence, which they did not yet want to make public. In September 2006, however, they were angered to learn from the police that there was not in fact enough evidence to prosecute anyone. The family vowed they would claim a judicial review. Nigel Heffron commented: 'If they think we will just let them forget about this they haven't learnt anything about our family. We will not be going away and will fight until justice is served.'

The family led a march from Brighton Police Station in John Street to Wild Park on October 10 to mark the 20th anniversary of the murders – and to protest that justice was not being done.

BADHAM, GEORGE

Alerted by an anonymous caller at 4.15 pm on Monday, 10 October 1938, New Scotland Yard was given the address of 43 Warleigh Road, Brighton as the scene of 'an accident' in which a woman had died. The man's call was traced to a kiosk near London Bridge Station. Brighton Police were contacted and officers were sent to the address. There, in a 'box settee', as the *Evening Argus* later described it, was the body of a woman, her head and shoulders covered by a rug. From the three ligatures round her neck, it was clear she had been strangled. The victim was Aline Ursula Marjorie Badham, a young mother of 25. Of her infant son there was no sign.

The mystery call had been made by 22-year-old George Alexander Badham, who had fled the scene that afternoon after one of the frequent quarrels between Aline and himself during their stormy two-year marriage. Now penniless and wretched in the capital, he spent the night following the tip-off at a Church Army hostel in Great Peter Street, giving his name as Albert Brown. The next day, in his search for his second night's accommodation, he was apprehended, having been identified from a photograph at Cannon Row Police Station. Much later that morning, he stood in the dock at Brighton Police Court, facing the charge of the wilful murder of his wife.

At Aline Badham's inquest, evidence was given that the cause of death was asphyxia due to strangulation. At the detailed second hearing of the case at Brighton Police Court on Thursday, 20 October, a much clearer picture of the background to the crime emerged. Increasingly, Badham came to be seen as a victim of provocation. Aline had had sex with another man while her husband was out looking for work. Testimony was given that Badham was very kind and good to his wife but she was always the boss and always on at him for not earning enough money. It was partly to seek better-paid work and partly through marital discord that Badham had gone to London on 21 September, leaving behind his wife and baby Alexander, aged 19 months. On his return and there-after, there were repeated quarrels. On Aline's last day on earth, Badham had learned of her conduct via his sister, whom he visited, and this tipped him over the edge.

He confronted his wife with what he had heard and she finally admitted that the report was true. He was utterly despondent, reminding her that this was not the first time she had strayed (the astounded court heard that Alexander was not his son, although he loved him as though he were, and that he had married Aline because she was going to have a baby). She then attacked him, having already slapped his face. 'She started punching me,' he stated, 'and I had to defend myself and just lost my head.' He had no recollection of tying the ties around her neck; but he was aware she was dead – and had to be concealed. Leaving the infant with his father-in-law's landlady, telling her he was going to look for work locally, he fled to London.

Badham was ably defended in his Assize trial by Norman Birkett KC (see MANCINI). Through a combination of his advocacy skills, the accused's own sincere and genuine character and the open admission of his guilt, the revelation of a startling family truth and the sympathy of the judge, the young husband came to be seen in an entirely new light. Mr Justice Atkinson, clearly impressed by the model prisoner, referred to the 'defence of provocation' and temporary loss of reason as grounds for a manslaughter verdict. George Alexander Badham was dealt with leniently. His sentence was a term of imprisonment – 12 months.

BATTLE OF LEWES ROAD – see UNREST, INDUSTRIAL

BEGGING – see VAGRANCY

BIGAMY
Mary Rowe, 1834
Mary Rowe, 31, was first married in Croydon on 2 November 1819 in the name of Mary Dogett to Francis Rowe. However, on 26 September 1825, she married one James Brown, a sergeant in the Coldstream Guards, in Brighton after knowing him for about ten weeks. She had passed herself off as a widow and was a model wife for six years but then changed, so that Brown left her in September 1834, when she took her trial at the Old Bailey. He did not discover she had been married until later. He was present when she was apprehended at No. 2, Stepney Green on 11 August of that year.

Rowe's defence was that she had not seen her husband since June 1822, when he left her with a young daughter. Hearing from several people that he was dead, she concluded this to be the case. She lived with Brown very comfortably for six years until his misconduct (not hers, she claimed) led to the split. Mary Rowe was found guilty, with a recommendation to mercy by the jury. She was sentenced to three months' imprisonment.

James Malcolm, 1885
When Emma Dash of 10 Broad Street, Brighton, married at Easter 1885, it resulted in two trials at the Old Bailey.

Some time previously, the 28-year-old had met a gentleman, one 'Captain McDonald', at a ball in London. Seeing him again in Brighton, she accepted his swift offer of marriage. The wedding took place on Easter Saturday at St James's Church (this once stood at the corner of Chapel Street and St James's Street but was demolished in 1950). After the wedding breakfast, the young couple went to Chichester, returning to Brighton on Easter Monday. The 'Captain' told his bride he had to leave for his ship to arrange for her to be received on board. He never came back. What the new Mrs McDonald and her mother did not know was that in 1877 this shameful trickster had married one Elizabeth Williamson in Aberdeen and she was still alive.

McDonald would have become a serial bigamist had he not been stopped, since after leaving Brighton, he introduced himself to another gullible Emma (surname Dickenson) in St Albans, luring her with an engagement ring.

Some months after the Brighton ceremony, a guest who had been at the wedding breakfast recognised McDonald at a garden party in Fulham. He accused him of being Miss Dash's vanished husband. The man denied it, saying his name was James Malcolm, but he was detained. Malcolm, a meat salesman at Newgate Market, received an excellent character and was described as the strictest of teetotallers. But the bride from Brighton was summoned and on 13 July promptly identified him as the man to whom she had – however briefly – been married.

Denying everything, Malcolm said he had never been to Brighton in his life and that he was married to somebody else. When the case came to trial at the Old Bailey, the bride, priest and all the wedding guests swore without hesitation – partly from a scar on his face – that Malcolm and McDonald were the same person. Yet Montagu Williams, defending, called a number of witnesses who swore, also without hesitation, that the prisoner was in London on the days when, according to the prosecution, he was courting Miss Dash and getting married in Brighton. The general defence was that Malcolm must have a double who could honestly be mistaken for him.

Williams would write about the case later in his reminiscences, *Leaves of a Life* (1890). Because he was prevented by illness from seeing the case through, a second hearing took place a month later, in October 1885. The trial was remarkable for the number of witnesses who, in more or less equal proportion, respectively asserted and denied that McDonald and Malcolm were one and the same man. The possibility of witness perjury for pecuniary advantage was not ruled out in what the judge called 'this painful and disgusting case'.

The jury took less than half an hour to find James Malcolm guilty. He was sentenced to seven years' imprisonment – the maximum possible for the offence of bigamy.

Albert Blake, 1937

Albert John Blake, 27, a wireless engineer of Jubilee Street, Brighton, was sent for trial by Brighton magistrates on 25 August 1937 on a charge of bigamy. He had married a Brighton girl, Winifred Edith Stephens, during the lifetime of his wife, Jessie May Blake, whom he had married at Lee on 25 October 1930 when she was 23. They had lived there until early the following year, when Blake came to Brighton and his wife returned to Eltham. He had not contacted her since 1933 and all he had sent her by way of money had been 10s.

Winifred Stephens had first met Blake in Brighton when she was 17 in November 1934. The following June they were married at St Nicholas' Church. They had two children, both boys. Not until a couple of weeks before the trial had she learned he was already married and became so distressed during the proceedings that she had to be taken out of court to recover. Blake, when arrested, said: 'Yes, I have been dreading it ever since I married her.' He was committed for trial at the Winter Assizes, at which, on 1 December 1937, he pleaded before Mr Justice Charles 'I only did it because I loved her'. The judge's stern response was 'That is not my idea of behaviour towards a person one loves'. The bigamist, who had described himself as a bachelor to 'a mere girl' (to quote his lordship), was sent to prison for four months.

BIZARRE CASES

Some strange cases have come before Brighton magistrates during the period covered by this volume. Others went undetected.

An example of the latter was one of the most heartless of burglaries. It took place in early November 1800. The Promenade Grove, west of the Pavilion, was for many years a place enjoyed by the public for its ambience and for the events and gatherings held there from time to time. Its ruined north wall collapsed under the effect of high winds just as a 19-year-old girl by the name of Coupland was passing it. She was a bridesmaid, accompanying a young couple she knew to church for their wedding. The intended bride and groom escaped unhurt, as they were a little way behind her. The young victim's mother, while assisting in retrieving the body from the masonry, had her house burgled and suffered the loss of a watch, a one-pound banknote and a seven-shilling piece.

More trivial were simple cases of people being ordered not to bathe in the sea again and two pensioners fined three shillings for 'making a noise'. For wandering abroad and pretending to be a shipwrecked sailor, William Reay was sentenced to serve in His Majesty's navy.

In an 1817 case, John Carpenter of Brighton was handed a 4-month prison sentence for breaking and entering Rottingdean windmill. The fact that he did not steal anything counted for nothing, judging by the sentence.

A case was brought against a parson two years later for 'preaching wrongly', people were charged for whispering in church and there was a case against a 'spirit man' making a disturbance in church; a more serious charge was that of stealing a corpse (see RESURRECTIONISTS).

In 1819, a man was committed for not providing a cart for a soldier's baggage and six years later a man was fined 3d for lying on his back in Regent Square. Up on the Racecourse a woman was charged in 1825 for lying in a wheat field.

A boy from Rochester who had 'a fit' was discharged providing he left town. Two girls, named Pitts and Moore, both 20 and described by *The Herald* as 'terrible characters', were likewise ejected from the parish. After walking some way, however, they 'suffered worn shoes', whereupon they returned, only to receive a 3-month sentence apiece. A man considered to be insane was sent to Ringmer for being found knocking on the door of the Pavilion at midnight demanding to 'see the inside as well as the outside'.

Two environmental/nuisance cases were heard at the Petty Sessions in 1825: one man was fined 6d for leaving an unprotected hole at Black Rock and another was fined £5 for leaving two gratings in a dangerous state in Union Street. Three defendants on separate charges of throwing rubbish into the sea at Pool Valley Gapp were all fined 10s each. In a nuisance case in 1839, Joseph Inkpen pleaded guilty to removing manure of an offensive description out of the town in daytime.

Women sometimes faced the sessions on strange grounds: one was fined in 1829 for 'not washing clothes properly'. In 1816, the mother of Charlotte Brown told the magistrate that she could not control her daughter's 'bad conduct' and 'drinking with soldiers'. The magistrate locked the daughter up for 28 days.

Wilhelm Goergs, 28, a music teacher, was charged in June 1866 with feloniously sending to Count Bismarck a certain letter threatening to murder him. The letter, which the prisoner admitted was in his handwriting, read as follows:

Brighton, 3, Hampton Place, Whitsuntide, 1866.

Sir, – Unfortunately you have escaped this time. Take notice, – there are still patriots which are not afraid to put a stop to your miserable existence.

My dear, never-forgotten friend, Ferdinand Blind, has taught me how not to miss you. You must expect now

"Dagger
"and
"POISON.

I do not miss you. Take farewell from the world. Curses and shame on your memory. Eternal hatred against all bearing the name Hohenzollern and Bismarck. I have sworn it!"

"WILHELM GOERGS,
"Late teacher and gymnast at Stolberg,
near Aix-la-Chapelle."

Several witnesses were called as to the prisoner's character.

After consulting for some time, the jury returned a verdict of Guilty, but with a strong recommendation to mercy, whereupon Goergs was sentenced to four calendar months' imprisonment without hard labour.

In April 1938, the strangest of maintenance cases came before the Brighton Bench. Although warned against committing perjury, Kathleen Josephine Hemmett, whose address was given as the Municipal Hospital, applied for an order against Joseph Hemmett of Buckingham Street on the grounds of desertion. The man strenuously denied ever having been married to her. She maintained they had wed at the Catholic church of the Sacred Heart, Hove, on 7 July 1937; the court adjourned while the certificate was sought there but it was not found. The banns had never been published and she had herself not received a certificate after the service. Despite her protests, the magistrates dismissed the case without hearing any further evidence.

BLACK HOLE

The local name given to the dungeon at Brighton's TOWN HALL.

It was first used with reference to a small cell in the first building to be known as the Town Hall which stood on the western side of Market Street. This two-storey gabled edifice was erected in 1727 and primarily used as a workhouse, although on occasions meetings of the Vestry and superintendents of the watch, the forerunners of the POLICE, were held there. A 'small cell' is also referred to in the 1938 brochure commemorating 100 years of the Brighton police. There, the 'clink' or lock-up in the eighteenth century is stated to have been at the back of the *Running Horse* public house in King Street. Yet Bishop records that in 1800 the inn, at No. 20, was called *The Hen and Chickens*. The change of name took place around 1840. It was still called the *Running Horse* at the time his *Peep into the Past* was published in 1892.

The Brighton 'Night Constable's Report' for 1822–23 reveals that extensive use was made of the 'Black Hole', for the majority of entries relate to drunken disturbances and overnight stays by the offenders, followed by quick summary justice the next day. There is some evidence from the reports that drunks from a high social status in the town were not confined to the Black Hole. After disturbers of the peace, the most numerous class of offenders were vagrants. After spending a night in the Hole, magistrates returned them to their original parish so that they should not become a burden on the rates. The Petty Session Minute Books for an earlier period (1816–18) show this to be so.

The building was demolished in 1823 to make way for the new market building and the site is now occupied by Bartholomew Square.

The present Town Hall, built in 1830–32, was visited by JD Parry when brand new. He was not greatly impressed, describing, in his *Guide*, the dungeons 'for temporary confinement, said to be dreary enough, and if ever to be used, not particularly appropriate to the present day.'

BORSTALS

In 1902 a wing of the convict prison at Borstal, now Rochester Borstal, was taken over for teaching young inmates a trade and preparing them to lead a new life on their discharge.

The borstal system was formally introduced in the Prevention of Crime Act 1908. The training regime, administered under a strong moral atmosphere, was based on hard physical work and technical and educational instruction. Inmates would work through a series of grades, based on privileges, until they were released. On discharge they were given special supervision through the Borstal Association.

The film *Boys in Brown* (1949) starred Richard Attenborough (1923–) as Jackie Knowles in a drama where a progressive Borstal governor tries to reform his boys.

In 1963, a borstal experiment was successfully tried at LEWES PRISON, which had been used throughout the 1940s and 1950s as a centre for Young Offenders. However, pressure on the London prisons meant that it had once more to be requisitioned as a London overspill.

In July 1964, two youths, one aged 20 and the other 17, were sentenced to a period of borstal training by Brighton magistrates following an orgy of destruction: they had stolen two cars and the property inside them, damaged another car by throwing bricks at it and also stolen some tools from a further vehicle. They had no insurance. No less than 22 further offences were taken into consideration. The 17-year-old fainted during the court proceedings.

In January 1969, a 17-year-old Portslade youth, Mervyn Herring, was sentenced to borstal training for falsely confessing to the murder of KEITH LYON, thereby wasting 200 hours of police time. 'I was a bit bored,' he said, 'nothing to do. I did it for a laugh.' He had made eight previous court appearances for other offences.

Borstals were abolished in 1983.

BOTTING, JAMES

James Botting of Brighton was appointed the nation's Public Executioner at Newgate Gaol, London, in 1817. The executioner of the misguided Cato Street conspirators (see ASSASSINATION, ATTEMPTED), he was the son of Jemmy Botting, the owner of some land immediately to the west of the bottom of Cannon Place known as Botting's Rookery from being the haunt of tramps of the lowest order.

Nearly five years after dispatching Ings, Botting also executed at Newgate, on 30 November 1824, the banker Henry Fauntleroy (see FORGERY). These were just two of the 175 'parties' he had ushered out of this world. So numerous were the crimes in the early days which attracted the death penalty that he executed no fewer than 13 persons in the space of one week at Newgate.

Due to contracting paralyis, Botting retired from his post of public hangman and lived on a pension of 5s a week granted by the Court of Aldermen of the City of London. He was a well-known character around Brighton, using what we would now call a wheelchair to get him about. Perhaps because few were keen to enjoy his company on account of his former occupation, he always appeared isolated from the world. He died in Brighton, according to Erredge, on 1 October 1837, reportedly when he fell from his chair at the corner of Codrington Place and Montpelier Road and no one would come to his aid. His demise was not, however, recorded in any newspaper for that year to which the author had access.

BOW STREET RUNNERS – see also POLICE

By 1800, Henry Fielding's Bow Street Runners had already been in existence for half a century. The original eight were London's first band of constables. Their functions included serving writs, detective work and arresting offenders. The Bow Street Runners gained a reputation for honesty and efficiency and they travelled all over the country in search of criminals. On a number of occasions they ran their quarry to ground in Brighton.

BREACH OF PROMISE

The local *Morning Herald* of 27 August 1805 reported that Townshend and Sayers, two Bow Street officers, arrived here that morning in search of an individual who had been guilty of a burglary in the metropolis. They had been here but a short time when their man, in laced livery, was seen by them to be crossing the Steine. They took him into custody and 'having ornamented his wrists with a pair of iron ruffles [. . .] bore him off in triumph to London.'

Erredge, in his *History of Brighthelmston*, refers to Johnny Townsend [sic] as 'the noted Bow Street Runner' – presumably Sayers' colleague – telling us that the *Albany Tavern* at the top of Duke Street, with a sea view down West Street, was for many seasons his lodgings when GEORGE IV was living in Brighton. He was for a good few years in constant attendance on him, both when he was Prince of Wales and King. West Street at that time was a place of fashionable resort, especially for equestrians. Members of the royal family frequented it daily, often visiting Townsend to lunch with him. The food for the occasion would be sent up from the Royal Pavilion. The historian tells us that

> *Townsend was a shrewd but illiterate man, a staunch politician of the Tory school, kind-hearted, generous, and charitable, an agreeable companion with his equals, a man who commanded the respect of his superiors and his inferiors; but he was a sore terror of refractory boys and girls.*

BREACH OF PROMISE
£200 for a broken heart, 1886
Among the civil cases before Mr Justice Hawkins at the Sussex Winter Assizes in Lewes in February 1886 was a suit in which an Italian lady named Katerina Aurelia Margherita Corio sued Ernest Frederick Salmon, son of a Brighton chemist, for damages for breach of promise of marriage.

The three issues involved were whether any such promise had been made, whether it was a promise conditional on the consent of his parents, and whether, if unconditional, it was to be fulfilled within a reasonable time and, if so, whether that time had elapsed.

Miss Corio worked as lady's maid to one Lady Vivian and met Salmon in Biarritz, where he was employed as assistant to the principal chemist in the town. In November 1883, he presented her with a pair of earrings and their romance continued to blossom over a period of five months, during which, the prosecution claimed, he promised to marry her. In April 1884, Salmon returned to England as did, subsequently, Miss Corio and her mistress. Here the 24-year-old suitor continued his ardent courtship, both in meetings and in correspondence, while studying for qualifying professional examinations. He was aware that his sweetheart was around 30 and therefore older than him but not by how many years. In a letter received in early October, Salmon wrote how he looked forward to making her his wife. At the end of that month, therefore, Miss Corio began preparing her trousseau for an Easter wedding but when more time elapsed with no firm plans for the ceremony, she grew anxious.

To set her mind at rest, she travelled to Brighton and saw Salmon. The meeting was an unhappy one, as he positively refused to marry her. She testified that in early 1884 he had said he would do so in two years' time. Salmon denied he became engaged to her in Biarritz and was in any case not now earning sufficient to undertake marriage. Moreover, his parents were very much against the marriage and he was powerless in the matter. The main reason he ultimately broke off the relationship, he admitted, was on account of the age difference, which he had learned from her in November 1884 was no less than 10 years. Yet for quite some time he had continued to see and write to her.

The jury found for the plaintiff in the sum of £200. Mr Justice Hawkins found this reasonable and gave judgment accordingly.

BRIGHTON ROCK
Film, 1947

> *Hale knew, before he had been in Brighton three hours, that they meant to murder him.*
> (*Brighton Rock* by Graham Greene, published in 1938)

Synopsis
In Brighton, between the wars, Fred Hale is killed by a local gang, led by 17-year-old Pinkie Brown, which holds him responsible for the death of their former leader. Fearing one of his men might be recognised by a young waitress, Rose, Pinkie asks her out on a date, warning her to keep silent.

Pinkie is patronised and sent away by a larger and more powerful rival gang when he visits its leader, Colleoni. Ida Arnold, an entertainer, is suspicious about Hale's death and decides to conduct her own investigations.

Pinkie, hoping to have his associate, Spicer (who complained about his leadership), killed, sends him to the races the next day to be murdered by Colleoni's men. In the event, both Spicer and Pinkie are knifed and make their way separately back to the lodging house, where Pinkie pushes Spicer over the banisters to his death.

Pinkie decides to marry Rose, who is now in love with him, so that she will not be able to give evidence against him. Following the hasty registry office wedding, she asks him to record his voice for her in a fairground booth. In his message, he confesses that he hates her. Fearing that Rose, who has been visited by Ida, might talk, Pinkie resolves to kill her by pretending to enter into a suicide pact. Taking Rose for a walk on the pier, he tries to persuade her to shoot herself. To save her, Dallow, a henchman, joins forces with Ida and the police to arrest Pinkie, who, during the drama, falls off the pier to his death. Rose's record has been damaged when Pinkie had tried to destroy it. When she does play it, the needle sticks on the words 'I love you'.

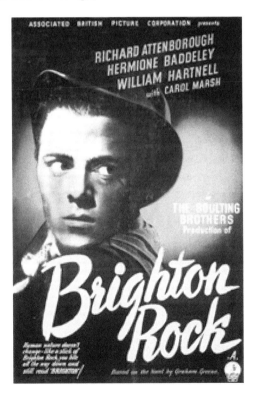

Details and comments
Director John Boulting was initially attracted by the way Graham Greene's pre-war novel so vividly evoked a sense of place. The film, produced by his twin brother, Roy, makes equally deft use of its locations. Harry Waxman's skilled and atmospheric cinematography enhances the authentic portrayal of Brighton's bar rooms, racetracks, cafés and boarding houses.

But the town's councillors were wary and defensive about how the place would be projected. And not for the first time. When Greene's novel had appeared, the *Brighton Gazette* had complained that it was

a gross libel on Brighton, which gives a totally wrong and damaging impression of the place. Its description of Brighton implies that ... it is the home of squalid crime, that its hotels are haunted by gangsters.

When the London *Evening Standard* serialised the book, it was the last straw for the *Gazette*: 'Mr Greene stuck a knife in Brighton's back, but it was only a little one – the *Standard* has come along with a bayonet.' In 1947, concerned that the town's image might suffer further, this time at the hands of filmmakers, the councillors imposed a preface to the film (which rolls over a scene of paddlers braving the Channel's surf), depicting the resort as 'a large, jolly, friendly seaside town in Sussex, exactly one hour's journey from London'. Fearing opposition to location shooting, the Boulting twins agreed to the disclaimer stressing the historical nature of the roguery depicted, thinking that 'in the circumstances', the concession was 'a fair one to make'.

Perhaps the councillors shot themselves in the foot for, despite the preface's ending, its substance serves only to resurrect grim memories of trunk murders and racecourse warfare best left undisturbed:

[...] *in the years between the wars behind the Regency terraces and crowded beaches there was another Brighton of dark alleyways and festering slums. From here, the poison of crime and violence and gang warfare began to spread until the challenge was taken up by the police. This is a story of that other Brighton – now happily no more.*

Brighton Rock, retitled *Young Scarface* for its American release, was a thriller in the tradition of the American gangster movie. Although a contemporary *Daily Mirror* reviewer accused it of 'false, nasty, cheap sensationalism', his was a minority view. The film was voted fifteenth in the British Film Institute's millennium poll of 100 favourite British films. It was the first of Graham Greene's adaptations of his own work and the precursor of classic crime films like *Get Carter* and *The Long Good Friday*. It also made Richard Attenborough a star.

Jake Arnott, writing in *The Guardian* (20 July 2002), describes Pinkie ('Attenborough's boy monster') as 'archetypal of the small-time nastiness of English criminality'. He also points out that it is Whitsun weekend by the Palace Pier when Pinkie's mob kill Hale – the same feast day and the same place that in 1964 would see Mods fighting with Rockers.

The ending of the film takes quite a different course from the novel. Greene rewrote Terrence Rattigan's happy ending, putting a scratch on the record that prevents Rose from hearing the awful message of hate from Pinkie. Greene saw it as a compromise, but a clever one: 'Anybody who wanted a happy ending would feel that they had had a happy ending', adding 'Anybody who had any sense would know that, the next time, Rose would probably push the needle over the scratch and get the full message.'

BRIGHTON STRANGLER, THE
Film, 1945
Synopsis
A prominent West End actor has been starring in a play about a maniacal strangler. When the theatre is bombed during the Blitz, he suffers a head injury. On waking, he is an amnesiac and begins wandering the London streets in a daze. Finding himself at Victoria

station, he overhears a chance remark from a stranger that is identical to one from the play. Now convinced that he really is a strangler, he takes a train to Brighton, where he begins re-enacting his stage role by embarking on a series of strangulation murders. The police are soon on his trail – but pay a price. Inspector Allison is murdered at his home in 'Rottingdean Way'. The same fate befalls the town's 'Lord Mayor', killed outside his home in Hove Terrace.

At great personal risk, the killer's lady love attempts to save the actor from himself.

Details and comments

The film was made by RKO in the USA from an original screenplay by Arnold Phillips and Max Nosseck, the director. Reginald Parker, the actor, was played by John Loder and the love interest was provided by June Duprez as April Carson.

With a running time of just 67 minutes, the production is tautly-paced and has been described as a 'neat little chiller'. Yet in terms of realism – particularly in the depiction of Brighton – it is a flawed work. The town is the Hollywood version, an attempted simulation on standard studio sets. 'Clearly,' remarks Chibnall in *Brighton Rock*, 'neither Max Nosseck nor his art director Albert D'Agostino had ever been to the town or bothered to research its distinctive appearance.' An internet observer writes that there are not even any library shots to set the scene in Brighton.

The unlucky Inspector Allison was attached to the 'Sussex Constabulary, Brighton Division', yet this is shown as being responsible to Scotland Yard.

Just two years after *The Brighton Strangler*, Ronald Colman won an Oscar for Best Actor in *A Double Life* by portraying an actor who becomes obsessed with the role of Othello he is playing – an obsession which turns into violence and insanity. The dramatic device of the actor becoming a murderer whenever one of the lines from his play is inadvertently recited was later used to greater effect than in *The Brighton Strangler* in Richard Condon's *The Manchurian Candidate* (filmed 1962).

The Brighton Strangler was shown on BBC2 on 6 January 2006. A reviewer awarded this 'odd, eerie little thriller' three stars.

BURGLARY

Burglary, formerly a capital offence, is committed by any person who enters a building or part of a building, as a trespasser with the intent to steal, inflict grievous bodily harm, rape, or commit criminal damage.

A father/daughter partnership, 1807

Harsh sentences were handed down in the early years. A father/daughter partnership was one of the more unusual cases to come before the courts. The daughter, Mary Tree, was apprehended on the strong suspicion of having, on the night of 29/30 January 1807, entered the dwelling house and shop of one Edward Jenkins of Castle Square and stolen two ladies' hats and ribbons, with a silk band and tassel for a lady's hat. She was taken to Lewes to appear before the Magistrates and committed to the House of Correction for further examination. On the same day that Thomas Pope was taken before the Lewes Magistrate on a RAPE charge, 10 February 1807, Mary Tree's father, Cephas, was committed from Lewes to Horsham for trial charged with being concerned in the burglary committed by his daughter. The Trees were among the 11 prisoners given the death sentence at the trials, although Mary and eight others were reprieved before the judges left town. That left Cephas Tree and another facing the gallows. It was, however, reported in the *Sussex Weekly Advertiser, or Lewes and Brighthelmston Journal* of 23 March 1807 that Tree had, a couple of days earlier, 'received a respite during His Majesty's pleasure'.

Cases from 1837

One night in February 1837, forcible entry was made into the slaughterhouse of George Matthews, butcher, of Church Street, the prize being the hind quarters of a sheep. In September of that year, rich pickings were obtained from two of the town's squares. Thieves obtained easy access to a house in Norfolk Square during the absence of the owner, Mr Hannam. Their haul included a large mahogany writing desk, a promissory note for £15, a large gold seal in the shape of a greyhound, two plain gold guard rings, and two dress coats. They apparently overlooked several valuable cloaks in the passage. In the second incident, in Bedford Square, a horse was actually stolen from the night cart of one Stanford while the house was occupied.

A warning to the public, 1851

The local press warned its readers on 1 February 1851 of a new system of burglary which had sprung up in Brighton. Thieves were making use of adjoining newly-finished uninhabited houses. On the evening of 31 January, access was gained by this method to the dwelling of one Henry Smithers at 6 Upper Brunswick Place. The thieves had to pass over the tops of three or four houses to get into the upper apartments of Smithers' house, from which they carried off a quantity of clothing and a brooch.

Some recent cases

- In the summer of 1998, Brighton police were hunting a tiptoe burglar nicknamed 'The Creeper' who sneaked into bedrooms and even spoke to his victims. One woman thought it was her son creeping into her bedroom in the middle of the night at her home in Rugby Road. When asked if it was him, the thief replied: 'Yes, just wanted to borrow your watch. Sorry to disturb you.' The thief stole the watch and £80 from the clothes of the woman's boyfriend.

- An area of mainly flats and bedsits between Brighton's Royal Alexandra children's hospital and the railway station was in early 1999 dubbed 'Burglary City'. A total of 43 burglaries had taken place in three months.

- A Brighton man whose home was burgled complained to detectives in November 1999 that his money had been stolen. But he added that his stash of cannabis had also been taken from the flat near Western Road. The man was soon 'helping police with their inquiries'.

- It was reported in August 2000 that burglaries and car crimes had been slashed in Brighton after a new crackdown. House break-ins were down by nearly a third, with the average weekly burglary toll being cut from 36 to 23.

BURT, WILLIAM – see also INFANTICIDE

Shortly before Christmas 1825, journeyman shoemaker William Burt assaulted his young wife, Harriet, at his mother-in-law's house, 13 Woburn Place, in the Carlton Hill district of Brighton. The couple had only been married five months and had been living in Kingston-upon-Thames since their wedding.

Harriet's mother, Ann Young, witnessed the incident on her return home. Her pregnant daughter was covered in blood and thereafter never lived with her husband. She stayed at her mother's until the birth, at the end of May, of her son, Isaac. Some weeks later, mother and baby transferred to Ditchling poor-house, returning to Woburn Place on the evening of Sunday, 20 August, at her mother's invitation. But her husband was on her trail, determined that she should share his life.

On the following Tuesday afternoon, Mrs Young was urgently summoned home from her work at the *Gloucester Hotel*. When she got back, the door was locked. She found her daughter at the house of a Mrs Isted, a neighbour. Harriet was covered in blood and it was clear that little Isaac was dying from injuries. Both had been attacked by William Burt.

The dreadful crime, usually dubbed the 'Carlton Hill Murder', had not in fact taken place at Mrs Young's in Woburn Place as might be expected but in nearby William Street. Mother and infant had gone in the morning to No. 32, the house of one Ann Loveridge, who had known Harriet for nearly a year. Following this visit, she returned in the afternoon but had been shadowed by Burt. He forced his way in and brutally attacked his wife and child in an upstairs room to which they had fled in terror.

Mrs Loveridge summoned help from a neighbour who, together with another, held Burt until the officers of justice arrived. Justifying his dreadful actions to his wife's friend, he said 'it is better for me to be hanged for her than that I should live such a miserable life as I do, because she will not live with me.'

Later, the injured Harriet told visiting members of the Coroner's jury what exactly had happened. He had stabbed her and the child in turn, plunging his shoemaker's knife several times into various parts of the infant's body. The stab to the abdomen had

William Street, which has today changed beyond recognition. Chris Horlock collection

been so ferocious that his intestines protruded. Isaac soon died from his injuries. Harriet suffered three wounds to the head and one on her right breast. Three of her teeth had been knocked out.

Following the inquest held on the day after the crime at the *George the Fourth* public house, a verdict of wilful murder was returned against William Burt. The next morning, he was conveyed to the county gaol at Horsham until the Winter Assizes, due to be held in Lewes in early January 1827.

He pleaded Not Guilty in the three-hour trial, scornfully dismissing Ann Loveridge's testimony. By law, Harriet could not be examined. In his defence, the prisoner produced two letters, one he had addressed to the judge and the other to the King, both of which were read out at the author's request. They were essentially an earnest appeal for mercy, pleading the unkind and indifferent conduct of his wife towards him in extenuation of his offence. During the readings, his eyes were frequently filled with tears.

These did not help him. The jury retired shortly before noon and after a few minutes' deliberation returned a Guilty verdict. Burt begged his wife to visit him before he died. Not only did she do so, but she forgave him for his actions.

A repentant William Burt was executed on Monday, 8 January 1827, before a crowd numbering nearly a thousand, a great number of them females. These, observed the *Herald*, were 'chiefly of the lowest class'. His body was used for dissection.

C

CAIRNS, ROBERT

Robert Cairns and his friend, Paul Maynard, stood trial in March 1998 for the murder of 19-year-old Justin Hayward at Duke's Mound two years earlier. Cairns was convicted of the killing and given a life sentence while Maynard was convicted of the less serious charge of causing grievous bodily harm and jailed for three and a half years. During the trial both men blamed each other for the killing. Hayward, from Copthorne, near Crawley, who had been treated for leukemia, was stabbed 40 times in the throat, neck and eyes during a frenzied attack following a row about the sharing of alcohol. His body was found by a passer-by on the day of the murder, 19 October 1996. He had been punched and kicked while on the ground as well as being stabbed.

Cairns' conviction was, however, later quashed by the Court of Appeal and a re-trial was ordered so that new forensic evidence could be presented. On the second day of the proceedings, the jury heard new DNA tests were carried out in 2000 on the waistband and pockets of the jeans, which were found in Maynard's room at the *Royal Promenade Hotel* in Percival Terrace, Brighton, where all three men were staying. Although there was no scientific evidence to connect Cairns with the jeans, the results showed they could have been worn by Maynard. A Swiss Army type knife, which had been washed, was later found in Maynard's room.

In December 2000, the jury, by a 10:2 majority, found Cairns guilty for the second time of the brutal murder and his life sentence was reinstated.

CAPITAL PUNISHMENT

In the 28-year period 1809–37, 2,338 people were hanged, of whom just 95 were women. The average number of executions was thus 83–84 per year with a peak of 219 in 1801.

A petition from Brighton was sent to the House of Commons in 1830 against the death penalty for crimes against property, which was deemed 'abhorrent to the feelings of humanity'.

In 1861, the Criminal Law Consolidation Act reduced the number of capital crimes to four: Murder, High Treason, Piracy and Arson in a Royal Dockyard (the latter ceased to be a capital offence, in fact any specific offence, in 1971).

In December 1969, Parliament confirmed the abolition of capital punishment for murder. In 1994, the last vote on the reintroduction of the death penalty was defeated by 403 votes to 159. On 31 July 1998, the Criminal Justice Bill removed high treason and piracy with violence as capital crimes, thus effectively ending capital punishment.

CARDING – see also PROSTITUTION

The practice of placing prostitutes' cards in phone boxes, once rife in Brighton and Hove. The boom began in the 1980s when a loophole in the law meant it was not technically illegal to advertise in phone booths. In 1999, more than 100,000 cards were removed by BT in boxes in the two towns.

As late as February 2005, the company was reporting that carding was a problem in Brighton and Hove (and Norwich) – this despite the fact that the widespread use of mobile phones has meant the virtual demise of the public call box.

CARLTON HILL MURDER, see BURT, WILLIAM

CHANDLER, GLENN (1949–)

> *Detective Inspector Steve Madden had an adage. Murders were usually what they seemed. This one didn't seem like anything. The phrase 'sex murder' always gave him pause for thought. Sex was a beautiful thing, or should be. Murder was not. In any form, it was a despicable act. That the two could be lumped together always scared him.*
>
> *(Savage Tide,* published in 2003)

Edinburgh-born playwright, screenwriter and novelist, Chandler began writing for the stage but became a television scriptwriter in the late 1970s. Although he worked on such memorable programmes as *Angels* and *Crown Court*, he is best known as the creator and writer of *Taggart*, now the longest-running detective series on British television.

In 2003, Chandler turned his attention away from the mean streets of Glasgow and penned *Savage Tide*, a highly-acclaimed thriller set around the Brighton gay scene. The hero is Detective Inspector Steve Madden and, unusually, in this first excursion for the Brighton cop, the victim is his own son, whom Madden discovers was working as a male escort. Madden's own guilt over his relationship with his son, and with his estranged wife, compounds the investigation.

Madden's second outing (2004) was in the follow-up novel *Dead Sight*, which delved even further into the bohemian side of Brighton, encompassing clairvoyants, witches, new age folk and a visit to the bonfire celebrations in Lewes. Madden's personal life is integral to both novels.

The *Daily Record* said of *Savage Tide* 'Quite simply, this book rocks' and *Dead Sight* was similarly described as a 'cracker'. It is hoped that a film or television series will follow.

Chandler, who now lives in Hertfordshire, spends much time in Brighton and got the idea while sitting on the beach eating fish and chips, watching a man in a crumpled suit and with a troubled expression pacing the sea-shore.

CHILD ABUSE – see KEPPLE, WILLIAM

CHILD SUPPORT – see also AFFILIATION
The fertile doctor
In an (undated) case recorded by H Wojtczak in *Women of Victorian Sussex*, we learn that no fewer than seven different summonses for child support were taken out by one Louisa Jane Hawkes against Thomas Stowell, a doctor practising in Church Street – one summons for each of the illegitimate children he had fathered by her. The doctor's defence counsel agreed to an order being made by the magistrates in the case, described by the prosecuting counsel (Mr Lamb) at the outset of the proceedings as one of the worst he had heard.

Little more than children, 1886
In February 1886, Harry Thomas, aged 19, of 59 Albion Hill, was summoned by Ada Elizabeth Phillips, who was only 17, of 58 Albion Hill, to show cause why he should not contribute towards the support of her illegitimate child, who had had to be born in the Workhouse on 4 January. The magistrate said the case was 'a shocking and melancholy state of things' and that the defendant (who did admit paternity) deserved the greatest punishment that could be inflicted. He ordered him to pay 2s 6d a week until the child was 13.

CLIFFORD, PERCY – see HOTELS AND BOARDING HOUSES

COLWELL, MARIA – see KEPPLE, WILLIAM

CONTRACT KILLING
The murder of Barbara Gaul, 1976

> *I went straight up to her and fired a shot. She half turned towards me with her hands raised and said 'Oh, oh, oh'. I thought I had missed* [and] *fired a second shot. I intended to hurt her in the left leg only.* (Roy Edgeler)

Millionaire London property dealer, (Alfred) John Gaul, 65, got away with murder. The much-married entrepreneur counted the Rainiers of Monaco among his friends and entertained them and other celebrities at Buchanan Park, a 264-acre estate in Sussex whose squire he became. He had, however, attracted police attention in October 1962, when he had been fined £25,000 for living off prostitution. He had been leasing flats to prostitutes for £20 a week, although only £8 8s was entered in the rent book.

His marriage to his 34-year-old fourth wife, Barbara Harriet Gaul, a former Mayfair model, was already over by the time she made her fateful visit to Brighton. She was shot at close range in the car park of the *Black Lion Hotel*, Patcham, on 12 January 1976 as she stepped out of her blue Fiat 126. She died in hospital from the injuries to her left arm, chest and stomach just over 10 weeks later, on 26 March – but not before she had whispered to detectives her belief that her husband was behind the shooting. It may have been a 'love grudge', as *The Argus* surmised, or Gaul may have feared his wife was about to disclose business secrets which could harm him.

Mrs Gaul – former model Barbara Peart – of Trimingham, Norfolk had come to Brighton to see her 3-year-old daughter, Samantha, who lived with relatives in the town. Her husband had known of her planned visit. The couple had been separated for more than two years and John Gaul considerately chose to sue Barbara for divorce when she had been in hospital 10 days.

On 4 March, seven London men and a mother of six children were committed for trial at Lewes Crown Court by magistrates at Brighton. Two of the accused were held to have played a key part in the attack: Roy Albert Edgeler, 49, a driver, of Clapton, East London, and his brother Keith Henry Edgeler, 34, unemployed, of Waltham Abbey, Essex. A third brother, Carl Edgeler, 28, an electrician, of Dalston, London, was accused of helping Keith in disposing

Barbara Gaul in her modelling heyday.
The Argus

of a Ford Cortina estate car on the day after the shooting with intent to impede his apprehension or prosecution. Also implicated in the crime was Roy Edgeler's son, Michael.

Lewes Crown Court heard that Roy Edgeler had accepted a £5,000 contract to shoot Barbara Gaul but there was no evidence that John Gaul had arranged it. Roy and his brother Keith, both denied murder and having a sawn-off shotgun to commit an indictable offence. The prosecution alleged that Roy did the shooting and his brother drove the escape car. Roy would not name his 'employer', whom he had met in a pub, but said it was not John Gaul. He had no money after coming out of prison in August the previous year and was offered the chance to earn some by 'a right villain'. He had not known it would involve shooting and feared for his own life if he failed to see the contract through. He expressed deep remorse for his actions. Yet stronger, rather than weaker, cartridges had been used in the 12-bore weapon and both barrels had been fired. The defence conceded that the shots had been fired but with the intention only of causing serious injury. The attackers had trailed their intended victim for more than 300 miles until the opportunity arose to shoot her.

Keith Edgeler said he had not known the woman's name until he had read it in a newspaper or even that his brother had a gun. Nor had he known who had put up the money or why, but Roy had told him his share would be £2,500. Six other prisoners denied conspiring to obstruct the course of justice.

Roy Edgeler changed his plea to guilty of shooting and admitted two shotgun offences. Keith admitted driving the getaway car but continued to deny knowing what his brother was going to do. The brothers were sentenced to life imprisonment and both were given concurrent 13-year sentences relating to the possession of a shotgun. Mr Justice Wien recommended Roy should serve 20 years before being considered for parole.

He told Det. Supt Maurice De'Ath, Head of Brighton area CID, who had been in charge of inquiries, 'This was brilliant police work conducted by dedicated officers.' The case was not closed, however, as Sussex Police wished to further question John Gaul, who

had fled abroad just hours before Sussex police issued a warrant for his arrest in connection with the murder. It would emerge that he had tried to kill Barbara once before by throwing her off a yacht; that his second wife Anne warned Barbara he intended to harm her; and that the Soho club-owner Vince Chercuti claimed he was offered £12,000 to do the shooting – by a man who looked like Gaul. Businessman Rory Keegan, a childhood friend of Gaul's son Simon, made a seven-page statement shortly after the murder in which he claimed that Gaul broke down and confessed to him, when they met at a Rio hotel, that he had arranged the killing. For years Keegan lived in fear of reprisals if he repeated his allegations in court.

John Gaul fled England and justice for the Mediterranean. Mirrorpix

John Gaul had fled the country taking with him 21-year-old Angela Pilch, the family's nanny. The pair seemed to vanish from the face of the earth. Despite numerous apparent sightings and a massive worldwide police manhunt, it was more than two years before anything was heard of him. In 1978, he suddenly surfaced in Malta. He had married Angela, they had a son, Xavier, and were living on board Gaul's £80,000 yacht *Lotus Eater* in Valletta harbour. For the next six years the British police tried unsuccessfully to have him extradited to face murder charges in England, but his investments in Malta were considerable. Not only did he have a £40,000 hilltop villa, complete with swimming pool, at Madliena, five miles from Valletta, but he had built a 240-room holiday hotel which he leased to a local operator. In the end the Maltese managed to veto every extradition request.

The case against John Gaul collapsed dramatically in 1984 when Keegan suddenly changed his evidence. Eventually he signed an affidavit altering his statement substantially. Gaul immediately applied to be allowed back in to Britain without facing arrest so that he could be treated for a heart condition. The Director of Public Prosecutions ordered the arrest warrant to be withdrawn and dropped the case on the grounds that witnesses could not be relied upon to remember accurately events that had happened eight years before.

John Gaul was free to return to Britain safe in the knowledge that a jury would never hear the incriminating evidence against him.

After that, the tycoon lived a quiet life travelling between his homes in Switzerland and Malta. But there was a bizarre twist when he died five years later at the age of 76. He was flying from Zurich to Malta when he had a heart attack. The plane diverted to Milan, where he was rushed to hospital in a critical state and died a few hours later. Nobody knew who he was and, despite attempts to contact next of kin, his body lay for a time in the mortuary unclaimed. When he did not show up in Malta he was posted as a missing person, and it was more than three days before his family tracked him down.

CORPORAL PUNISHMENT
Whipping
The whipping of women was absolutely prohibited in 1820 by the Whipping of Female Offenders Abolition Act. There were, however, numerous statutes authorising the imposition of a sentence of whipping on male offenders, namely adults who were incorrigible rogues (Vagrancy Act 1824), who discharged firearms, etc., with intent to injure or alarm the sovereign (Treason Act 1842), who were guilty of robbery with violence (Larceny Act 1861), or offences against 21 of the Offences Against the Person Act of 1861. The Garrotters Act of 1861 authorised the ordering of more than one whipping in the case of an offender over 16 years of age. In the case of males under 16, the penalty was authorised in any of the above cases and for many statutory offences, such as larceny and malicious damage. If a boy was over seven and under 12, not more than six strokes could be inflicted, while if he was over 12, but under 14, not more than 12. The birch-rod was to be used and the punishment administered by a police constable in the presence of a superior officer, and of the parent or guardian if he desired it.

Early local cases
The *Sussex Weekly Advertiser* reported that on 20 January 1800 in Brighton, William Newnum, a boy, was convicted of stealing a silk handkerchief and a swan's skin waistcoat, the property of John Hutchins, and ordered to be re-committed for 14 days then to

be publicly whipped and discharged. Elizabeth Taylor was found guilty of stealing three silver teaspoons, the property of Mr Henwood of the *New Inn*, Brighton. She was ordered to be re-committed for six months and to be once privately whipped. Joseph Pullen, tried for stealing two bundles of coals belonging to Mr Gregory of Brighton, was found guilty and sentenced to six months' imprisonment and to be publicly whipped on a market-day in the town.

Members of the MILITIA were, of course, flogged by their own kind. In March 1812, three Privates attached to the 89th Regiment stationed in Brighton were flogged at the Barrack Yard in Church Street. One received 200 lashes and the others 150 each.

Bishop notes that a cruel statute from the time of James I, whereby a beggar was to be 'stripped naked, from the middle upwards, and to be whipped until his body was bloody, and to be sent from parish to parish, the next straight way to the place of his birth', was being applied in Brighton as late as July 1819, when, as reported in the *Brighton Herald*, judicial business began with three vagrants being brought up and ordered, by the sitting Magistrates, 'to be flogged until their backs were bloody'. The sentence was duly carried out the following day but 'the flagellation was comparatively light' due to the Beadle's inexperience in inflicting such a punishment. In the same year, Sarah Beatie was imprisoned and whipped for stealing before being transported.

Mercer records that whipping continued to be a fairly common punishment in the 1820s, but only in the case of males. James Best was privately whipped for stealing, while James Catling was publicly whipped in 1820 for the theft of a tea caddy. Two years later Thomas Clarke was given nine months' hard labour and three private whippings for stealing a pencil case worth 2d and silver worth 6d. Sir David Scott, who handed out this savage sentence, had only qualified as a magistrate the year before. Edward Chapman was given four months' hard labour for theft in 1823 and five years later a further three months and a private whipping for 'leaving his family'. For stealing a chair valued at 3s in 1827, James Coates was given hard labour and a public whipping in the Market Place. Magistrates Scott and (Samuel) Milford (see VAGRANCY) were the greatest advocates of the use of the whip in Brighton.

Birching

The Royal Navy introduced birching for its boy seamen (following the use of a junior version of the cat-o'-nine-tails) in the 1860s – a short time before some schools started abandoning it. The last birching of boys in the Navy was in 1936, although as a general day-to-day punishment it had been replaced by the cane in 1906. In schools, it took a long time for the birch to disappear altogether. Eton College is thought to have last used it in 1963.

In reformatory schools (later known as 'Approved Schools'), the changeover to the cane or tawse was completed by the mid-1920s. Birching as a judicial punishment for young offenders in Britain was abolished in 1947. The last prison birching was in 1962.

The *Brighton Gazette* of 19 December 1925 revealed the severe physical punishment still being meted out to violent offenders. An armed robber was sentenced to receive 25 lashes of the cat-o'-nine-tails and five years' imprisonment for armed robbery in Brighton.

A July 1964 survey among 300 students of Brighton Technical College showed 54% in favour of flogging for sex crimes.

COUNTERFEITING – see also FORGERY

This type of crime was relatively rare in Brighton. An early case was that of John Fuller (see PILLORY) in 1811. Mercer notes he was fined for fraud in that year.

In the following year, a case for counterfeiting and uttering was brought against Catherine Smith, whom Magistrate Harrison sent to Horsham Gaol for 12 months.

In the period between 1812 and 1836, according to the Quarter Session report, seventeen offenders were heard before the Bench for counterfeiting or coin uttering. JOHN HOLLOWAY engaged in it, but no record has been found of him being brought to book for the offence.

Sir David Scott sent Matthew Taylor, a gardener, to prison for six months and four weeks' solitary confinement in 1835 for passing a half-crown coin.

Counterfeiting was often the work of small gangs. Four years later, for example, *The Herald* reported on five persons being summoned for uttering forged banknotes.

In 1843, Edmund Sayers, a fishmonger, received a 12-month sentence, while one of 18 months was imposed in the following decade (1851) on Hugh Saunders.

COURTS – see also JURIES, MAGISTRATES

Magistrates' Court

Petty offenders were for centuries dealt with by the Hundred Courts. In the case of Brighton, this was the Court of Whalesbone. This came to be replaced by the Bench at Lewes and it was under the aegis of the County Bench that Brighton's first magistrates' court was established.

The *New Inn* in North Street (later the *Clarence Hotel* and now the *Royal Pavilion Tavern*) was in 1808 the first place in which a local magistrate's sitting was held. The magistrate was in attendance every Monday, Wednesday and Friday, from noon till one o'clock or until the business was finished. Should a second magistrate be required, his attendance, stated the clerks' announcement, 'will be procured, *if possible*' (author's italics).

The first Petty Sessions at the *Old Ship* were held in September 1812, with Mr Serjeant Runnington (see also UNREST, CIVIL) as Chairman.

Brighton petty sessional records start in 1816, at which time they were regarded as being private papers. An analysis of the Petty Sessions Minute Books 1816–30 provides a fascinating snapshot of criminal life in the town.

The sessions were transferred for a short time to what Bishop describes as the 'miserable' old TOWN HALL, twice a week, Mondays and Thursdays, before moving back, six years later, to the *Old Ship*.

The *New Inn* was again used in 1823. Almost the last court held there was on 4 March of that year, when there was a special sitting to enquire into the mysterious death of one Williams of Brighton, whose mutilated body had been washed ashore between Rottingdean and Newhaven. The verdict of 'Accidentally Drowned' returned at the inquest at the former place was deemed unsatisfactory, foul play being suspected. Despite the offer of a reward of 200 guineas for information leading to the murderer(s), and Peel, the Home Secretary, promising a free government pardon to one accomplice, no further light was ever shed on the crime.

The sessions then remained at the *Old Ship* until around 1832, when the new TOWN HALL in Bartholomews accommodated them.

In January 1854 the first borough bench of magistrates sat with the mayor as chief magistrate.

The Old Ship – *a pleasant venue for judicial proceedings.* Author's collection

Quarter Sessions

Two months later, on 26 March, Borough Quarter Sessions commenced. These were periodic courts held in each county and county borough in England and Wales. When the Bench was displaced during the reconstruction of the Town Hall in 1897–9, it sat in the public library building.

Criminal cases heard at the Quarter Sessions covered very nearly every felony possible but did not have jurisdiction to hear the most serious crimes, most notably those which could be punished by capital punishment or, later, life imprisonment. These crimes were sent for trial at the periodic Assizes. The Quarter Sessions also had some limited civil jurisdiction, and until 1888 also had an important administrative function in their respective counties.

Mercer estimates that between 1810 and 1839, there were around 3,000 cases involving felons from Brighton, some of whom were transported for less serious crimes than those for which short custodial sentences were given. According to Davey, the vast majority of cases heard at the Quarter Sessions – say 98% from 1830 onwards – were concerned with larceny. This was often of very minor items, such as that by Charles Clarke in 1835 for stealing pickles, for which Sir David Scott gave him a 14-year TRANSPORTATION sentence.

The Courts of Quarter Sessions were held until 1972 when, together with the Assize courts, they were abolished by the Courts Act 1971 and replaced by a single permanent Crown Court of England and Wales.

Assizes

The Assizes, or Courts of Assize, were criminal courts held periodically around England and Wales. They heard the most serious cases, which were committed to them by the Quarter Sessions.

In Sussex, they were held at East Grinstead, Horsham, Chichester and Lewes. East Grinstead ceased to be an assize town in 1799. From 1830, the Spring Assizes held at Horsham were moved to Lewes for good.

County Court

A county court joined the petty sessions at Brighton Town Hall in 1847 but by 1850 was at 151 North Street, whence it removed to Prince's Street. It was intended to provide a means of recovering small debts and to give, in a limited number of cases, similar remedies to those obtained in a High Court.

On the Prince's Street site, a large red-brick building was built in 1894 as the Brighton Parochial Offices for the Board of Guardians and Registrar. Following the dissolution of the Guardians in 1930, the offices were taken over by the Council's Public Assistance Committee. They were occupied from 1974 by the county's social services department. In 1986–89, they were used temporarily as a magistrates' court while the Edward Street building (see below) was being refurbished. In 1994, the empty premises were taken over by squatters (see SQUATTING) from the 'Justice?' collective. Today, the building, whose existence as a courthouse was admittedly brief, is made up of six apartments.

Brighton's new county court building, of red brick with stone dressings and a royal coat of arms over the western entrance and containing two court rooms, was opened in 1869 at the bottom of Church Street, taking over from the original Prince's Street building. It was used for nearly a century (until 1967), when it became a library store. Today the Old Court House, as it is called, contains offices connected with Brighton Museum.

As you enter the building, the Registry would have been on the right hand side, and forward of that, the Judge's room and the High Bailiff's Office. On the left hand side was the Public Entrance and Public Office. The corridor led forward to the Court Room, dominated by the Judge's throne. It is being converted into a lecture room at the time of writing. Also on the ground floor was the Female Waiting Room and the Public Waiting Room. Upstairs was the Office Keeper's bedroom and living room and additional sleeping accommodation. The building retains its slate roof.

Today's County Courts nationally deal with civil cases, most of which involve debt, personal injury claims, the possession of land or housing or disputes over contracts. They additionally handle family issues, such as divorce or adoption, and insolvency.

Today's Courts

Brighton's modern court complex, in Edward Street and John Street, was opened by the Lord Chancellor, Lord Gardiner, on 3 November 1967. It was designed by Percy Billington and cost £665,000. It comprised juvenile, magistrate, coroner, county and quarter session (later crown) courts. An extension to the high court and county court was opened in William Street on 23 October 1985 by senior circuit judge Granville Wingate.

The complex was refurbished between 1986 and 1989 and it was formally reopened by the Chief Justice, Lord Lane, on 27 April 1989. The new facilities included eight Magistrates' Courts and three Crown Courts. Today, the number of Magistrates' Courts remains unchanged but there are two Crown Courts.

Nowadays, 95% of cases nationally are completed in Magistrates' Courts, a branch of which is the Youth Court, where specially-trained magistrates hear cases. Members of the press and members of the public with some connection to the case can be allowed into the court with the magistrates' permission.

The ornate archway of the former bastion of justice. The author

Crown Courts are for more serious offences, such as rape, murder or burglary. The term is a misnomer, since strictly there is only one Crown Court, which sits in about 90 centres throughout England and Wales.

A well-attended Open Day was held at Brighton Law Courts on 11 March 2006.

The old County Court on the north side of Church Street. The author

COURTS-MARTIAL

In the wake of the Hunt EMBEZZLEMENT case of 1800, Lieutenant-Colonel Dacre of that regiment was court-martialled. He stood charged of conduct unbecoming an officer and gentleman and was acquitted. He was, however, found guilty of other charges relating to the misapplication of moneys received for the payment of his troop and was dismissed from His Majesty's service. The court, however, having regard to the confused state of the Lieutenant-Colonel's accounts caused by Hunt absconding, recommended the King to reinstate him, but this he refused to do because of a number of frivolous charges preferred by Dacre against one Colonel Everett of the same corps, who had recently been tried by a General Court-Martial at Chelsea College and honourably acquitted.

The Castle Tavern. JG Bishop. Author's collection

On 11 July 1810, a court martial held at the *Castle Tavern* on Corporal Robert Curtis of the Oxford Militia found him guilty of endeavouring to excite disaffection amongst his regiment, and he was condemned to receive 1,000 lashes. He bore 200 of them; the remainder were remitted.

The Reynolds case, 1840

In the summer of 1840 the 11th (Prince Albert's own) Hussars were stationed in Brighton as a guard for the Royal Pavilion, under the command of the notorious James Thomas Brudenell, 7th Earl of Cardigan. Pilloried by his critics as one of the arch-villains of Victorian England, his private life was a public scandal. He was even tried for intent to murder by the House of Lords.

While the troops settled in, some at Preston Barracks and others in Church Street, near the Pavilion itself, Cardigan and his aristocratic officers took up residence in the luxurious *Royal York Hotel*. Cardigan later leased the best available mansion in Brunswick Square, Hove, as a residence and there he held lavish parties for his friends and the local gentry.

At one such gathering, on 25 August, a fashionable guest, Mrs Cunynghame, enquired of her host why two young captains, both called Reynolds though not related, were not present. His gruff response was: 'As long as I live, they shall never enter my house.'

John Reynolds was in disgrace for simply bringing a black bottle (of Moselle) to the regimental mess 'which should be conducted like a gentleman's table, and not like a tavern or pot-house', while Richard Anthony Reynolds was a well-known opponent of Cardigan and openly contemptuous of officers who had served in India (as Cardigan's had), regarding them as lax in discipline and probably poor because they could not afford to exchange to another regiment.

When Cardigan's words at the party were relayed to Richard Reynolds, he wrote his commanding officer a letter in which he described the report as highly objectionable and 'calculated to convey an impression prejudicial to my character'. He therefore asked his lordship to be good enough to authorise him to contradict it. Cardigan took Reynolds aside the next day, telling him he had no reply to his letter, which he considered to be of 'an improper nature'. Reynolds protested but was shouted down.

Dissatisfied, the young officer wrote challenging the earl to a duel. Cardigan was in a dilemma: to refuse the challenge would be the action of a coward, but to fight would be a breach of military law and etiquette. He had Reynolds placed under arrest to await a general court-martial. This meant his removal from the *Royal York Hotel*, where most of the Earl's supporters lived, to *Edlin's Gloucester Hotel*.

The day set for the hearing, 25 September, was a field day for the press and Brighton society. Reynolds had a lot of backing from many quarters. He took his trial in a hospital ward at the cavalry barracks which was temporarily converted into a courtroom. A huge throng of journalists and sightseers pressed into the corridors and around the windows when Reynolds was charged with conduct 'unbecoming an Officer and a Gentleman, prejudicial to the interests of the Service, subversive of Good Order and Military Discipline'. Cardigan, as prosecutor, reportedly wept with rage against the imputation of cowardice against him in the second letter. Reynolds' defence was that Cardigan had provoked the challenge by ruling the regiment by arrogance and insult. The hearing was adjourned but the debates in the press raged on.

When the proceedings resumed on 1 October, there was pandemonium. An unexpectedly large and determined crowd besieged the courtroom. As it surged down the corridor, the door was torn off its hinges and the glazed panels either side of it were smashed. The room rang with applause and cheering lasting several minutes when Reynolds concluded his speech by saying: 'I hope by your verdict of "Not Guilty" you will prove to Lord Cardigan that wealth and rank do not license him, although the commanding officer of a regiment, to trample with impunity upon honourable men, who have devoted their lives to the service of our country.'

Cardigan denied provoking the anger of his officers and ever having said at his ball that the Captains Reynolds would never enter his house. Mrs Cunynghame, the sole witness, was (conveniently) away on the Continent.

There was national indignation when, on 20 October, it was announced that Reynolds had been in breach of 'The Articles of War' and was sentenced to be cashiered. Large and violent demonstrations were reportedly held against Cardigan, whose opponents extolled Reynolds as a hero. Public meetings were held in support of him, penny subscriptions were raised all over the country, and the papers were filled with letters championing his cause.

The campaign against the abuse of military power ended in the anti-climax of Reynolds publicly admitting that he had 'greviously offended' against army regulations by challenging Cardigan to a duel. There was, he felt, no justification for a subordinate 'breaking from the strict line of respectful submission'. After two years away from the limelight, he was gazetted a captain in the 9th Lancers in 1842.

Cardigan remained as unpopular as ever. This was strikingly manifested in Brighton when he appeared in a box at the Theatre Royal. For half-an-hour, hisses and groans held up the beginning of the performance. The earl impassively weathered the storm of insults, but finally withdrew, to the accompaniment of 'three cheers for Captain Reynolds' and 'three groans for the Earl of Cardigan'. In the Guy Fawkes celebrations that year, in place of the traditional guy, a dummy dressed in the Hussars' uniform was paraded through the streets.

Although controversy and scandal continued to follow Cardigan, he redeemed himself by twenty minutes of heroism in the Crimea when he led the Light Brigade in their futile charge against the Russian guns in 1854.

COWELL, WILLIAM

I went to see the body. I done it. I don't know what made me do it [. . .] I can't tell you how
I done it and I am not going to. I shall soon meet the Almighty. That's all I've got now.
(William Cowell, 1939)

Very early on the morning of Wednesday, 27 September 1939, a 25-year-old gamekeeper, William Hudson, came across a woman's body in a ditch, covered with brushwood and branches. The discovery was made in Shaves Wood, near Muddleswood, not far from Hurstpierpoint and some seven miles north of Brighton. The body was badly decomposed and there were indications that it had been dragged to the spot. The severe wounds to the skull and the attempt at concealment pointed to a clear case of murder. A letter in a nearby handbag immediately revealed the victim's identity. She was 33-year-old Annie Farrow Cook, who had been employed at the Red Cross Hospital for Officers at 3–5 Percival Terrace, Brighton.

Among the staff from whom statements were taken was 38-year-old William Charles Cowell, a night orderly at the hospital, whose wife and son lived in straitened circumstances in Tunbridge Wells. He had apparently made arrangements to meet Cook on the night she vanished. Some time after 7.30 pm on 22 August, he walked into Brighton police station and made a voluntary statement saying their rendezvous was at the central recreational area known as The Level. Annie seemed preoccupied and asked to borrow 15s to attend to a matter. She then went to the station to catch a train. When she did not return that night, the matron, after speaking to Cowell, contacted the police.

It was learned that in 1937 Cowell had lived in a cottage in Muddleswood – only a few hundred yards from the wood where the body had been found. He gave up his job at the

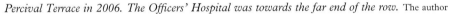

Percival Terrace in 2006. The Officers' Hospital was towards the far end of the row. The author

hospital and moved to 18 New Steine without telling the police, then to 1 Southover Street, where he was traced. Meanwhile, a butcher's roundsman from Hurstpierpoint reported he had actually seen Cowell at the edge of Shaves Wood shortly after midday on 22 August and positively identified him from a photograph.

More lies from Cowell to the police followed, then his startling admission of guilt. After several police court hearings, the last of them on 29 November during which an affectionate letter from him to Annie was read out, Cowell took his trial at Lewes on 6 March 1940. There it emerged that Annie had been a quiet girl and had for some time been a professional dancer with a touring company but had given this up when the 'Talkies' became popular. The cause of her death was a fracture to the skull. Cowell never explained why or how they had travelled to the woods in the first place but did admit in his statement that he had killed Annie by striking her with a large piece of wood after they had argued. He also described how he had visited the body each day from 22 to 26 August to make sure it was well hidden and undiscovered.

The jury took just 40 minutes to find Cowell guilty. Before sentence of death was passed, he said: 'All I can say is that I am not guilty.' Following an unsuccessful appeal, William Charles Cowell was hanged at Wandsworth on 24 April 1940.

CRIMINAL PETITIONS

The National Archives' class numbers HO17 (1819–39) and HO18 (1839–54) contain the original petitions of convicted criminals appealing against, or for a reduction in, their sentence, which might range from a few weeks' imprisonment to death. Although the amount of information provided is very variable, many petitions are very detailed. They were sent from every county in England and Wales, with a smaller number from Scotland and Ireland. An example of a case is that of Alexander Cole (see VAGRANCY).

CRUELTY TO ANIMALS

On the afternoon of 19 March 1800, some boys throwing stones from off the Eastern Cliff wantonly and maliciously killed a small dog belonging to a lady of the town. A reward of two guineas was put up to catch the culprits and was to be paid by Mr Donaldson at his Library on Marine Parade.

Young Henry Roxby was fined 10s and costs, or, in default of payment, ten days' imprisonment with hard labour, when he appeared before the Borough magistrates on 22 February 1866 for working a pony which was in an unfit state. The local officer of the Royal Society saw him the previous evening driving the animal, attached to a cart laden with linen, along King's Road. The pony was in a most miserable condition, quite worn out and unfit for any kind of work. It appeared to be completely paralysed on one side and was nothing but skin and bone. Roxby actually maintained – to the disbelief of the magistrates who had gone out to see the animal for themselves – 'I have always fed him well'.

On 8 June 1878, George Salvage, 18, was charged with being drunk and pulling off the head of a live duck, the property of Mark Hollingdale, keeper of the *West Hill Inn*, West Hill Street. He went to the house in question and asked to go into the back yard, where he was seen decapitating the young bird. He was charged with the offence, which he denied, and ran away. PC Blackman later apprehended him in Surrey Street, when he admitted his guilt. Magistrates ordered him to pay 1s 6d, the value of the duck, and 3s 6d costs or, in default, seven days' hard labour.

Before the same bench was 18-year-old Jesse Smith who was seen in Market Street by an officer of the RSPCA to be in charge of a horse attached to a wagon belonging to

Mr Pannett, florist, of Chailey. The animal, which had fallen lame at Cooksbridge on the way to Brighton, was much affected in the near foreleg and it was a great cruelty to work it in such a state. A fine of 10s and costs, or in default, 10 days' hard labour, was imposed – the same as in the Roxby case 12 years earlier.

CRUELTY TO CHILDREN – see also KEPPLE, WILLIAM

On 2 June 1938, and on various previous dates, RAF Leading Aircraftman Stanley Parrack appeared before the magistrates charged with assaulting and ill-treating his 7-year-old son, Dennis. He pleaded not guilty but was convicted. The penalty of £25 (or 3 months' imprisonment in default of payment) would have been far more severe had he not been given a good character by his Pilot Officer and in consideration of his wife and family.

Parrack, of Picton Street, was prosecuted on behalf of the NSPCC, whose representative alleged 'a continued course of deliberate and ruthless cruelty' and one specific act of 'almost inhuman barbarity' – namely placing the boy's hands in the fire. When at home on some weekends, Parrack beat his son unmercifully, resulting in a multiplicity of bruises all over his body. The lad appeared in a state of terror. An assistant teacher at Elm Grove School had reported marks on the boy to the head teacher. She found him very intelligent and quite well-behaved. A visiting inspector found his hands bound with rags and on examining them found they had been severely burned.

Dennis Parrack, who had been recovering in hospital, himself gave evidence to the Bench, standing on a chair.

On the following day, an angry crowd of well over 500 people were held back by a cordon of police outside Parrack's house, 11 Picton Street. The mob, who included long-standing neighbours (some of them ex-schoolfellows) gathered at 6 pm and shouted for him to come out. There was no reply. The crowd rattled the windows and doors but could not get in. They were infuriated by what they considered was a lenient sentence passed by Brighton Bench. The police, who had problems in clearing the growing crowd, denied knowing if their quarry was indoors or not. Some protesters thought he had escaped via a back passage and gone to where his wife had been staying since the court case.

D

DEFAULTING BANKERS

The case of the Brighthelmston Bank is not one of default but rather of neglect. William Wigney started as a draper in town, but by 1814 his business had evolved into the New Bank of Rickman, Wigney and Co in Steyne Lane. He died somewhat depleted of wealth, but his successor, Isaac Wigney (Member of Parliament for Brighton from 1842 to 1857), disregarded this fact, preferring the high life in London – to the bank's cost. Customers left and in March 1842, after losing the confidence of the town, the bank suspended all payments.

The Brighton Savings Bank was established in Duke Street, at the top of Middle Street, in 1817, with George Sawyer as Actuary. His successor, Richard Buckoll, became a defaulter, and absconded.

Some decades later, the same fate befell the Bank of Deposit. This had branches across the country and a head office in London's Pall Mall; for some years it enjoyed public

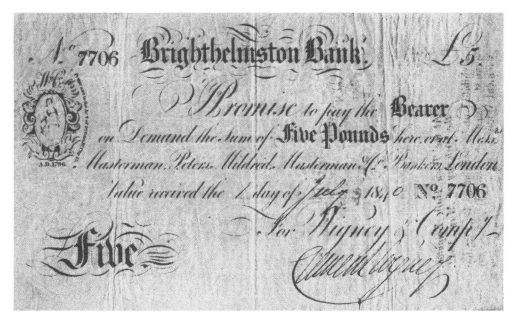

A £5 note of the Brighthelmston Bank. It is endorsed 'At the Town Hall, Brighton, the 1st day of May, 1842. Exhibited under a Fiat in Bankruptcy against Isaac Newton Wigney and Clement Wigney.'
Author's collection

confidence but in 1861, when Peter Morrison, the manager, became a defaulter and a bankrupt, and eventually absconded, many hundreds of depositors were irretrievably ruined.

The District Savings Bank, adjacent to the Odd Fellows' Hall in Queen's Road, closed abruptly in the same year after attracting some considerable notoriety and involving many small capitalists in financial difficulties.

Today's Alliance & Leicester Building Society began life in Brighton in 1863 as the Brighton and Sussex Equitable Permanent Building Society. In 1909, the secretary vanished with much of the Society's cash. Panic set in among the investors when the news leaked out. Battling against the heavy withdrawals, everyone did their bit: the new secretary agreed to a reduced salary and the landlord lowered the rent. The Society survived to go on to greater things.

DESERTION

In January 1837, the magistrates had before them one Weist from the 38th Regiment of Troopers and in September, William Wheeler of the Royal Marines. The *Patriot* reported that Wheeler had received the customary shilling and then said: 'Now I have got the shilling, I will give them the double, and they may catch me if they can.' Unfortunately for Wheeler, they did and he was 'delivered to the custody of the Recruiting Officer'.

Charles Stanford was on 31 May 1878 charged with being a deserter from the 107th Regiment. He had been taken into custody for committing an assault on a constable two years earlier. When Stanford was taken to the police station, it was found he was missing from his regiment without leave. He was detained until sent for.

DNA

DNA technology has made huge strides in crime detection possible. Cases whose solution seemed all but hopeless are now under a new spotlight – witness the LYON case, in which a DNA match might even yet identify the perpetrator(s).

Brian Cook, the head of the scientific support branch at Sussex Police, has described DNA profiling as vital to police investigations and the best thing to have happened to criminal investigations since fingerprints.

In October 1989, a 39-year-old American woman was woken and raped in her University of Sussex bedroom in Brighton. Two months later, a University of Kent student was raped and another indecently assaulted in similar circumstances. The attacker was finally identified through DNA technology as Paul Collings of Icklesham, near Hastings, who was 23 at the time. He was jailed for life in March 2006.

At the time of writing, almost 75,000 adults and 8,000 children – about one in 20 residents in Sussex – have their DNA records held by Sussex Police.

DOPING – see also RACECOURSE/RACES
The end of a gang, 1963

> *You are guilty of an extremely serious conspiracy, in that the amount of drugs which you alone supplied could have undermined the whole horse racing system of this country.*
> (Charles Doughty, Brighton Recorder, to Richard McGee)

An important part in uncovering the nationwide activities of an unscrupulous racehorse doping gang over the previous nine years was played by Brighton's police in 1962. The ring was shut down the following year.

While Brighton Racecourse was only one of the locations where the associates operated (others included Epsom, London, Newmarket and Newcastle), it was here that one of the key players, a 59-year-old from Surbiton named Edward Smith, was arrested. The two gang members who appeared with him before Brighton magistrates at the end of November 1962 were both Londoners – Richard McGee, 49, a tablet production manager, and Lipman Leonard Steward, 29 (known as 'Darky'), a stable boy turned salesman.

Ten other men, including two bookmakers, were implicated. An attractive 25-year-old blonde Swiss lady, Michele Lugeon, who was in reality employed as a domestic help, spied for the gang by visiting no less than 30 training establishments posing as a wealthy French racehorse owner looking for a suitable trainer to take over her horses. She would later be brought before Brighton magistrates.

During the court proceedings, a dramatic description was given of a 3 am raid by six gang members on stables at Newmarket on 1 April 1960. There, the filly *Treasure Hunt*, favourite for the Cannon Yard Plate race run at Windsor later the same day, was nobbled. A racing lad was given £50 to show where the animal was stabled, while two other men received £50 for their assistance.

It was McGee who supplied the drugs. The source was Winthrop Laboratories, initially when they were at West Mosley then later when they moved to Newcastle. Smith had also worked for the company at one time and was very friendly with McGee. The gang made their money up and down the country by doping horses which were favourites. By making them lose, they could lay odds against them winning.

Their activities came to light through the vigilance of Brighton police. DCI G Dunstan and DC Hovey went to the licensed bar at Brighton Racecourse where they saw Smith having a drink. Before being questioned outside, he was caught trying to conceal a bottle

of sodium amphetamine and brought in for questioning. He had it on him ready to hand over to one of the gang outside the *Metropole*. He feared the gang and now wanted to come clean. When Smith's home in Surbiton was searched, an arsenal (to use the prosecution's term) of doping products was discovered.

The whole case proved too much for the suspect. The day before he was due to appear at Brighton Quarter Sessions, Smith threw himself off the first-floor balcony at Lewes Prison, fracturing his skull, thigh and left wrist. For 45 days he lay in the Royal Sussex County Hospital. There, on 13 February 1963, he died.

Like Smith before him, McGee – admitting, 'I have made a mess of things' – came clean. A family man with four children, and no interest in racing, he pleaded guilty to stealing drugs from his employers. Sentencing him to two years' imprisonment, the Recorder said: 'You supplied the technical advice from your own professional knowledge.'

Steward denied being mixed up with horse doping, claiming, 'I would never have anything to do with horse doping. I love animals too much.' On the window sill of his flat, however, police found several books on racing, a ready reckoner and a copy of *Practical Animal Husbandry* which fell open where a corner of a page, describing how to give pills to horses, was turned down. Steward was in fact an expert on the theory and practice of administering dope. He testified that he had made £1,500 on one horse, *Faultless Speech*, in the William Hill Gold Cup race; and he had known a stable lad who had made £3,700 from one punter. Badly frightened and agitated in the dock because he feared reprisals against his family – and particularly his girlfriend – he refused to help the police bring the rest of the doping gang to justice. Charges against him of being an accessory after the fact and of stealing and receiving were withdrawn. He was, however, found guilty of conspiring with others to administer drugs to racehorses to affect their performance and of stealing a quantity of drugs and poisons to give them. He was sentenced to four years' corrective training.

Referring to the gang collectively, the Recorder remarked that 'if their activities were allowed to continue, it would not be worth anyone's while to own a racehorse, to train a racehorse or to ride a racehorse'. The aptly-named prosecution counsel at the Quarter Sessions, Mr Owen Stable, expressed strong views on the crime they were dealing with. 'Doping,' he declared, 'is still a very serious matter to trainers and could destroy the entire sport of racing in this country. It is the curse of racing.'

DORGAN, JOHN

John Joseph Dorgan was a decorated 46-year-old veteran of the First World War. Finally discharged in 1931, he obtained employment as a waiter, then a potman, at the *Arlington Hotel*, Marine Parade. But in July 1943 he lost his job. This meant he needed to raise money, and raise it fairly quickly. To do this he began selling possessions – mainly his wife's. They had married in 1927. Florence Elizabeth Agnes, 60, had been married before and had two grown-up children from that union, but none from her unhappy marriage with Dorgan. She had for the past five and a half years been employed as a cleaner at Barclays Bank. The couple shared a basement flat at 8a Madeira Place (now a guest house) with a man named Charlie Fife, a waiter and fire watcher at the *Old Ship Hotel*.

Dorgan was a drinking man and pubs were the natural place for him to sell personal and household effects. These included, on 29 July, a clock to an employee and a camp bed and a suitcase full of lady's clothing to the licensee's wife. She, however, became suspicious. The following day, Dorgan managed to sell off some more garments at the *Queen's Head*, near the Old Steine. That evening, with a suitcase of possessions, he went to *The Aquarium* inn in the same vicinity. He then went back to the *Queen's Head* round the corner, where he negotiated the sale of a wireless to a friend, Ernie Beazley. To be sure it was in working order, Beazley returned with Dorgan and another man to the flat to listen to it. Meanwhile, his stepdaughter, Beatrice Primrose Blaker of 72 Hollingdean Terrace, had called twice and found no one in. On returning, this time with her husband, words were exchanged, with Dorgan asking with feigned concern about his wife, who, he understood, had left earlier to walk to Beatrice's house. After going back to the pub for a while, Dorgan returned and told his still-waiting stepdaughter that he was going to bed, locking the door against the couple.

Very early the next morning, Dorgan went to the *Norfolk Arms*, and treated two Canadian soldiers to a few drinks. There he arranged for the potman to take a large barrow he owned round to Madeira Place to be loaded up with items he had sold and wanted delivered. These were duly dropped off to Beazley at the *Queen's Head* to be taken away in a taxi to his house in Hove. The drinking continued at the pub all morning through to late lunchtime, with Dorgan insisting on paying for rounds. Back at the flat, Charlie Fife had returned from work – and discovered Mrs Dorgan's body in a bundle under his bed. The police were immediately informed and the victim was eventually identified formally by her son, Sidney Ernest Pentecost, at the Royal Sussex County Hospital mortuary.

Dorgan was out visiting his favourite haunts, but the police caught up with him in Steine Street, where the taxi he was in had to stop because of an obstruction. Superintendent Pelling conducted him to a waiting police car and when seated in it, Dorgan said: 'I have done the old woman in. I have done it properly this time.'

The Aquarium *inn, which stands at the seaward end of Steine Street, was one of the public houses favoured by Dorgan.* The author

At the station the prisoner made a full written statement of his actions. He claimed that he and his wife had not been getting on well for quite some time. There were constant arguments about money and because of interference from her stepchildren. This had affected his health. He had in the past suffered from malaria and had been shot in the head on active service in the First World War, during which he had been classified as suffering from shell shock. The stress within the family only added to his problems. On the day Florence died, Dorgan had asked her to be quiet but she continued to nag him. He had grabbed her by the hair and the next thing he could remember was dragging her into the front room and pushing her body under the bed.

Dr LR Janes gave the cause of death as asphyxia due to strangulation by manual pressure and the tying of a necktie round the neck. He thought she had been strangled on the settee in the middle room of the flat. Her blood, belonging to the rare group AB, matched that found on the accused's trousers and shirt. Since his blood group was B, it linked him directly to the crime.

At the Sussex Assizes in Lewes in late November, it was not disputed that Dorgan had killed his wife but an attempt was made to show that he was insane at the time. It was claimed by a physician that the war veteran had been unstable ever since he had been a young man, an instability aggravated by his experiences in the trenches in France. The jury were not swayed, however. After a short deliberation, the prisoner was found guilty and sentenced to death. There was to be no appeal and no reprieve. On Wednesday, 22 December 1943, John Joseph Dorgan was hanged at Wandsworth.

DRINK/DRINKING – see also INNS AND PUBLIC HOUSES
Beer shops

The 1830 Sale of Beer Act was partly intended to reduce the public demand for gin, although the response from publicans was simply to open more gin palaces; hence the beer house, which fell outside magistrates' jurisdiction, came into being. Only two, from the multitude which opened, have survived: the *Regency Tavern* (originally *The Gate*), and the *Druid's Head*. Under the Act, anyone whose name was on the rate books could, from 2 October 1830, pay a two-guinea fee to the excise office and open their house as a beer shop and brew beer on the premises. Nor did the proprietors have to show proof of financial stability or good character. The Act set opening hours (5 am to 10 pm, apart from Sunday service times) and abolished beer duty. In the first week of October 1830 alone, 100 licences were granted.

Three years later, the Poor Law Commissioners for Sussex described beer shops as 'receiving houses for stolen goods, and frequently brothels'; they were thus 'most mischievous' because they 'allow of secret meetings' and were run by 'the lowest class of persons'. The prostitutes would often lodge with the landlady above the shop.

In *Brighton As It Is* (1860), 'a Graduate of the University of London' told how the poor, in their despair and squalor, turned to the shops for solace:

> *The houses of the poor in Brighton, which are situated in narrow streets and courts, are for the most part ill-ventilated, and badly drained, if at all. The numbers which are huddled together in them render decency and decorum next to impossible. Many of them being built with inferior bricks and mortar made of sea-sand are wretchedly damp so that even the walls are covered with lichens, and the miserable tenants, unable to endure the depression of spirits which is the necessary result, try to drown their uneasy sensations in the neighbouring beer shops.*

There were in fact as many as 479 liquor shops in that year compared with 541 provision shops in the whole of the town.

The author also described the effects of alcohol as observed in Church Street:

Go along there any night and you will see hideous old women, drunken old men, young men, and sometimes mere boys, hopelessly intoxicated, reeling and staggering in the road. There is also of course the usual amount of cursing and blaspheming, which is sometimes followed by an occasional fight, which terminates in the ordinary manner, with broken heads and black eyes.

The 1869 Wine and Beerhouse Act restored the power of local magistrates over the licensing of premises.

Excessive drinking in public has been a constant social problem. The police spent an increasing proportion of their time dealing with drunks in the street and supervising the conduct of public houses, whose opening hours had been restricted on Sundays in 1839 and at night in 1864. By 1870 a quarter of the work of the magistrates involved drink cases in some form.

Until 1872 mere inebriation was not actually an offence. The Licensing Act imposed penalties for being drunk or disorderly, rather than both together, and for being in charge of a vehicle or a firearm while under the influence. At the same time, the police were encouraged to be much more rigorous in their application of the law. The number of summary convictions relating to the excessive consumption of alcohol was three times higher in the mid-1870s than it had been two decades earlier – a rise which took place at a time when the incidence of other offences was beginning to fall.

Briggs *et al* note that at the beginning of the final quarter of the nineteenth century, recorded alcohol consumption reached its all-time peak and 43% of national revenue was derived from the sale of drink. Thereafter the proportion declined, although even as late as 1939, one pound in every eight of taxation was derived from this source.

Some cases from 1837

A published study of the year 1837 in Brighton records that there were numerous cases of both men and women arrested for being drunk and disorderly in the street. The usual fine for being drunk was 5s. If the charge included disorderly behaviour, there would generally be additional costs to keep the peace.

An amusing case came before the Bench of Magistrates on 29 June 1837. Shabbily-dressed Charles White, his scarf tied in an enormous knot round his neck, had been charged by PC Shoulders with drunkenness. The officer stated that the prisoner had been very drunk and had used disgusting language on the previous evening in North Street, so as to prevent people from passing. When asked to 'move on', he became very abusive and had thus been brought to the Town Hall. White's response was that 'he was not drunk: that is, not *particularly* drunk' and that he had been told to go home in a very rough way, which he thought an insult. He 'didn't like to be spoke to as a dog' and of the policeman said: 'I thought I was as good as he.' White, a self-employed shoemaker, was told by Seymour, a magistrate, that he worked for a bad master. He was fined 5s and costs and was given a week to pay. He thanked the Bench, muttering as he left the bar that he still thought himself as good as the policeman.

The same sentence was handed down by Magistrate Seymour on one John Owen who appeared before him charged by a policeman with being drunk and disorderly at the bottom of Regency Square. Owen frankly admitted he had been drunk: 'I had some beer with my Lord's servants and it got the better of me. I know I was very drunk, sir; I very often gets tipsy, but I never abuses anyone, and I *never* gets drunk on a Sunday' (laughter in court). Seymour reminded him, when learning it was his first appearance in court, that if a man was fined for drunkenness a second time, he was made to find securities; if he failed to do so, he was sent to prison.

In another case, a boy apprenticed to a local tailor and hatter, who absented himself from his employer 'to frequent the beer shops and cricket' was sent to the House of Correction for fourteen days' hard labour.

Two notorious female offenders, 1886

On 9 February 1886, Annie Opheris, 37, appeared before Brighton Borough Police Court on a charge of being drunk and disorderly the day before. She had not long previously been charged with the same offence and had brought a serious – but the magistrates considered unfounded – accusation against Police Sgt Warr of assaulting her. The latest incident came just after her release from Lewes Prison after serving a term of imprisonment for drunkenness. PC Austin found her lying on the pavement in Castle Square. Thinking she was in a fit, he obtained assistance to help her up but she became very violent, throwing herself down again and alternately praying, singing and screaming. When brought to the Town Hall, she abused Supt Gibbs, calling out 'Oh! You villain, you are the cause of my ruin.' After further abuse and begging for money, she was remanded but it was established after a quiet night that she was willing to go into a home. She consented to go with Mr Cooper, the Town Missionary, to seek admittance in person at the Rev Wagner's Home in Queen's Square. Following her charge against Sgt Warr, orders were issued that thenceforth when the cell bells were rung, two constables had to attend to the wants of prisoners.

In the same week, Eliza Chapman, one of the most frequent visitors to the Court, was sentenced to another term of 14 days' hard labour for being drunk and disorderly. An offer to get her admitted to a home was received by her in silence.

The following week, Opheris was back before the Bench on charges of being drunk, using obscene language and stealing a pair of boots from a shop kept by a furniture dealer named Tully in Glo'ster [sic] Street. She pleaded guilty to the second charge, saying she went into the shop to buy the boots and as no one was there she took them and intended to call again and pay for them. With regard to the other charge, she had apparently entered a beer shop on Carlton Hill drunk and, when liquor was refused her, she became very noisy and had to be ejected. She then caused a great disturbance. She had gone to Wagner's Home as she had promised but had to be dismissed owing to her bad behaviour. She was sentenced to a month's hard labour for stealing the boots and to 14 days for the other offence, the sentences to be served concurrently. On leaving the dock, she told the Bench she would be fifty times worse in the future.

An inebriate of good family, 1930

Thomas Baden-Powell, 30, of independent means, was charged on 23 June 1930 with being drunk and disorderly in North Street Quadrant the previous evening. He pleaded guilty. PC Plank said the accused was staggering about the pavement, bumping into pedestrians and eventually fell against the Clock Tower. When arrested, he became very violent and 'made use of obscene expressions'. FH Carpenter, for the defence, said the man came of extraordinarily good family but had unfortunately become addicted to drink. He had been before the court 21 times before, the last being in April that year when he was sentenced to 21 days' hard labour on a similar charge. Baden-Powell was contemplating going abroad and to this end suggested he be bound over. The Chairman, however, questioned whether he would get a passport if all the facts were known. It was imperative that he be kept off alcohol and he therefore sentenced him to one month in prison.

An uncooperative alcoholic, 1969

Alan Till, of Vine Place, Brighton, was left a large sum of money when his companion died. Unable to cope with his loss and his addiction, Till would down two bottles of whisky a day. A verdict of 'Death from chronic alcoholism' was recorded by the Brighton coroner on 9 January 1969. Till had been a companion and secretary of a John Richard Jupp of Clifton Hill, whom he had known for 15 years. Jupp had died two years earlier. Till had left the area in 1966 and was hospitalised in Hampshire, where he discharged himself against medical advice. He returned to Brighton in 1967 and his condition deteriorated. After two months in Bevendean Hospital he again discharged himself, against advice, as soon as he could walk, and carried on drinking. He died at the Lee House Nursing Home, Brighton, on 29 December 1968, from bronchial pneumonia following sclerosis of the liver due to chronic alcoholism.

Oblivion outside the Dome. Chris Horlock collection/Evening Argus

DRUGS

According to police figures, Brighton and Hove has the highest rate of deaths from illicit drugs in Britain – 32 per 100,000 of population, compared to 17 in London, the second highest. This means one person is dying in the city from drugs every five days.

The Argus, 27 April 2002

The same report pointed out that drug barons, their middlemen and street pushers did not care that 80 per cent of burglaries, thefts and robberies in the city and nearly 70% of all retail crimes were drug related, and that addicts would resort to robbing anybody to feed their habits – mothers, brothers, anyone. The previous week, officers found £200,000 worth of crack cocaine, cannabis resin and 60 cannabis plants at an address in central Brighton, the largest haul in years. With it, officers discovered a shotgun and 17 cartridges, suggesting dealers had begun arming themselves to protect their trade areas.

Brighton and Hove had had a high death rate from problem drug use since the early 1990s. In 1999, the National Programme on Substance Abuse Deaths identified Brighton as having a death rate typically about five times higher than the neighbouring areas of East Sussex and West Sussex. The following year a peak rate of 32.3 per 100,000 population aged 16 and over was recorded. In 2006, the unenviable title of Britain's drugs death capital was earned for the fourth year running.

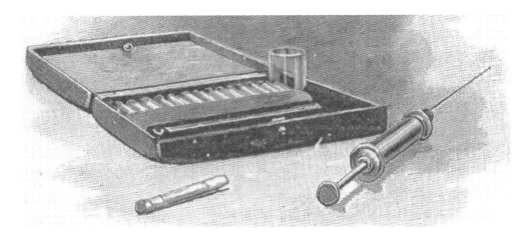

Although there has been a downward trend in recent years in deaths where **heroin** has been implicated, that drug has always figured largely in the statistics.

Another great social menace has been **crack cocaine**. It was in 1988 that the first 'crack factory' in Britain was discovered, in Peckham, South London. A smokable form of cocaine, crack had already gained a notorious reputation in the States for causing almost instant addiction from the intense 'high' it gave (despite this lasting only about 15 minutes). The drug was introduced into Britain by Yardies – Jamaican gangsters with a deserved reputation for violence.

A century earlier, **laudanum** and **opium** were being widely used. Cocaine even acquired an element of respectability: Sigmund Freud, an early enthusiast, described it as a magical drug, writing a song of praise in its honour; he practised extensive self-experimentation. To Sherlock Holmes, cocaine was 'so transcendentally stimulating and clarifying to the mind that its secondary action is a matter of small moment'. Robert Louis Stephenson wrote *The Strange Case of Dr Jekyll and Mr Hyde* during a six-day cocaine-binge, while intrepid polar adventurer Ernest Shackleton explored Antarctica propelled by tablets of Forced March. Doctors dispensed cocaine as an antidote to morphine addiction (unfortunately, some patients made a habit of combining both). The drug was soon sold over the counter. Until 1916, one could buy it at Harrods.

Key legislation
Legislative interference began with the Poisons and Pharmacy Act of 1868, which restricted the sale of dangerous substances and required that less harmful drugs (including opium) should be labelled as poisons. The Act's impact on consumption levels was, however, negligible since it excluded patent preparations, which, like alcohol, were a source of government revenue.

Recognising the dangers of the drug trade, the Government passed the Dangerous Drugs Act in 1920; this set out to curb the cocaine and opium menace that was spreading through British cities.

Banned in the UK in 1956, **heroin** was, and remains, the curse of inner cities. Before the passage of the Drugs (Prevention of Misuse) Act 1964, which controlled amphetamines in the UK in advance of international agreements and was later used to control LSD, it was possible for heroin addicts to be prescribed enough of the drug to manage their addiction without being forced to buy from the black market, for example.

With regard to **cannabis**, the ground-breaking Wootton Report of November 1968 accepted that the drug was not risk-free but declared 'the existing criminal sanctions intended to curb its use are unjustifiably severe'. Its recommendations included: no prison sentences for possession of small quantities of cannabis, no legal penalties for allowing private premises to be used for consumption and the separation of the legal status of cannabis from that of heroin. The report is thought to have led to the *de facto* decriminalisation of cannabis in subsequent decades.

The report was welcomed the following year in *Wine Press*, the weekly newspaper of the University of Sussex Union. Its editorial remarked that

> *If cannabis were to be legalised, its distribution would cease to remain tied to a great extent to the tender mercies of the drug underworld. [...] The sooner cannabis is legalised the better – after all, you don't have to smoke the stuff if you don't want to.*

By contrast, the report was deemed 'appalling' by the Rev LOC White, assistant priest at All Saints' Parish Church, Hove, in January 1969. He stated publicly:

> *Anyone who suggests lessening the extreme seriousness of taking soft drugs, which almost always lead to hard drugs, is living in cloud-cuckoo land [...] I hope we will speedily see an end to this swinging, sex-ridden, drug-taking Britain, which in some aspects is frighteningly like conditions at the end of the Roman Empire.*

At the end of June 2006, the Government's downgrading of cannabis from Class B to Class C (meaning possession of the drug was normally no longer an arrestable offence) was criticised by the Executive Director of the UN Office on Drugs and Crime (UNODC), who, without naming the UK, said such countries got the 'drug problem they deserved'. He suggested cannabis was as harmful as cocaine and heroin.

It was in fact indirectly through the UN, via US influence, that all drug use was criminalised, ending the UK's relatively liberal drugs policy before 1971. The Misuse of Drugs Act of that year controls the possession, use and trafficking of narcotics in the United Kingdom. Although often presented as little more than a list of proscribed drugs and of penalties linked to their possession and supply, the Act in practice establishes the Home Secretary as a key player in a drug licensing system. Therefore, for example, various opiates are available legally as prescription-only medicines and cannabis (hemp) may be grown under licence for 'industrial purposes'.

The Act created three classes of 'controlled substances', and ranges of penalties for illegal or unlicensed 'possession' and 'possession with intent to supply' are graded differently within each class. The lists of substances within each class can be amended 'by order', so the Home Secretary can list new drugs and upgrade, downgrade or delist previously-controlled drugs with less of the bureaucracy and delay associated with passing an Act through both Houses of Parliament.

A Victorian misadventure
In 1870, a year-old infant died after swallowing a pill of opium, a drug to which his mother, Elizabeth Moore, had been addicted for 17 years. The Brighton coroner recorded death by misadventure.

The Withdeane Hall eccentric
Together with drink, it was opium that was the downfall of one of Brighton's most bizarre characters.

Count Erik Magnus Andreas Harry Stenbock was born at Thirlestaine Hall, Cheltenham, on 12 March 1860, of an aristocratic Swedish family with royal connections. He would, in time, inherit vast ancestral estates in Estonia. His father died young the following year. Eric lived in Cheltenham with his mother, who by 1864 had remarried. Her second husband, Francis Mowatt, eventually rose to be Permanent Secretary at the Treasury. Over the next ten years the Mowatts had six children – three half-brothers and three-half sisters for Eric. Thirlestaine Hall was sold in 1874 and the family moved to Withdeane Hall at Patcham near Brighton.

Erik was educated abroad until the age of 19, in Germany, Russia and Estonia. Then, in 1879, he went up to Balliol College, Oxford. It was Shrimpton of Oxford who, two years later, published a slim volume of the aristocrat's verse – *Love, Sleep and Dreams*. In April, he dropped out of Oxford. The census of 3/4 April found him at home in Brighton with the Mowatt family and their ten servants.

After travel in Europe and continuing to write poetry, Stenbock made his way back to England. He was taken ill in the spring of 1882 in St Petersburg and spent weeks in bed writing letters to his friends in England. It is here that we see the first hints of delusion that were to plague his last few years. It may have been at this time that he was treated with opium to which he became addicted.

Three years later, on the death of his grandfather, he inherited extensive estates in Estonia. He became more and more eccentric, adopting conspicuous clothes, such as a bright green suit with an orange shirt, and smoking increasing amounts of opium. One huge room of his house in Kolga was wallpapered poppy red and he kept a menagerie of animals, including snakes and a monkey. His huge bedroom was painted peacock blue and covered in the trappings of esoteric and occult beliefs. There was a pentagram over the bed and an altar over the fireplace dedicated to Eros. By now he had also evolved his own religion comprising a mix of Buddhism, Catholicism and idolatry.

He missed England, however, and returned in July 1887, renting a house in fashionable Belgravia. He never returned to Estonia. Three years later, on the top of a Piccadilly horse bus, he first met, and was smitten by, 16-year-old Norman O'Neill, who would later become a composer of theatre music.

The winter of 1893/4 found Stenbock staying with his family in Brighton and working on his short story collection, *Studies of Death*, which was published in December 1894. But he was by then very ill and progress was slow. His increasingly eccentric behaviour and violent outbursts made the Mowatt children somewhat afraid of him. It was rumoured that on 26 April the following year, he flew into a rage and struck out at someone in the house with a poker. Overbalancing, he hit his head on the grate and died. His death certificate, however, cites 'hepatic cirrhosis' as the cause. No head injury is mentioned and his half-sister, Mary, is listed as informant and as being present at his death.

Count Erik Stenbock (1860–95). Author's collection

He was buried on 1 May in Brighton's Extra Mural Cemetery, but before burial his heart was placed in a jar and sent to the family church in Estonia.

Stenbock's grave is now in very bad condition. The crucifix has been toppled by a rampant growth of ivy and the whole grave is in danger of sliding down the hill. Members of Brighton Ourstory (see HOMOSEXUALITY) are campaigning with The Lost Club (a society devoted to reclaiming the reputations of unjustly forgotten writers) to have the grave restored.

An unusual addict, 1958

Fifty-five-year-old Michael Fulton, of Ladbourne Parade, Lower Bevendean, Brighton, who was addicted to paregoric, became so agitated after his arrest that a detective had to obtain three bottles of the drug for him to drink, Gloucester Assizes were told. He was sentenced to eight years' preventive detention for breaking into a dispensary at Gloucester health centre and stealing a quantity of drugs. Sentencing him, Mr Justice Elwes said: 'You have been a drug addict for 31 years. All your convictions since 1935 have been for stealing opium and morphine tablets and being in possession of dangerous drugs. Everyone must have sympathy for you. If there were any other way of dealing with you I would take it. But you must be locked up for your own protection and the protection of other people.'

Some 1960s incidents

The popular perception of this being a drug-hazed decade is disproved by a scrutiny of the local press. There were few reports of drug problems, although the impression is gained that incidents may have been swept under the carpet to avoid tarnishing the town's image.

An early specific mention of drugs in Brighton was in connection with the case of a 16-year-old grammar school boy from Bristol who, around Easter 1966, was fined £10 for carrying a knuckleduster and a further £20 for possessing drugs. Two other 16-year-olds caught in possession of 'French Blues' (a methaqualone/amphetamine mixture which featured in QUADROPHENIA) were also fined £20 each.

The first *Brighton and Hove Herald* for 1967 carried the headline YOUNGSTERS IN SEARCH OF DRUG ADDICTS. It reported that a team of young people would be searching the streets around the Clock Tower the following day for drug addicts, teenagers and beatniks with nothing to do. These Christian crusaders, who called themselves 'The Fishers', were the reconnaissance groups in a big campaign against addiction which was being waged by an organisation headed by local clergymen. Their aim was to invite as many youngsters as possible back to a hall at the (now demolished) Union Church for refreshments and a talk. Already they could claim one victory: a young girl drug addict on the run from the police who gave herself up and started a new life after attending one of their meetings. Rev David Copestake, a 26-year-old Methodist minister, one of several of the committee of church people behind the scheme, said drug addicts needed more than just medical care, they needed some sort of spiritual power inside them. This was what they were trying to give them. However, the *Herald* was quick to point out in the same article that the minister had himself been found guilty of illegal drug possession the very same week ...

In May 1969, six Sussex University students were fined a total of £445 on LSD drug charges. One called what he had taken a 'Strawberry Field'.

The Katrina Taylor murder, 1996

The murky world of modern drug-dealing and addiction led to the fatal stabbing of 19-year-old Katrina Taylor in St Nicholas' churchyard, Brighton, on 4 July 1996.

London drug dealers Trevor Smith, 27, and Fergal Scollan, 25, were convicted and jailed for life for the crime at Lewes Crown Court in 1997 but cleared after a retrial at the Old Bailey. Their barrister successfully argued there was no case to answer, claiming there was no evidence of what happened in the churchyard and nothing to point to who was holding the murder weapon.

Katrina, the mother of a baby daughter, Kyia, was stabbed six times, once through an arm and five times in the chest, in a revenge attack for her part in a burglary. This had taken place on 9 May 1996 at 10 Bolney Road, Moulsecoomb, the home of mother-of-two Neisha Williams, across the street from Katrina's own family home. Katrina had acted as lookout for two thieves (John Cosham and her boyfriend Matthew Laurie) who, in their search for drugs, stole valuables, smashed up furniture, piled clothes in a room and set fire to them and pulled a washing machine out from the wall, leaving the house to flood. Katrina, an addict, later sold some of the haul of jewellery for a paltry £20 heroin fix. She was charged with burglary a month later.

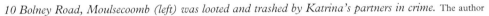

10 Bolney Road, Moulsecoomb (left) was looted and trashed by Katrina's partners in crime. The author

Meanwhile, mechanic Trevor Smith, Williams' former live-in boyfriend with whom she was still in touch, and his associates sought revenge. The posse included Smith's close friend, Fergal Scollan, and Williams' brothers, Jason and Simon (who was growing cannabis from his council house in Centurion Road). The two Londoners had their own operation in Cricklewood for growing 'skunk', a potent form of cannabis. They had big ideas and expected to earn £120,000 from their operation.

When Cosham was traced, he was beaten and stabbed in both legs with a screwdriver. A friend who was found with him was stabbed in the face, beaten with a hammer and repeatedly kicked in the head. The posse then moved on to track down Katrina Taylor.

When the vigilantes caught up with their slight and frail quarry at a Brighton hotel, they took her to Neisha's new home at 77 Centurion Road where they held and threatened her. She was then taken to nearby St Nicholas' churchyard and murdered.

Neisha and Simon Williams were tried along with Smith and Scollan in 1997. Both were cleared of murder but Neisha was sentenced to two years for false imprisonment, a charge of which her brother was cleared.

For legal reasons, neither gave evidence at the retrial, taking out pieces of what was a prosecution puzzle built on circumstancial evidence.

In 1986, the future murder victim, whose youth was marred by sexual abuse by one of her mother's ex-boyfriends, had taken part in a police murder reconstruction posing as 9-year-old Nicola Fellows, one of the BABES IN THE WOOD. At Falmer School, Katrina did well in sport, especially netball, but was below average academically. Often in conflict with teachers, she left as soon as she could, with few qualifications. She took to drugs, dabbling first in soft substances and then heroin. Before her death, she was taking three 'shots' a day, costing nearly £200 a week. Her addiction was funded by crime – mainly thefts and burglaries. It was the drugs which Trevor Smith sold from 10 Bolney Road that Katrina was looking for on the night of the break-in which sealed her fate.

Mark Kenyon says sorry

Mark Kenyon, 48, was one of the most prolific burglars in Sussex whose criminal career spanned 30 years. Sixteen years of his life were spent in prison. In early 2006, he chose, through the medium of *The Argus*, to say sorry to all his victims. He was a heroin addict for most of his criminal career and needed lots of cash, as he spent at least £300 a day on heroin and sometimes splashed out £500 for a night on crack cocaine. The hauls he made to fund his addiction included silverware worth £1,500 from a house in Haywards Heath, antiques worth £50,000 from a house in Wales and further silverware, worth £5,500, from an address in High Salvington, Worthing. He was mainly based in Brighton and Hove, where he associated with the most notorious criminals in the county. At one time he was hunted by the FBI in the US where he was thought to have absconded while on bail.

He was the first to complete the Brighton and Hove Prolific Offenders Supervision Scheme run by the Probation Service and Sussex Police started in 2005, having been put on the scheme immediately after leaving prison in December 2004 after doing more time for burglary. He was prescribed the heroin-substitute methadone, housed in a council hostel and assigned a key worker who liaised with Probation. At the time of writing he is making good progress and acknowledges that the programme may have even saved his life.

E

EDMUNDS, CHRISTIANA

Christiana Edmunds, Brighton's 'Chocolate Cream Poisoner', was aged 43 when her case came to trial (although she persisted in giving her age as 34 in the proceedings). She was of good birth and lived for some years in perfect respectability with her mother in lodgings – long since demolished – at Gloucester Place, Brighton.

She conceived an inordinate fondness for Dr Charles Izard Beard, whose surgery stood obliquely across the square at 64 Grand Parade and who had attended her. In the summer of 1870, she unsuccessfully attempted to kill his wife by a poisoned chocolate cream, with the result that the doctor would have nothing more to do with her. To clear herself of suspicion, she embarked on a scheme of poisoning on a wide scale. She bought strychnine from Mr Isaac Garrett, chemist and dentist of 10 Queens Road, on the pretext that she wished to poison dogs and cats.

She then sent a number of children on separate errands to buy chocolates from Maynard's famous confectionery shop in West Street. When the children brought back the sweets she would say that they were the wrong sort and would have ones containing strychnine returned to the shop instead. She even left a bag of them at a grocer's shop in Church Street kept by a Mrs Harriet Cole, whose son gave one of the sweets to a Mrs Walker. This lady later complained that it had made her very ill and almost killed her.

However, no fatality arose from this malicious distribution until 12 June 1871, when Charles Miller, the uncle of a 4-year-old boy named Sidney Barker (both were staying in

The shop in West Street where Edmunds bought her chocolate creams. One caused the death of young Sidney Barker. Chris Horlock collection

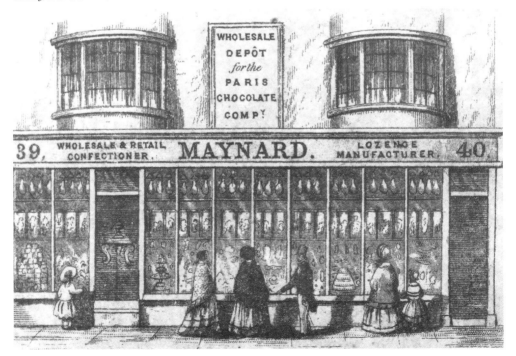

Brighton), bought some of the chocolates which had been tampered with and gave one to his nephew. The lad died very rapidly but in great agony.

The jury at the inquest found the youngster had died by misadventure. To appear as an innocent party, Edmunds even went herself to Maynard's to complain, as was recorded at the inquest on her victim. She said she was going to have the creams tested because a lady friend of hers had eaten some chocolates bought at the shop and they had made her ill. Edmunds went so far as to write anonymous letters (which were proved at the trial to be in her handwriting) to the little boy's father, urging him to take proceedings against Maynard. In one of these she had the effrontery to write: 'Had I lost my child in such a sad way, as a parent I should feel myself in duty bound to take proceedings against the seller of the sweets.' By comparing these with the reply to a letter he himself sent Edmunds, Inspector Gibbs was able to establish that it was she who had written the letters to Barker.

In August 1871, Edmunds devised her second extraordinary and diabolical scheme whereby, at one and the same time, a number of respectable families in Brighton (Mrs Beard's, of course, among them) received presents of cakes, sweetmeats and fruit, some of which were so crammed with arsenic as to cause the death of anyone, of whatever age, eating them.

In January 1872, the *Brighton Gazette* recorded that one of Dr Beard's servants was still suffering the effects of having eaten a portion of cake sprinkled with arsenic. It also reported the circumstances leading to the poisoner's apprehension:

> *... she went to the Brighton police office and complained that* she *had received a parcel of poisoned fruit. This communication, coupled with her appearance at the Coroner's inquest in the preceding June, aroused the suspicions of Inspector Gibbs. Instructed by his chief, Mr White, to wait upon Mrs Beard with respect to the poisoned present received by that lady, he asked her if she was acquainted with Miss Edmunds? Mrs Beard replied she was, and then, after a pause which indicated the terrible suspicion that flashed on her mind, she disclosed to the Inspector the facts of the previous attempt to poison her by Miss Edmunds ...*

This link, together with the handwriting evidence, meant the game was up for the devious poisoner. Her trial was ultimately removed from Sussex to the Old Bailey, owing to the great local prejudice and excitement surrounding the case. The unbalanced spinster was found guilty and condemned to hang, but she pleaded, in order to stay execution of her sentence, that she was pregnant. A jury of matrons was empanelled (for the first time for many years) to try that issue, but when it became obvious that the prisoner's plea was groundless, her distress – she had been calm throughout the whole trial – became terrible. 'Oh, how shall I sleep to-night?' she wailed. The jury of matrons wept around her. Ultimately, the Home Secretary appointed two medical men to enquire into her mental condition, resulting in her being sent to Broadmoor, where she died in 1907.

EMBEZZLEMENT – see also DEFAULTING BANKERS, FORGERY

The fraudulent conversion of property of another by a person in lawful possession of that property. Crimes of this nature have generally involved a position of trust and confidence on the miscreant's part, such as that of agent, fiduciary, trustee, treasurer, or attorney.

The serious case of Lieutenant Hunt, 1800

Hunt, a Lieutenant and Paymaster in the Hampshire Fencible Cavalry stationed in Brighton, decamped from the town at the end of February 1800 with regimental property worth £6,000 – an immense sum in those days. The day before he left, he drew from the Old Bank, on the credit of the regiment, the sum of £400 and from the New Bank, £500. Shortly after leaving Brighton he boarded a vessel lying in readiness to receive him off Rottingdean. His wife remained in Brighton.

A clerk in disgrace, 1866

Sutherland Walker, 22, a cashier, was indicted at Brighton's Midsummer Quarter Sessions in July 1866 for having embezzled, on 25 January that year, the sum of £294 17s 6d from his employers, the Hampshire Banking Company. Initially, he pleaded not guilty.

The company's head office was in Southampton. They had a branch in North Street, Brighton, at which Walker worked as a counter-clerk. In that capacity, he received deposits from the company's customers. The party whose account had been tampered with was the eminent wine merchants, Messrs Findlater and Co. On the day in question the manager of the Brighton business deposited £20 in notes, £96 in cash and six cheques representing £178 17s 6d. This money was received by Walker but not accounted for to the bank. Through his position, he had been able to charge these cheques as if they had been cashed at different times for Findlater. He was without doubt well aware that the client did not often compare the counterfoils with their pass book, so that in April when their pass book was sent to the bank, he doctored it to make it look as if the £294 17s 6d had been credited. It had actually been omitted from the detail of deposits – an omission calculated to appear merely as a clerical error. Fortunately, the embezzlement was discovered before Walker could falsify the entries in the ledger. He had been in the company's employment for three years, during which time he had been a model employee and always regarded by his employers as strictly honest. On Walker changing his plea to one of Guilty, he was sentenced to eighteen calendar months' imprisonment with hard labour.

More hard labour, 1888

A sentence of hard labour also awaited Daniel Murrell Johnson as he left Brighton Quarter Sessions on 9 January 1888. The manager of the Bodega Company (Limited) at Brighton, he had been found guilty of embezzling his employers' money to the tune of £2 11s and £9 11s, both in November 1887, and £35 18s in December 1887.

An accountant makes amends, 1975

Peter Myatt, a 48-year-old accountant who stole from his clients, took £9,000 into Brighton Crown Court on 28 November 1975 to pay off some of his debts. Myatt, of Florence Road, Brighton, admitted at a hearing six months earlier that he stole £19,000 from clients and dishonestly obtained £1,000. He asked for 11 further offences to be considered. Sentence had been deferred to enable him to make efforts to pay the money back. The court had heard in June that Myatt joined his father's accountancy firm, W Myatt and Son, of Norfolk Square, Brighton, in 1952, becoming principal in that year when his father died. But he misused the respectable reputation of the firm in recent years and stole money from some clients by saying he was using their cash for investments which were, in fact, bogus. Sentencing him to two years' imprisonment suspended for two years, Judge Haddow Forrest said Myatt had clearly made every effort he could to pay back his creditors.

F

FALSE PRETENCES
Three cases from 1800
At the sessions for the Eastern Division of Sussex which ended in Lewes on 19 July 1800, William Budd was tried and found guilty of having obtained, under false pretences, money from Sarah Grimes and Ganey Graley, servants of Mr Barrett, surgeon, and Mr Attree, draper, respectively, in Brighton. Budd was recommitted for twelve calendar months and ordered to be publicly whipped (see also WHIPPING) on the last day of the month.

It was reported on the 18th of the following month that a woman had recently been going around Brighton collecting money under false pretences. She would obtain the names of residents and details of their connections and by these means had succeeded in collecting various sums by pleading that her children had been taken into care out of humanity by some people. She was making her way eastward and had reached Alfriston, saying she would be going on to Ashford in Kent.

Three months later, someone passing himself off as a clergyman appeared in Shoreham and Brighton soliciting donations, claiming he had long been out of employment. The *Sussex Weekly Advertiser* warned the public against assisting him until his identity and situation had been satisfactorily authenticated, especially since 'his conduct was not very exemplary at either place'.

No hiding place, 1811
John Batis Shuckard, a swindler, was on 10 August 1811 committed to Lewes House of Correction for having defrauded, among others, Leonard Shuckard, master of the *Old Ship Tavern*, at Brighton (no mention was made in the *Sussex Weekly Advertiser* of any family relationship between the two men – they may simply have shared a rather unusual surname). The fraudster had cheated his namesake of £21 by passing him fictitious banknotes and had thereby unlawfully obtained credit for, and acquired, two gold watches owned by James Irish, a watchmaker of North Street. He also used two sealed documents which he falsely claimed contained banknotes to the value of £550 as sureties for obtaining credit from other townsfolk. When he was searched in the House of Correction, one of the gold watches and some pawnbrokers' duplicates slipped from under his rupture truss. He was sentenced to six months' imprisonment in Horsham Gaol, that being the greatest punishment the Court could inflict.

Non-existent parcels, 1830
Thomas Stollen was sentenced to jail at the Assizes in 1830 for obtaining money under false pretences by undertaking to deliver parcels which proved to be fictitious.

Shady dealings at Marine Gate, 1938
In July 1938, estate agent Randolph Bernard Hider, aged 48, of Brunswick Place, Hove, appeared at Brighton Quarter Sessions at the Town Hall charged on three counts of obtaining money from local traders by false pretences with intent to defraud. He pleaded Not Guilty.

In March at Black Rock, Kemp Town, the block of 125 flats called Marine Gate was nearing completion. Hider told local retailers he was the letting agent and offered to introduce residents in the flats to them so that the shopkeepers might get a substantial share of the custom. The traders paid him various sums of money 'up front' with this in mind. Following later misgivings on their part, however, the police were called in.

Hider, a First World War veteran who had two hard labour sentences on his record (for false pretences and embezzlement respectively) maintained he had acted honestly, with no intention to defraud the traders. But he was found guilty on all three counts by the jury. Reminding him of the convictions in 1934, the Recorder ruled, 'You must go to prison for nine months with hard labour.'

Crooked ways in a soft drinks firm, 1969

This has been worrying me. It might sound silly, but I am glad I am caught ...
(William Bourne, London, December 1968)

A former manager of the Brighton depot of a soft drinks firm, 60-year-old William Bourne was jailed for seven years on 21 January 1969 when he admitted frauds and theft involving more than £14,000. Sentencing Bourne, of Wheatfield Way, Brighton, the Recorder (Mr Charles Doughty, QC), told him: 'Ever since 1928 you have been living dishonestly for a large part of the time, except for the last few years. You obtained an excellent job but even then you could not go straight. When you went in for these false pretences and tricking your friends out of sums of money which they could not afford you went into it in a big way.'

Bourne, who had eight previous convictions up to 1952 when he received a sentence of eight years' preventive detention, pleaded guilty to two charges of obtaining a total of £2,249 by false pretences from Henry Leslie Jellicoe, an 84-year-old retired Hove accountant, and stealing £365 from his employers, Canada Dry (UK), Ltd. He asked for 25 other offences involving more than £11,500 to be taken into consideration. Twenty of these were for obtaining cheques by false pretences and five for obtaining cash in a similar manner.

Bourne and his family became tenants of a bungalow in Wheatfield Way owned by Jellicoe, with whom they were friendly. The scam he operated related to the purchase of replacement lorries for his firm, which he had joined on his release in 1959 and which was later merged with Canada Dry. Bourne had been promoted to foreman, departmental manager and depot manager. In connection with the vehicle purchases in 1966, Bourne persuaded Jellicoe to part-fund his phased purchases of the old lorries which could be later resold at a profit, to the benefit of both of them. Additional sums were obtained from him on the pretext of, for example, purchasing road fund licences. Time went by and Jellicoe saw no return for his outlay, despite pressing Bourne. He finally saw him on 13 August 1968 at his home, but Bourne said it was too late to go to the bank then and promised to go the following morning. But he did not turn up the following day and went off with £365 belonging to his employers.

On 15 August, Bourne wrote to Jellicoe from London, where he lived pretending to be an antiques dealer, telling him that he had swindled him out of the money but asked him not to go to the police. However, he was arrested and taken back to Brighton to answer the charges against him. To Bourne's credit, about £3,600 was returned to his victims.

The bogus curator, 1969
Peter Terence Keating, 37, of Birdham Road was jailed for two years for obtaining, and attempting to obtain, old coins and other articles by posing as Curator of Brighton's Museum Administration Department. He asked for 16 similar offences to be taken into consideration.

FLOOD, JOHN – see MILITIA

FORGERY – see also EMBEZZLEMENT
A travelling suspect arrested, 1807
The *Brighton Herald* reported, on 23 May 1807, that a person named Hayes had been apprehended at the *Royal Oak*, Milbourn St Andrew, Dorset, on a charge of issuing fictitious bills 'to a large amount' (purporting to be of the Ipswich and Suffolk Bank) in Salisbury and its environs. These notes seemed similar to those which had been passed in Brighton, 'in which the names of Holden and Winckley are introduced'.

Death penalty for a forger, 1824
Henry Fauntleroy was a partner in a leading banking-house, who forged securities to the value of no less than £170,000. He was executed at Newgate in 1824.

The case attracted enormous interest at the time, not least on account of the vast sums involved. He was apprehended on 10 September 1824, following information being lodged against him at Marlborough Street Police Office.

The firm with which Fauntleroy was connected was that of Marsh, Sibbald, Stracey, Graham and Fauntleroy (Marsh, Sibbald & Co.) of 6 Berners Street, London, in which he had become a partner in 1807, succeeding his father.

Fauntleroy's arrest on one charge was followed by the discovery of his having sold out stock to the above staggering amount since 1814, all of which he had converted to his own use. So apprehensive were the public about what degree of misconduct might be revealed that a run on the banking-house took place. To counter this, payments were suspended and its bankruptcy followed.

During his years of high living, Fauntleroy owned large, finely-furnished houses and carriages and kept expensive mistresses; one was 'Mrs Bang'. This was the sobriquet of Mary Bertram, or Kent, a notorious woman of pleasure, the original of Pierce Egan's Corinthian Kate (Egan was a successful Regency sporting writer whose hugely popular *Tom and Jerry* is a picaresque journey around London's high and low life pleasure haunts). Fauntleroy installed her for some years in an imposing Brighton villa named Hampton Lodge, a delightful single-storey neo-classical building situated at the lower end of Hampton Place, which was the site of a post office for many years until its closure in March 2004.

It was when he tired of the woman's fondness for gin and display that he turned to the youthful Maria Forbes. She was still at boarding school and he installed her in a house in Lambeth, settling no less than £6,000 on her. He got her with child and before long a second baby was born. Other mistresses included a Mrs Disney, the wife of the Somerset Herald, who happened to be one of the customers at the bank.

Fauntleroy was tried at the Old Bailey on 30 October 1824 on indictments including forging a power of attorney for the transfer of stock in 3% consols in the sum of £5,000 with intent to defraud a bank customer, one Frances Young of Chichester, in 1815.

Amazingly, in one document found in a tin box among his private papers, the forger acknowledged his guilt and gave a reason

Hampton Lodge. Henry Smith collection

for it. The manuscript detailed large individual sums of money and the persons involved, who included Lady Nelson (£11,995 consols). His statement read:

> In order to keep up the credit of our house, I have forged powers of attorney for the above sums and parties, and sold out to the amount here stated, and without the knowledge of my partners. I kept up the payment of the dividends, but made no entries of such payments in our books. The bank began first to refuse to discount our acceptances, and to destroy the credit of our house: the bank shall smart for it.

In court, the accused read a long document in his defence, then sat down and wept. No fewer than 17 gentlemen gave him the highest character and felt him incapable of a dishonourable action. Their opinions, however, counted for nothing with the jury, who took just 20 minutes to return a verdict of guilty of uttering. Sentence of death was then passed.

Fauntleroy's execution, the last for the crimes of forgery and embezzlement, took place on 30 November 1824 before a crowd estimated at nearly 100,000; every window and roof which could command a view of the dreadful scene was occupied.

Forged notes, 1838 and 1839
In 1838, Thomas Thompson, an attorney in West Street, was placed before the bar on three separate occasions for forgery. After a long and complicated trial during which time he was refused bail, he was finally discharged for lack of evidence to defraud.

Small gangs were active in uttering forged notes and in 1839 the *Herald* reported on five persons being summoned for uttering forged bank notes.

A young forger, 1938
A 16-year-old boy was bound over for six months on 20 July 1938 for forging a postal order. The order had been sent by a lady in Lewes to a Brighton hospital and made payable to the Appeal Secretary, crossed and marked 'and Co'. The boy was employed by the Secretary in a nearby office. He admitted to a detective that he had found the order loose among letters he collected at the hospital. Later, with an ink eraser, he removed the payee's name and the name of the hospital and inserted in their place the name of a company to which he should have sent a similar sum. The Secretary gave him a good talking to and was prepared to have him back. His character had been excellent.

FRAME, MARGARET (victim)
As Margaret Frame hurried through the darkness of Stanmer Park woods, she was struck over the head from behind and stabbed in the back. The weapon, a thick-bladed knife, cut through the back of her suede jacket, penetrated her rib cage and sliced into her heart. She was then raped. The 34-year-old mother had been making her way towards her home in Saunders Hill, Coldean, having just left nearby Falmer Comprehensive School where she worked as a cleaner. The date was 12 October 1978.

The killer left her for dead, but returned to the scene later. He then stripped Mrs Frame and dragged her naked body 500 yards before burying her, face down, in a shallow grave and covering the spot with bracken and branches. He had walked to the end of a field and picked his way through heavy undergrowth before digging the makeshift burial mound. In what police believe were efforts to conceal her identity, an attempt was made to sever her head and all her rings were removed. The corpse, its shoulder poking out, was discovered by police searchers ten days after she disappeared. The murderer was thought by detectives to be a local man, but no one was ever charged. He may well have moved the body to an area that had been searched, thinking the same ground would not be covered twice.

Peter Frame, the victim's husband, joined the search for his wife, together with his son Andrew, who was just nine when his mother died. He had the dreadful task of telling him his mother was dead. The former taxi driver realised suspicion would fall on him, but was resigned to the fact. He had nothing but praise for his neighbours on Saunders Hill and in Hawkhurst Road.

Twenty-two years later, the police re-opened the hunt for her killer. A team of detectives was assembled at Brighton police station under Detective Superintendent Peter Kennett to review the case, code-named Operation Harbour. He said: 'Files such as these are never closed and we will be doing all we can to bring the person behind this crime to justice.' A dedicated number was set up for callers who might have information. Regrettably, however, no developments have been reported in connection with the case since the review.

FRAUD
A marine insurance scam, 1802

William Codlin, a native of Scarborough and an excellent seaman in the north coast trade, was executed on 27 November 1802 for scuttling the *Adventure*, a brig of which he was Captain, off Brighton on 8 August of that year.

The vessel was nominally bound to Gibraltar and Leghorn and Codlin was indicted at the Old Bailey for feloniously boring three holes in her bottom with a view to defrauding the underwriters. As officers of the ship, he and one Read were charged for committing the action, while Messrs Macfarlane and Easterby, as owners, were charged for procuring it to be committed.

The Old Bailey trial on 26 October 1802 commenced at 9 am and went on until midnight.

The vessel, with a crew of five, two of them boys, had left Limehouse already part-laden for Yarmouth and thence reached Brighton via Deal. Codlin instructed T Cooper, a seaman, to bore two or three holes as close down to the bottom of the vessel as possible. Cooper did as he was asked. The water came in slowly at first, so Codlin ordered the holes to be enlarged.

When the vessel began sinking, Codlin refused offers of help from nearby vessels. The *Swallow* revenue cutter then came up and took the brig in tow, fastening a hawse to the mast; the brig, which before then lay on her beam-ends, immediately righted and went down.

On landing, Codlin and the whole crew went to the *Ship Tavern* at Brighton. Some time later they were joined by the owners. Some incriminating carpenter's tools had been brought from the vessel, which was driving into shore. Easterby told Cooper he should go out and plug the holes and said Codlin was a d–d fool; he had botched the job, which he would have been wiser to have done on the French coast anyway; given the good weather, he might have made the shore of either country in the ship's boat.

A brig. Author's collection

Macfarlane and Easterby ordered the Captain and Cooper to go to London together and take private lodgings. Macfarlane paid their fare. Cooper stayed in London two nights and then went to his mother, near Saxmundham, in Suffolk. Having no money, and failing to get a ship after several applications, he walked the whole way – 88 miles. She told him he was a wanted man, whereupon he gave himself up to the local constable. His testimony was corroborated by the other crew members. One declared the purpose of the voyage had been to defraud the underwriters, even though several witnesses gave Read and Macfarlane a good character. As Read had apparently taken no active part in the business, he was acquitted. The rest were found guilty. Between five and six guineas had been given to Codlin in Brighton and he had been urged to go off, although being assured that if he was taken he would be hanged. Sentence of death was indeed passed on him and he received it firmly and undaunted.

On Saturday morning, 27 November 1802, he was brought out of Newgate to undergo his sentence at the docks at Wapping. He calmly ascended the ladder to the scaffold and his body, after hanging for the due length of time, was cut down and carried away in a boat by his friends.

A disgraced policeman, 1968

PC David Fisher, of Montpelier Crescent, a father-of-one, was on 18 November 1968 fined £80 and given a suspended prison sentence of six months on four fraud charges. Fisher pleaded guilty to obtaining £5 10s from Mr Ivor Ward, the steward of Brighton police's social club, by falsely pretending a cheque was good. He also pleaded guilty to two other similar charges, one of them relating to the purchase of a car using a dud cheque, and to incurring a fraudulent £85 liability with Barclays Bank Ltd. He asked for six other charges involving cheques to be taken into account. He confessed to being very ashamed of what he had done. He acted without thinking and had ruined his career. He was dismissed from police service.

G

GAMBLING – see also GEORGE IV, RACECOURSE/RACES

The Betting Houses Act of 1853 attempted to prohibit ready-money gambling with bookmakers, and further legislation in 1874, and especially in 1906, sought to deal with the growing volume of street betting. Hostility to the practice was based on a patronising moral criticism and social concern about the diversion of money away from the family economy on the one hand and attention away from the workplace on the other (a commentator noted in 1936 that, paradoxically, a man with a telephone and credit could personally attend racecourses and bet with impunity, whereas a man without those facilities who engaged in exactly similar transactions for cash in a street was guilty of a criminal offence).

The Street Betting Act of 1906 replaced a tangled mass of statutes and by-laws and was a response to the remorseless increase in gambling. Initial zeal on the part of the police was in some cases followed by the acceptance of bribes from bookmakers and by magistrates resorting more often to fines than to imprisonment.

With the rise of dog racing and in particular the football pools, which by the 1930s were attracting ten million customers a year, all hope of eradicating gambling from the working class disappeared. After the Second World War, a royal commission confirmed that the law was in disrepute and that the harm caused by gambling was far less than had once been feared. The subsequent Betting and Gaming Act of 1960 finally legalised off-course betting by the mass of the population.

Nonetheless, between 1968 and 2005, UK gambling was the most regulated in Europe.

Gentle gaming in the Steine's libraries

Gambling in the early days was often carried on at the popular subscription libraries in the Steine. In that run by Donaldson Jnr at the opposite corner of St James's Street, 'the dice are often rattled to some tune, and bank-notes transferred from one hand to another with as little ceremony as bills of the play, or quack doctors draughts to their patients', according to HR Attree in his *Topography of Brighton*.

In September 1810, an attempt was made to constitute the card game of Loo an illegal act on account of the way Walker, a library proprietor, conducted it but the case collapsed when the defence argued that an 1806 Act deprived magistrates of all jurisdiction and control in such matters. The case was dismissed and Loo was enjoyed even more for a further seven years, until the magistrates, seeing how much sway the game held among ladies in general, got their own back by outlawing it in the libraries, claiming competence on the basis of an obsolete Act of Henry VIII. Its disappearance was accelerated by changes to the Steine which in turn affected the patronage of the establishments where it was played. Some of them, in its absence, became failures.

Cards on the beach, 1901

William Goble, a shoeblack, was on 21 June 1901 charged with gambling with cards on the beach near Junction Parade. He had several previous convictions and was sentenced to one month's hard labour.

A 1930s snapshot

Although off-course cash betting was illegal, there were over 14,000 bookmakers operating in Britain in the early 1930s. The gaming laws, intended to protect workers from the temptations of gambling, were unpopular and discriminatory. The unpleasant spin-offs from the £400 million-a-year industry were the involvement of extortion gangs and the corruption, in some cases, of the police. Protection money was earned by racketeers collecting gambling debts for the bookies, with clerks and tick-tack men doubling as bodyguards.

Stated to have had 38 betting slips in his possession when arrested, Leslie Smith, 24, a clerk, of Montpelier Road, Brighton, was fined £5 at Hove on 23 August 1937 for frequenting Brunswick Street West and Western Road on the 19th for the purpose of betting and receiving bets. Smith pleaded guilty. Thirty-three of the slips related to horses running that day.

The Metropole Casino

This was opened with a flourish in 1962. It was not only Brighton's first casino but the first one in Britain too. Some 800 people, all wearing evening clothes, used to patronise it every night, and at different times included celebrities such as heavyweight boxer Billy Walker, the band leader Ambrose, the singing star Kathy Kirby and author Ian Fleming. Diana Dors was once turned away because she was wearing trousers. Her offer to take them off was refused. Enormous sums were won and lost in the gold-leafed splendour of the Clarence Room but two events accelerated the Casino's closure: new

Chris Horlock collection

legislation in the 1970s based the licence on the rateable value of the premises, which for the Clarence Room came to £45,000; and in 1982, the rival *International Casino Club* was opened in Preston Street by the Metropole organisation. The *Metropole* Casino closed in 1985 and the casino division was bought by the Brent Walker Group two years later.

The *Rendezvous,* at Brighton Marina Village, opened in 2001 and is the biggest casino in Sussex.

GEORGE IV (1762–1830)
The future King George IV became Prince Regent in 1811 and ruled in place of his father (George III) until the King's death in 1820. His court, meanwhile, was renowned for its decadence. There, the fashions of the day called for flimsy dress fabrics, low-cut bodices and virtually no imagination. His companions were the elite, and the most dissolute, of the nobility of the day.

On a visit in 1813, Leigh Hunt, writing for *The Examiner*, found himself in trouble for writing too frankly about the Prince Regent, describing him 'as a violator of his word, a libertine over head and heels in debt and disgrace, the companion of gamblers and demireps'. Mercer writes that, perhaps unknowingly, the Prince Regent was the first role model for some classes of the town's criminals, as it could be argued that his incurable extravagance and indebtedness – amounting to some £375,000, wiped clean by his father on the Prince's later marriage in 1795 to the tactless Caroline of Brunswick to ensure a Protestant succession – were criminal in nature.

So notorious were the goings-on at the Pavilion that Lord Chancellor Edward Thurlow (who died in Brighton in September 1806) refrained from calling on the Prince – even though his own conduct was hardly blameless. While walking on the Steine one day, he was met by the Prince in company with Lord Barrymore, Sir John Lade and other raffish friends of his. The three Barrymore brothers were amongst the most notorious of the Regent's cronies; Richard was known as 'Hellgate', his younger brother, Henry, had a club foot and was dubbed 'Cripplegate' while the youngest brother, Augustus – ordained but irreligious – was known as 'Newgate'. The brothers' elder sister, Caroline, was known, due to her foul language, as 'Billingsgate'. Sir John Lade's wife, Letitia, was one of the most abandoned women of the Court and equally foul-mouthed. 'Thurlow,' said the Prince, 'how is it that you have not called on me? You must name a day when you will dine with me.' The Lord Chancellor, looking at the Prince's friends, said: 'I cannot do so until your Royal Highness keeps better company.'

The Prince was once outdone by one of his profligate companions, Col George Hanger, known familiarly as the Knight of the Black Diamond, the wit and satirist of the royal clique. Both men fell for the same attractive, but illiterate, female – Charlotte Fortescue. Believing she was eloping to London with the Regent (while having been conducting a relationship with Hanger), she was outwitted by the Colonel dressed as her royal lover. Seated on the coach-box and unrecognised until their arrival, he thus bore his mistress – herself in the disguise of a footman – off to the metropolis.

It was in London that the Prince would visit the fashionable brothels of King Street and King's Place (where he and his brother, the Duke of Clarence, were said to be regular visitors to Mrs Windsor's establishment) in the company of Charles James Fox, the Whig leader, and other dubious companions. One caricature of the Prince shows him being dunned by brothel-keepers who are holding up itemised bills, including £1,000 for 'uncommon diversions'.

'With every fresh amour,' wrote Robert Huish in his *Memoirs of George the Fourth* (1831), 'his appetite appeared to be sharpened – like the bee he roamed from flower to flower, sipped the honey, but never visited that flower again.'

The Prince, in disguise, and his friends used an underground passage from the Pavilion to the Stables for going to, and returning from, their nocturnal rambles. It connected directly with the royal suite of rooms by means of a trap in the floor of one of the apartments, beneath which an intricate staircase afforded him a means of ready exit as the occasion demanded.

George Street, off Edward Street, is home to the *King's Arms* public house. Built in 1790, this establishment was reputed to have served as a brothel for Prinny and his chums. Legend has it there is a tunnel linking it to the Pavilion. The function room upstairs boasts a ceiling design similar to one seen in the Pavilion.

'*A VOLUPTUARY under the horrors of digestion.*' *A stipple engraving by James Gillray (1757–1815) published in 1792.* The Royal Pavilion, Libraries and Museums, Brighton and Hove

In later life, the Prince's other great vice, gluttony, caught up with him: the nine-course meals that could last four or five hours, plus his heavy drinking, led to him becoming so gross that he needed a hoist to mount his horse. Not for nothing was he dubbed the 'Prince of Whales'.

The accompanying caricature says everything about the Prince of Wales's profligate lifestyle.

The location can be identified as his lavish London residence, Carlton House.

The obese heir to the throne is depicted sprawling in an armchair, his waistcoat barely held together under the strain of his expanding stomach. Instead of a timepiece at the end of his watch chain there is a corkscrew, implying his constant eating and drinking. His coarse behaviour is represented by him picking his teeth with a fork, not a toothpick – even before the cutlery has been removed. The remains of a meal can be seen on the table, including decanters marked 'Port' and 'Brandy', while empty wine bottles are heaped beneath the table cloth. The circular portrait on the wall extols the virtue of a moderate diet and lifestyle, in sharp contrast to the scene depicted below. Even his coat of arms on the right is represented as a crossed knife and fork, while the sconce contains a bottle and a glass which hold the candles.

On the shelf below stand a small pot 'For the Piles', a bottle of 'Drops for a Stinking Breath'; remedies for the Prince's implied sexual excesses are the box of 'Leakes Pills' and bottle of 'Velnos Vegetable Syrup', these being well-known as supposed cures for venereal disease.

The brimful chamber pot, whose position conveys the Prince's uncouth behaviour, is used to weigh down a number of (unpaid) bills. On the ground, dice can be seen, together with notebooks 'Debts of Honor Unpaid', 'Newmarket List' (referring to the Prince's interest in horse racing) and 'Faro Partnership', showing the consequences of the Prince's love of gambling. The 'Faro Partnership' reference implies that the Prince had a financial interest in a faro table – a card game in which bets are placed on the order in which cards will appear. Fashionable women kept faro tables as a means of generating income.

In 1827, George IV – as he had become by then – abandoned the Palace and the town forever.

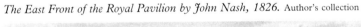

The East Front of the Royal Pavilion by John Nash, 1826. Author's collection

GILL, VICTOR

I am crazily in love with her. She promised not to do it again. She has been fooling around. I caught her with a guy in an American bar. I shot her. I have to admit it – I killed her and I will die for her. (Victor Gill to the police, 1943)

With many of Britain's menfolk serving overseas, the Canadian soldiers stationed here during Hitler's war had their pick of the girls. But relationships can be blighted, and a life even lost, by jealousy.

The tragic drama which unfolded outside the SS Brighton leisure complex in West Street on the night of 16 February 1943 involved 21-year-old Canadian dispatch rider Victor Eric Gill, a married man, and his girlfriend, Ivy Eade. The attractive daughter of a hairdresser from Camelford Street, she was shot in the Stadium car park in the blackout. Immediately after the shooting, Gill rode on his motorcycle to the police station under the Town Hall and gave himself up.

During the proceedings before the magistrates, it was learned that Ivy had been a waitress and then a clerk with the National Fire Service, whose crews were being called out night and day in those critical times. She had met Gill when working in a Brighton café in 1942 and become his regular girlfriend. She had been told about his wife and adopted family. When she became pregnant by Gill, he wanted to marry her and tried to obtain a divorce.

Prosecuting counsel Edward Robey – brother of comedian George Robey – told how Eade had been friendly with another Canadian soldier, Private Stanley Morey, and a mutually affectionate relationship had developed between them. Gill, who was jealous of Morey's earlier relationship with the girl, pleaded not guilty to murder.

The car park of Brighton Sports Stadium. Chris Horlock collection

On the fateful night, he found Ivy was out when he called at her home to pick her up (she was in fact with Morey and his brother). After another fruitless visit at about 9 pm, he eventually discovered her in the long bar at the Sports Stadium. Following a fierce argument, during which Ivy called him names and he slapped her, he took her outside and shot her with his service revolver. She was found dying from a bullet wound in the centre of her forehead. Although still breathing, she died in the ambulance on the way to the County Hospital.

At the Sussex Assizes at Lewes in March, the defence argued that Gill had suffered such provocation that he had lost control of his actions, being 'overwhelmed with apprehension and jealousy'. Gill, telling his own story from the witness box, claimed he did not know what he had done and had never intended to kill the girl. He was surprised to learn through his defence counsel, Eric Neve KC, that Eade had actually been seeing Morey two or three times a week. But John Flowers KC argued that the drama had been 'short, simple and tragic' – a calculated murder caused by jealousy.

After considering their verdict for nearly two hours, the jury unanimously found Gill not guilty of murder but guilty of manslaughter. Mr Justice MacNaughten sentenced him to six months' imprisonment, remarking that the prisoner had suffered great provocation. It was, however, impossible for the court to overlook the offence, which had resulted in a life being lost.

Gill was lucky. That same week, a fellow Canadian, a young regimental policeman by the name of Charles Gautier, shot dead an unfaithful housewife he was seeing in Portslade, west of Hove. His appeal against his death sentence was rejected and he was hanged at Wandsworth on 24 September 1943.

GRAND HOTEL BOMBING – see ASSASSINATION, ATTEMPTED

GRIFFITH, GEORGE (victim)

Like Frederick Gold, George Stonhouse Griffith was a worthy Brighton citizen who met his death while travelling, well away from his home town. He had moved to Brighton in

November 1845 to join Isaac Sewell, Manager of the Branch County Bank at Brighton, as principal partner in the brewery business, Griffith & Co. Its 'Rock Ale' was well-known throughout the town and across the county.

Griffith, a highly intelligent man who won many friends, became an active member of the town's Commissioners. He lived in a substantial residence, 25 Montpelier Crescent, with his wife and two sons, aged 8 and 10. On 11 January 1849, his chief clerk, William Shubrick Martin, received a strange anonymous letter postmarked Trafalgar Street. It was written in a disguised hand, with (probably deliberate) spelling errors, warning Martins [sic] to be on his guard as some parties intended to rob him the next time he went to Horsham.

George Griffith, as depicted in a chalk and charcoal sketch by J Watkins, 1845. Glenn Chandler collection

In the event, Griffith himself insisted on undertaking the next journey across the county, visiting customers, taking orders and collecting moneys owed. He set out on 6 February, arming himself with two pistols (one loaded and the other not), two powder flasks and some bullets. He declined Martin's offer to accompany him.

By late evening, he was back in Horsham, having passed through in the morning and made a number of calls during the day. He then drove in his gig to Henfield, where he had one last business call to make at the *White Hart*. After a meal he set out briskly on the last stage home at about 9 pm. There were two turnpikes on the road to Brighton: Terry's Cross Gate and, some three miles further south, Dale Gate. The road was lonely, rough and steep, sloping up to the Downs on one side. Griffith had to walk his horse up the hill towards Newtimber Church, and again up the following ascent, which was just a quarter of a mile short of Dale Gate in Pyecombe parish.

Sounds of alarm and distress were heard by residents in the vicinity. Two of them in separate locations heard firearms going off at around 9.30 pm. The lifeless Griffith was discovered at about 2 am by two brothers from Hove, Charles and James Hodson, and their companion Charles Kirton, who had been dining in Woodmancote. To their horror, they recognised Griffith as an acquaintance of theirs. They put the body into the cart to take to the *Plough* public house at Pyecombe. There they observed the single fatal pistol shot wound in the chest and immediately informed the nearest constable.

Griffith had clearly fought for his life and had taken off a glove to reach for one of the pistols in his pocket. In the heat of the moment, however, he had unfortunately drawn out the wrong weapon, since the loaded pistol was found in his coat pocket. A subsequent police examination indicated that an attempt had been made to use the unloaded firearm.

The assailant's booty consisted of some £20 – a very substantial sum in those days – in cash, a £5 Brighton Union Bank note, a cheque for £13, various coins and a gold watch. The gig had been turned back in its tracks and was discovered at Poynings.

Brighton police and a great number of townsfolk – many of them personal friends of the deceased – visited the murder scene, which was about seven miles from Brighton. Despite the offer of a very substantial reward of £300 and a free pardon to an accomplice for information leading to the conviction of the culprit(s), no clue to the perpetrator(s) of the murder was ever discovered. The inquest verdict was 'Murder by persons unknown'.

Strangely, Griffith's watch was found some years later by some workmen cleaning out the mud from a pond close to the road along which he had passed. They had acted on the advice of a helpful passer-by. No one thought to question the stranger further and he was not seen again.

H

HALL, Sir EDWARD MARSHALL

Edward, (later Sir Edward) Marshall Hall, KC, MP, one of England's foremost lawyers who became known as 'the Great Defender', was born at 30 Old Steine, Brighton, in 1858. The house, a stone's throw from where the Palace Pier would be built, is (aptly) occupied by a firm of solicitors and Hall is commemorated on a dark grey plaque by the entrance. A city bus also bears his name.

Over seven decades, Hall was involved in some of the most notorious crimes tried in his native Sussex, at the Old Bailey and elsewhere.

His father, Dr Alfred Hall, was a well-known Brighton physician who practised locally until his death in 1897 at the age of 85. He gave Hall his middle name 'Marshall' in honour of the eminent physician and physiologist, Marshall Hall (1790–1857).

Edward had an enduring love of firearms which stood him in good stead in his career.

His interest in the law was awakened by attending the local proceedings against CHRISTIANA EDMUNDS, the 'Chocolate Cream Poisoner'. He wagered – successfully – that LEFROY, the Brighton train murderer, would hang. He actually saw Lefroy arrive at Brighton Station, dishevelled, bloody and fresh from his crime, on 27 June 1881.

On leaving Rugby, where he won a mathematics prize, Hall went to Cambridge, leaving with a pass degree in 1882.

He was a keen cricket player and passed his weekends in his younger days playing at Hove for the Gentlemen of Sussex.

After working briefly and joylessly in a London tea-broker's office, spending time in Paris and travelling to Australia and elsewhere, he was called to the Bar in 1883, having married a childhood sweetheart the previous year.

He enjoyed early successes when working as a junior on the South-Eastern circuit and the Sussex Sessions. His first criminal defence was at Lewes Assizes for a fee of only 15s, which was all the prisoner could afford. He secured an acquittal.

Probably his first attendance at Lewes Quarter Sessions was in 1884, when he defended two men for receiving varnish they knew to be stolen. Sustained by recognising a fellow-cricketer among the jury, Hall obtained a Not Guilty verdict by his eloquence and said many years later: 'I think I felt prouder then than I have ever felt before or since.'

When the son of one of the outdoor servants at Horsted Place was indicted for apparently having kicked his wife to death on the Downs, Hall got the charge of murder reduced to manslaughter in the first of a long series of brilliant defences of capital offenders.

In 1887, two co-defendants named Barker and Hughes employed Hall and the eminent Charles Gill to defend them before the Recorder of Brighton in the notorious 'Love Home' case. The defendants had attacked the Edward Street premises (a converted stable) of a strange sect known as the 'Army of the Lord', run by a charlatan named John

William Wood. The misappropriation of funds, bankruptcy and sexual exploitation of younger female followers by this self-styled 'King Solomon' undermined his position and Hall won an acquittal for his clients.

In 1900, he appeared at Lewes Assizes, powerfully defending Brighton publican Tom Packham, who had killed his wife Lucy after a drunken quarrel on their premises, the *Marlborough Hotel* in Prince's Street (see p. 96). Hall's skills reduced the almost inevitable murder verdict to one of manslaughter and a sentence of four years' penal servitude.

Inevitably, there were failures: the impossible task of defending Dr Crippen, the wife-killer

Marshall Hall in 1903. Vanity Fair

(1910); the trial of the arrogant and miserly Frederick Seddon, who murdered his lodger for her money (1911); the infamous Brides in the Bath case (1915); and the Crumbles beach murder at Eastbourne (1920), in which two young ex-servicemen named Field and Gray were hanged for murdering an attractive 17-year-old typist.

Perhaps Hall's greatest disappointment was the Birkenhead case of Lock Ah Tam, one of the most influential of the Chinese community in England, who in December 1925 shot his wife and both his daughters. Tam was so popular locally that £1,000 was collected for Marshall Hall to defend him. The prosecution case was too strong, however, and the killer was hanged.

Yet Hall's successes during his long career were, without question, numerous, with the occasional dramatic defence. One such was his last capital case. Alfonso Smith was charged with murdering his friend, John Derma, whom he had indeed shot dead. Yet the barrister, dramatically producing a revolver in court, demonstrated that the shot could have been accidental. He secured for Smith a sentence of one year's imprisonment with hard labour.

Marshall Hall's final, and losing, battle came in early 1927, when he contracted bronchitis and pneumonia following influenza. He fought on for a month, during which time many of the enquiries as to his state came from the King himself. When he succumbed, the flag over the Inner Temple flew at half-mast, and the notables of the English bar met in the Lord Chief Justice's court to honour the memory of one of Brighton's most renowned sons.

HAMILTON, PATRICK (1904–1962)

English playwright and novelist, born Anthony Walter Patrick Hamilton in Hassocks, near Brighton. After a short career as an actor, he became an author in his early twenties with the publication of *Monday Morning* (1925), written when he was nineteen. *Craven House* (1926) and *Twopence Coloured* (1928) followed, but his first real success was the play *Rope* (1929). The *Midnight Bell* (1929) is based upon his falling in love with a prostitute, and was later published along with *The Siege of Pleasure* (1932) and *The Plains of Cement* (1934) as the semi-autobiographical trilogy *20,000 Streets Under the Sky* (1935).

In 1941 appeared Hamilton's *Hangover Square*, a grim study of a schizophrenic named George Harvey Bone who lives in the lower depths of Earl's Court, London. His mental deterioration is worsened by his love for a feckless whore, Netta Longdon, who is unfaithful to him with his best friends. Bone's agony forces him to revenge. Who can forget the memorable and brooding pen-portrait of Brighton the book contains?

While Brighton slept – North Street, West Street, East Street, Western Road, Preston Street, Hove, the hotels, the shops, the restaurants, the movies, the baths, the booths, the churches, the Market, the Post Office, the pubs, the antiques, the second-hand bookshops – slept and gleamed and climbed up from the sea under the dark blue dawn, the enormous gloomy man walked along the front, hardly visible in the darkness, seemingly the only wayfarer, the only one awake. And he looked out at the sea and wondered what it was he had to do. When he remembered he was about opposite the Grand. He remembered without any trouble, any strain. He had to kill Netta Longdon.

Behind the story was Hamilton's unrequited passion for the actress Geraldine Fitzgerald in the mid-1930s.

Hangover Square, judged his most accomplished work, was filmed by Twentieth Century-Fox before the end of the Second World War, but commercial considerations persuaded the makers to eliminate the Brighton locations and substitute the Edwardian age for the book's contemporary setting.

His Gorse Trilogy – three novels about a devious sexual predator and conman, the character of whom owes something to the psychopath Neville Heath – is not generally well thought of critically, although Graham Greene said of the first (*The West Pier*, 1952) that it was 'the best book written about Brighton'.

Hamilton, twice married, had begun to drink heavily while still relatively young. After a declining career and depression, he died in 1962 of cirrhosis of the liver and kidney failure in Sheringham, Norfolk.

Continuing the strong recent revival of interest in his work, BBC2 screened an adaptation of *20,000 Streets Under the Sky* in September 2005. It was reshown on BBC4 in January 2006, alongside a documentary account of Hamilton's life.

HIGHWAY ROBBERY

On 20 October 1800, a man by the name of Edwards who drove a vehicle described as a stage cart from Lewes to Brighton, was stopped on his return journey near the two-mile stone by two footpads (one in a soldier's uniform), who knocked him from his cart and, after robbing him of more than £10, made off. Edward's dog attacked one of the robbers but suffered for it, being wounded in the head – apparently with a bayonet.

A 'technical' highway robbery of between no less than £3,000 and £4,000 – a fabulous sum in those days – took place on 5 February 1812 from Messrs Crossweller and Co's Blue Coach between London and Brighton. The money was in the form of Brighton Union Bank notes which mysteriously vanished *en route*.

Messrs Brown, Hall, Lashmar, and West, of the Union Bank hired by Messrs Crossweller and Co, of the Borough, Southwark, placed the notes in the cash-box to be forwarded, as usual, to Brighton. When the coach arrived in East Street, John Pocock (Brown and Co's clerk) discovered, on unlocking the seat of the coach, that the box had been broken open and its entire contents removed. The only light the coachman could shed on the business was that six persons were booked for inside places. Two – a couple – appeared when the coach started and two gentlemen were collected on the road; the others never showed up. When Sutton was reached, the lady was suddenly taken ill and had to alight at the inn, where the coachman left her and her husband. At Reigate, the two other men inside left the coach to enquire – they said – after a friend; they quickly returned, however, and told the coachman that a gentleman that they supposed was at Brighton had returned to town, so there was no point in them continuing their journey...

A reward of £300 was immediately offered for information whereby the parcel could be recovered, a sum subsequently altered to 100 guineas for 'information of the offender' and £300 'upon the recovery of the whole of the above property, or 10 per cent, upon the amount of so much thereof as shall be recovered'. An addendum to a coach advertisement in the *Brighton Herald* in the week following the theft stated: 'Not accountable for any parcel above £5, unless entered as such and paid for accordingly.'

The perpetrators were never discovered, nor were the notes – although about twelve months later, an attempt was made to put them into circulation.

In September 1821, a portmanteau belonging to one of George IV's footmen and containing the Royal State liveries, a large stock of linen, etc., was robbed near Tooting.

HOLFORD, HARVEY

He loved my mother very much and he never ever got over her death and what he had done. He felt deeply that he had destroyed all that he had.

(Karen Beaumont, née Holford, June 2006)

At Christmas 1959, 18-year-old Christine Hughes from the Brighton suburb of Saltdean met 31-year-old local clubowner Harvey Holford at his club, the *Blue Gardenia*. Following an unsuccessful attempt at elopement in July 1960, they finally married in November 1960. In May 1961, a daughter was born, whom they named Karen Lesley Tracey. Initially they were tremendously happy, but Holford was disturbed by his wife's flirtatious tendencies. He himself was flamboyant and successful, earning well from his clubs, the *Whisky-a-Go Go*, the *Blue Gardenia* and the *Calypso* at 4 Queen Square. His enormous scarlet Pontiac Parisienne – often with his motor boat and trailer in tow – was a familiar sight around the town's streets.

Everything changed in the summer of 1962, when Valerie Hatcher, their 19-year-old live-in nanny, persuaded Christine to go on holiday to France with her, leaving the baby behind. Holford had no objection.

Soon Christine was being unfaithful, initially – and by arrangement – in Paris and Cannes with a young Swiss waiter who had been sacked from the *Blue Gardenia*. He was succeeded a fortnight or so later by a German drummer in a band and an Italian restaurateur. She was then introduced to the extremely wealthy entrepreneur, John Bloom, and became besotted with him – and his wealth. At Cap Ferrat, they became lovers.

Bloom was married but wanted to make Christine his mistress. He promised her a flat in Mayfair and another in Monte Carlo, plus, reportedly, £20,000 a year. Utterly naive, the young mother thought her husband would approve of this arrangement and consider it a good deal. He, meanwhile, was missing her greatly, drinking and losing interest in his business.

By 11 August – his birthday – Holford had had enough. He flew to Nice and there he was told about Bloom. Two days later, he and Christine were back in Brighton and even got on tolerably well for a time. But Christine's heart was not in the marriage. There were fearful rows and Holford found her diary containing incriminating names. He beat her particularly badly and cut off her hair, yet gave her a primrose-coloured Ford Anglia on her 21st birthday. Her frequent mentions of Bloom were a constant provocation, however.

On the night of 14/15 September, the police were called to the Queen Square flat and found the couple in bed apparently sleeping. But Holford had overdosed and

Christine and Harvey. Their happiness was short-lived. Mirrorpix

87

his wife was dead from six bullet wounds. She had been shot three times in the head and three in the body and lay in a pool of blood. The clubowner kept firearms, partly out of interest and partly for protection. It later emerged that the final provocation he had endured was being told that Karen was not in fact his child.

Not until 82 hours after the discovery of the couple in bed did Holford recover consciousness at the Royal Sussex County Hospital. When questioned on 18 September, he could not tell the police anything, even though he appeared rational. He was remanded in Lewes Prison where, in December 1962, he fractured his skull in a suicide bid, jumping from the safety wire on the first-floor landing. He was kept under 24-hour surveillance and his trial was postponed until March.

Concerning the shooting, Holford testified: 'It is like a dream. How many times I shot her I do not know ... I just wanted to die ... I took all the tablets I could find ... I now regret doing this.' He told the court about the improvements he made to the flat, including the penthouse he helped to build, claiming there was nothing he would not do for Christine. 'I was building a palace for my princess,' he said.

On 29 March 1963, to applause and clapping from the public gallery, the verdict returned by the jury following the 7-day trial was manslaughter on the grounds of provocation and diminished responsibility. Mr Justice Streatfeild stated 'there must be few men indeed who have been subjected to greater provocation than you were.'

Harvey Leo Holford's sentence was three years' imprisonment for manslaughter. He was paroled on 2 October 1964.

Changing his name to Robert Keith Beaumont, he turned to estate agency. From 1974 he directed much of his life to the MARIA COLWELL Memorial Fund which he set up in that year to fight for legislation to protect children from abuse. Also in 1974, he stood twice – unsuccessfully – as a candidate in both general elections, polling 428 votes in the first as an independent candidate for the Brighton Pavilion constituency and 155 votes in the second as the English National Party candidate for Brighton Kemp Town. One of his election messages was that convicted child killers should be executed.

Harvey Holford died of leukaemia on 27 June 2006 at the age of 77.

HOLLOWAY, JOHN

Brighton's first 'trunk murderer', John Holloway, was born in 1806 in Lewes. In 1818, his family moved to Brighton to seek work. There, in his teens, he turned to petty crime, drinking and womanising. At the age of 17 or 18, he met his future victim, the singularly unattractive Celia Bashford.

Bashford, a native of Ardingly, West Sussex, was born in 1800, one of 10 children. She met Holloway at Brighton Races and became deeply attached to him. Although he despised her, not even wishing to be seen with her till after dark, he nevertheless made her pregnant. He refused, however, to marry her. Bashford thereupon applied to the Overseers of her parish for relief for herself and her unborn child, naming Holloway as the father-to-be. The Ardingly Poor Law authorities had him imprisoned in Lewes until he agreed to marry her. This he did after five weeks, when they bailed him out. 'I married through fear of lying in prison', he later recorded. 'I did not marry her for love ... I loved her as a friend.'

They returned to Brighton, where they lived in various lodgings and Holloway obtained work. He grew increasingly resentful, however, believing the child – which was in any event stillborn – had been fathered by someone else, something Bashford would always deny.

John Holloway in Horsham Gaol, painted at the particular request of his mother by J Perez of Brighton. Author's collection

Ann Kennett as she appeared at Holloway's trial. Drawing by J Perez. Author's collection

Relations between the couple deteriorated and Celia's brother took her back to Ardingly for a time. Holloway went to sea then returned to Brighton, where, strangely, the couple resumed their relationship and Bashford again fell pregnant, although the infant girl died in infancy.

Holloway was away when this happened, having joined the Naval Blockade Service in 1827. When based at Rye he met, and bigamously married, Ann Kennett. Only 20, she had already had two illegitimate children. She became pregnant by Holloway but miscarried. As the pregnancy had been the main reason for their wedding, history bizarrely repeated itself.

The couple returned to Brighton, where they took up lodgings at 7 Margaret Street. Holloway found work as a painter on the Chain Pier, while Celia, learning of his return, promptly applied to the Brighton Poor Law authorities for relief. In June 1831 the Overseers imposed an order on the errant husband to pay two shillings a week maintenance, but he could not keep this up. In

The lovers dismembering Celia Holloway at 11 Donkey Row. Author's collection

LIFE, Trial, Confession and
EXECUTION
Of JOHN Wm. HOLLAWAY,
Who was EXECUTED at HORSHAM. For the MURDER
OF CELIA HOLLAWAY, HIS WIFE

A Copy of Verses

Written on the above Occasion.

O did you ever hear a deed,
so barbarous and severe,
As Hollaway did of late commit,
n his Virtuous Wife so dear.
He mangled her most barbarously,
er limbs from off her bod- tore,
nd nearl eight months gone with child,
She weltered in her gore.

He in a privy first placed her limbs,
here also put her head,
ow barbarous he used her,
efore that she was dead,
ut Justice did him overtake,
And that right speedily,
nd for the same his day did end,
Upon the gallows high.

It was upon last Wednesday,
They placed him at the Bar,
To hear the Murders tried,
Honestly wandered from afar,
his heinous did beside him stand,
With Hollaway she was tried,
she said in hard I'm innocent,
I am innocent she cried.

When Holla ay was tried and cast,
he Judge to him did say,
You must return from whence you came,
and a wait the awful da ,
Your do s must end on Frida next,
Upon the fatal tree,
And for your bad for our cruel deeds,
Must then dissected be.

When on killed poor la ful victim,
You could no mercy give,
nd n t it s orld no longer no ,
You can expect to live,
but nothing did ing seem to s ock,
Ho s awful for to pen,
When the Judge did pass t is sentence
he Murder er cried amen.

Ma old and young was going take,
Be his unjoined fate,
I ook on t e e imes of Hollawa ,
And repent befo e too la e,
Le t e now de of is haw ful i e,
Fo t is d cad el c uel y:
He died exposed o Public gaze,
Upon the al tree

JOHN WM. HOLLAWAY, alias, Goldsmith, aged 25 & Ann KENNARD was placed at the Bar on a Charge of Wilful and barbarous Murder, Committed on the Body of CELIA HOLLAWAY, the Wife of John Hollaway. — *Wednesday Dec 14th 1831.*

David Maskell sworn:— I live at Brighton and am a labourer, On Monday afternoon, in July last, I went into a place called "the Rottingdeam," in Preston, which lies on the side of the high road, in the plantation, of Mr Standford's Farm, and in a sort of hollow, overhung with branches of trees a little on the left of a narrow footpath up the hill, leading from the "Hole in the Wall," to the Church hill, I stooped to the earth, and fancied some of it had been moved. I poked some of the mould away with my stick and saw a piece of red cotton, sticking through the earth, I took no particular notice of it then; but went home, and mentioned it to my wife, who said it might be a small child buried there. I mentioned it to several persons, but I did not go and tell the Magistrates. I mention'd it to a Mrs. Gillam, and on Friday Night myself and her husband went to the spot between 6 & 7 o'Clock, Gillam scratched the dirt a-way, and the piece of red cotton was still there. We poked the stick into the earth which smelt very strong and nasty.

Several other witnesses proved that the prisoner, had often threatened to ki l his wife and treated her in a most brutal manner.

After the evidence had been gone through the following Confession signed by Hollaway was read.

When at four o'clock in the afternoon on Thursday 11th, of July, Hollaway took his wife from her lodgings, they went straight to the house, North Steine Row, which he had hired expressly for the commission of the Murder; and to which he had just before taken her things. On Hollaway opening the street door, his wife first entered, and was going up stairs, when without fastning the door he approached her, as though he was going to kiss her, and suddenly tying a cord and threw himself upon her back

and exerted all his force to strangle her, the poor creature in resisting fell to the bottom of the stairs, where she continued strugg ling; Hollaway, with an end of the cord in each hand, called to Ann for assistance, and Geo. I knows she assisted me by taking hold of each end of the rope, untill the poor girl dropped I then held the cord myself and Ann made use of this expression—"Do not let your heart fail you." After having committed the Murder, the next question was what was to be done was to be done with the body.—Holla ways, first idea, was to cut it up at once, and then remove it peacemeal. He then dragged the body to the closet beneath the stairs where he hung it on a nail for the night.

The next day Hol away went to the h ouse, and having taken down the body, cut off the head, then the legs and afterwards (for the convenance of packing the trunk in the box) the arms and thighs; he then put the head away, and legs, in the tocking. It was then a reed that he should go but with his bag to the privy in Margarets Kennet followed to see if any blood oozed out The first attempt he said failed. They returned to Dankey we and put the head and limbs into a small box, and then mix then took and carried them away. Kennet followed him

Mr. Justice Patison summoned up the e dence, and the Jury without hesitation found the prisoner Guilty Death, on hearing the verdict, the prisoners face assumed a pallid hue and his hands appeared shor con. He stood up firm in the Dock and evidence of death was being passed. When his Lordship concluded by praying the Lord to have mercy upon his soul, he d as in a tone, "Amen." He was sentenced to be hanged on Friday and his body to be given for Dissection.

At an early hour on Friday morning the Town of Horsham nd the roads leading from Brighton, and all parts of the Coun try eaten, were thronged with spectators, to witness the fix cut on of John Wiltren the luny, alias Goldsmith,

At the usual hour the unfortunate man ascended the Pla tform ctied by the clergyman and the Executioner, and after a few mo nts being spent in prayer the bolt was drawn and he was ushe t om Eternity, amidst thousands of Spectators.

[Printed by]
CARPUE
Rose Lane,
Spitalfields.

A broadside chronicling Holloway's crime. It contains the testimony of David Maskell, who discovered Celia's body, and a confession by Holloway. The 'Rottingdean' to which it refers is a location in Preston, near Brighton, and not the village some three miles east of Brighton. The Argus/Press Association

addition, there were occasional confrontations between the two women. Holloway saw only one way out of his predicament.

With another child due within a fortnight (fathered, incredibly, by Holloway), Celia was persuaded to go with him to a mean dwelling at 11 Donkey Row, or North Steyne Row, where he said they would live and where, on the pretext of kissing her, he strangled her on the stairs – assisted at one point by Kennett, who had concealed herself in the house.

The following morning, they dismembered the body and took the head and limbs to Margaret Street, dropping them in the common privy. That night they conveyed Celia's torso in a wheelbarrow to Preston Village, north of Brighton, thence to a copse near a track known as Lovers' Walk, where it was placed in a shallow grave.

Although clues to the burial were discovered on 25 July, it was not until mid-August that the parish constable was called in and uncovered the torso, with a male foetus protruding from it. Holloway and Kennett had meanwhile moved to High Street, Brighton, but the privy at 7 Margaret Street was soon made to yield its grisly secret.

Holloway gave himself up and Kennett was apprehended. The inquest jury returned a verdict of Wilful Murder against the killer and he was removed to Horsham Gaol. There he tried more than once to commit suicide and finally confessed (in three versions) to his crime. Kennett, meanwhile, was detained in Lewes House of Correction.

At the couple's trial at Lewes Assizes on 15 December 1831, however, the murderer pleaded Not Guilty although by the end of the day the jury gave their verdict to the contrary. John Holloway was hanged on 21 December and his body was displayed at Brighton Town Hall for 24 hours, where it attracted no fewer than 23,000 spectators. It was then removed for dissection.

Kennett got off lightly. Fainting and tearful, she was dismissed early in the Assize trial, the judge's opinion being that she was Not Guilty. She was also found Not Guilty at the March 1832 Lewes Assizes on a charge of concealing and harbouring Holloway. With her baby, Ann, in her arms, she won the judge's sympathy and this rubbed off on the jury. Yet his lordship's words: 'No wife can ever be found guilty of assisting her own husband ... the law cannot touch her ...' strike us as astonishing today.

Celia Holloway, the tragic victim, is remembered on a wall plaque in the churchyard of St Peter's, Preston, Brighton.

HOMOSEXUALITY

Brighton, in fact, is ten or twenty watering places rolled into one ... so much larger, grander and gayer than all the sea-bathing resorts in England as to well deserve the title of their queen.
(From *Mattins and Muttons* (1866) – with apologies to the author, 'Cuthbert Bede' (Reverend Edward Bradley))

Perception and legislation
Buggery was until recent times a criminal offence – and formerly a capital one. Not until 1861 was the death penalty for indulging in it abolished, although the last two men to be hanged for the offence had been John Smith and James Pratt in 1835.

Under the Criminal Law Amendment Act of 1885, almost any sexual contact between males was made a serious criminal offence, punishable by up to two years' hard labour. Because it paved the way to blackmail, contemporaries dubbed it a 'blackmailer's charter'. The criminalisation of male soliciting dates from the Vagrancy Act 1898. It remains a crime for a man to 'persistently solicit or importune in a public place for immoral purposes'.

In 1912, Havelock Ellis observed that England possessed the most draconian laws against homosexuality, but in contrast to countries such as Germany used them more sparingly.

Changes were made to the law following the Wolfenden Report of 1957 whereby homosexual acts between adult men (homosexual acts between women were never illegal) were legal if they took place in private. Ten years later, the Sexual Offences Act exempted gay sex from criminal prosecution if it took place between two consenting males aged 21 or over in private. Procuring homosexual acts remains illegal, in most circumstances, under those Acts.

Section 28 was a controversial amendment to the United Kingdom's Local Government Act 1986, enacted by the Local Government Act 1988 on 24 May of that year and repealed on 18 November 2003. The amendment stated that a local authority 'shall not intentionally promote homosexuality or publish material with the intention of promoting homosexuality' or 'promote the teaching in any maintained school of the acceptability of homosexuality as a pretended family relationship'.

In 1989, there were some 2,500 prosecutions of gay men for consensual acts, but this figure fell sharply within the decade. In 1994, the gay male age of consent was lowered from 21 to 18 and in 2001 to 16.

Key dates in homosexual history, from 1290 to the present, are set out in detail at: http://www.stonewall.org.uk/information_bank/history_lesbian_gay/89.asp

Early cases

In August 1822, George Wilson, a servant from Newcastle-upon-Tyne, was accused by a soldier of the Third Regiment of Light Dragoons he had met in the *Duke of Wellington* public house in Pool Valley of having offered him a sovereign and two shillings to 'go with him to the beach and there commit an unnatural crime'. The soldier called in a night constable. The offender's only excuse was that of intoxication. He was sent to gaol for two years.

Stanley Stokes, a London solicitor who had been making sexual approaches to a groom at the *New Ship Hotel*, was in May 1836 mobbed and tarred. He cut his own throat in East Street and died two days later. In January the following year, according to Brighton Vestry, a man who had 'made a proposition of a disgusting nature' to a Grenadier Guard on sentry duty at the Royal Pavilion was allowed to escape by the arresting officers (they may have been mindful of the recent Stokes' case).

Brighton's present gay capital, Kemp Town, was where the 6th Duke of Devonshire, a bachelor, enjoyed an unusually close friendship with his butler, who for 25 years occupied a small house connected to the rear of the Duke's home.

Early lesbian relationships included that between philanthropist Angela Burdett-Coutts (1814–1906) and her companion Hannah. They spent part of each year on holiday at the *Royal Albion Hotel* and were socially recognised as a pair. They even sent joint Christmas cards. When Hannah died in 1878, Miss Burdett-Coutts mourned the passing of 'the companion and sunshine of my life for 52 years'.

Miss Harriet Rowell was a teacher of swimming at Brill's Baths in Pool Valley under the name of Miss Elphinstone Dick in the 1870s who won a series of public swimming feats. She fell in love with a Brighton woman, Alice Moon, and the couple emigrated to Australia, where they started a women's gymnasium and taught gymnastics.

The Brighton Man/Woman
Lillias Valerie Arkell-Smith (1895–1960), aka Lillias Barker, left her husband and Australian soldier Ernest Pearce Crouch in 1923 to begin a life as a man under the assumed identity of Victor Barker. She checked into the *Grand Hotel* in Brighton as Sir Victor Barker and as Colonel Victor Barker married Elfrida Haward later that year at St Peter's church. They honeymooned at the *Grand*. Lillias, regarded by Radclyffe Hall (author of *The Well of Loneliness*) as a 'mad pervert of the most undesirable kind', was found guilty of describing herself as a bachelor in a register of marriage and sentenced to nine months' imprisonment. The *Evening Argus* commented 'there are obvious difficulties in discussing the case'. She then pursued careers as an actor, boxing club manager, dog kennel manager, dairy farmer, café owner and fruit picker. In 1929, as Captain Leslie Ivor Victor Gauntlett Bligh Barker, she found work as a hotel clerk. After service in the Home Guard as Jeffrey Norton she lived as the husband of Eva Norton.

Gay meeting-places
By the 1930s, pubs in and around Brighton with a lesbian or gay clientele were flourishing – among these, the *Star of Brunswick* in Brunswick Street West and Pigott's bar at the *St James's Tavern* in Madeira Place were especially popular with the boys and girls respectively. Playwright and local historian John Montgomery later wrote:

> From London in the thirties we used to roar down to Brighton in fast sports cars ... The main rendezvous was the Star of Brunswick *pub in Hove, outside which Rolls Royces, Daimlers and MGs were parked far up the street. There was also the* New Pier *Tavern, long since gone, with its noisy honky-tonk piano, thick atmosphere of tobacco and sprinkling of red-coated, pink-faced guardsmen, and sailors from Portsmouth.*

The war and after
Although Brighton was closed to casual visitors during the Second World War for reasons of national security, there was compensation for gays in the wide availability of soldiers. The Sussex Arts Ball, held annually in the ballroom of the Aquarium (now Brighton Sea Life Centre) was started in 1947 and became a magnet for cross-dressing gays of both sexes, including flamboyant drag artist, Betty Lou. Another popular gay venue was the *Marine Hotel* (see ARSON).

There was, however, a reluctance to go to gay bars and clubs in the 1950s and '60s – the police were known to raid such haunts, taking names and addresses of those present. People usually kept a 'club name' for these occasions. Yet Brighton was the premier destination for British gay holidaymakers until the late 1960s, when the cheap package holiday changed the face of tourism. Venues ranged from the lavish *Regina Club* in North Street and the very select *Argyle Hotel* in Middle Street to the *Belvedere* and *Fortune of War* pubs on the seafront.

The *Forty-Two Club* at 42, King's Road was Brighton's longest running gay venue, opened in the Fifties by the licensee of the *Greyhound* in East Street, which had a gay bar upstairs.

The Sussex Gay Liberation Front (SGLF) was established in February 1971 by a group of Sussex University students and lesbians and gay men from the town. They organised the first gay demonstration in Brighton in October 1972 and the first Brighton Gay Pride march in July 1973. Only a tiny minority of the town's gay population was ready to take to the streets, however, and there was not another Brighton Pride until

1991. What was to become Brighton Gay Switchboard started in 1975 at the Open Café, a centre for alternative politics in Victoria Road.

In 1985 the Sussex AIDS Helpline was set up and soon its activities expanded to include training for volunteers who would deliver a home care service for people living with AIDS.

Public meetings in opposition to Section 28 were held in Brighton, the first of them in February 1988. One of the spin-offs of the campaign was the setting up of the lesbian and gay history group 'Brighton Ourstory Project'. Throughout the 1990s and beyond, it produced shows, exhibitions and books based on interviews with a wide variety of gay people about their lives.

Brighton Pride has grown into a major attraction for residents and visitors alike. The first Pride in the Park took place in 1992, organised by a group of community activists called Pink Parasol. The organisers of Brighton Pride '95 were the first to attract major sponsorship and bring the pubs, clubs and drag artists on board. Thereafter, the event went from strength to strength with Pride 2000 and 2001 reporting 60,000 visitors.

HOOGSTRATEN, NICHOLAS VAN (1945–)

I deal with people in cold blood, not hot blood. (1992 interview)

Nicholas Marcel Van Hoogstraten (he added the 'Van' later) is a wealthy local business-man and property owner whose dealings and methods have earned him a notorious reputation. Judges have variously referred to him as a 'bully' and a 'self-appointed emissary of Beelzebub', but he holds them in contempt (he was once brought to book for calling magistrates 'trash'). Others he scorns include tenants, whom he has branded 'filth' and 'scum', and the Ramblers' Association, with whom he engaged in a long-running feud concerning a 140-year-old right of way which runs across his land and which he obstructed. Spells in prison resulted from organising a grenade attack on a debtor's home and, more recently, for manslaughter.

He was born in 1945 (not 1946 as commonly reported) in Shoreham-by-Sea, the son of strictly Catholic Marcel, aka Charles, Hoogstraten, who worked for the Dutch East India Trading Company. From the age of 14, Nicholas was educated at a Jesuit school in Worthing, attending senior school in a three-piece suit and carrying a copy of the FT to study his mining shares. He refused to go to certain classes, instead sitting alone in empty classrooms attending to his business.

Taken out of school at 16, he joined the merchant navy and stayed in it for a year. During his voyages as a lift boy he saw how Florida was being developed and started his property business in Bermuda using the £30,000 or so proceeds from the sale of a valuable stamp collection as initial finance.

In 1963, aged 18, Hoogstraten spent £40,000 on mining claims and land in the southern African country of Zimbabwe (then Rhodesia) striking up a friendship with magnate Tiny Rowland of Lonrho. He became a financial backer for the Zanu–PF party as it fought for liberation from the colonial Government. Over the years he contributed hundreds of thousands of pounds and in return his properties, which covered more than a quarter of a million acres, remained untouched, although by 2002 three of his prime properties had been seized and others invaded.

By 1967, when he was only 22 and Britain's youngest millionaire, Hoogstraten had 300 run-down properties in Brighton, all of them bought dirt-cheap at auction. He would sometimes even buy up whole streets. Eventually he would own 2,000 properties. After refurbishing them with government grants, he would sell them on with vacant possession at a vast profit. Existing tenants, often on low rents, were an inconvenience and their lives made unbearable. Repairs were not carried out and power might be cut off for extended intervals. One elderly couple who complained of litter in the garden of the house where they had lived for 32 years woke to find Hoogstraten had shipped in a mound of garbage and lorryloads of horse manure.

Other local business interests included ownership of a nightclub and a partnership in a Brighton fashion boutique. This venture failed and he fell out with his partner, David Braunstein, in a dispute over money. Hoogstraten's men visited Braunstein's house and lobbed a hand grenade through the ground floor window, although luckily the intended victim, his wife and their six children were upstairs and were uninjured. 'Mr H', as he has styled himself, was in August 1968 jailed for four years for the attack. He was simultaneously sentenced for five years for housebreaking, larceny, burglary and receiving more than £7,000 worth of stolen property. Minutes after his release in 1972 he was arrested and later jailed for 15 months for bribing a warder to smuggle luxuries into his cell. On his release following a successful appeal, his first visit was to an accountant who, he believed, had stolen £14,000 from him while he was inside. The man was shipped off to France where he was forced to work off his debt in isolation, living on a diet of sardines for a year.

'Accidents' befell tenants who complained. In 1974 he was fined £3,000 following a harsh eviction exercise in Vere Road, dubbed the 'Battle of Brighton', during which he smashed up furniture and removed windows. He famously told the *Evening Argus* 'This is the best bit of fun I've had in ages.' He even took the roof off a house in Portslade, contemptuously dismissing the occupants as 'squatters'.

In 1978 he was back in the headlines when a company of which he was director, Getherwell Finance Ltd, barricaded 12 elderly people in a nursing home, holding siege as they attempted to take possession.

In 1980 he made the *Guinness Book of Records* for being served a £5.3 million bill for unpaid tax – the largest independent bill ever sent out by the Inland Revenue. It was paid in two years.

He then turned to activities abroad, investing in other fields which included mining interests in Nigeria and, again, in Zimbabwe (mainly acquired from the Lonrho conglomerate). Nearer home, he has land holdings in Cannes, Cap Ferrat, Monte Carlo, Maryland, Florida and Barbados.

In 1985 he began building a sumptuous home, Hamilton Palace, on the old High Cross estate near Uckfield in East Sussex, thought to be the largest private dwelling to be constructed in the UK in the twentieth century. The vast edifice, named after the capital of Bermuda, is intended to house his collection of art and includes his mausoleum. A good description of the structure and works in progress in 2000 is to be found in a site visit and interview with the tycoon by Emma Brockes ('Even Nastier Nick', *The Guardian*, Friday September 8, 2000). By 2002 the cost had risen to around £35 million.

In 1992 Hoogstraten was linked, via a network of companies, to 11 Palmeira Avenue, Hove, where five people died in a fire. Three jumped to their deaths because there was no fire escape. He initially denied any connection with the building but, after an investigation by *The Argus*, admitted it was linked to him in 'some way'.

In July 1999, a former business associate of his and notorious Brighton slum landlord, Mohammed Raja, 62, who had been in the process of suing Hoogstraten for fraud, was shot and stabbed at his home in Sutton, Surrey. Evidence pointed to the two murderers, David Croke and Robert Knapp, being hired by Hoogstraten. In 2002, Hoogstraten was sentenced to 10 years' imprisonment for manslaughter. Although found not guilty of

Nicholas Marcel Van Hoogstraten – a tycoon in and out of trouble during the last four decades. Press Association

murder, he was convicted of manslaughter. The conviction was overturned in July 2003 at the Court of Appeal, however, due to a technical flaw in jury instructions in the Old Bailey trial.

In an exclusive interview for *The Argus* soon after his release in December 2003, Hoogstraten revealed to reporter Adam Trimingham that he had become a Samaritan when serving 12 months of his 10-year sentence at Britain's most secure jail, London's Belmarsh. There he had also honed his legal expertise and used it to help secure the acquittal of a fellow-inmate charged, like himself, with manslaughter. He claimed he was now the second leading expert on manslaughter after Sir Stephen Mitchell, the judge at his last hearing.

Although £30 million of his fortune had been sequestered and £90 million frozen, he gave the impression there was plenty more, much of it held in gold. He also denied reports that Hamilton Palace was depreciating drastically and succumbing to the elements. He revealed that a second – smaller but still substantial – palace was being built by him in Zimbabwe, where he still had plenty of farmland (although not the million acres he once possessed) and that he had bought a coal mine with one of the biggest reserves in the world. He continued to be on good terms with president Robert Mugabe and with all his own five children from three different African mothers, none of whom he had ever married.

On the humanitarian side, he had given huge sums to charity but specified only the former Royal Commonwealth Society for the Blind (now Sightsavers International) as a beneficiary.

In a surprising statement, he said his tenants had been overjoyed at his release and that he had received scores of supportive letters from them. He had never evicted any of them, claiming his actions had been confined to 'illegal occupants'. He also denied ever being a slum landlord.

HOTELS AND BOARDING-HOUSES – see also ARSON
With increasingly large numbers of visitors being catered for in Brighton since the earliest days of the period under review, it is inevitable that a few of the town's many hotels and boarding houses will have been the location of crimes of all kinds.

The Grand Hotel
For the *Grand Hotel* Bombing, see ASSASSINATION, ATTEMPTED.

Marlborough Hotel, *Prince's Street*
PC Mullins was on duty in Prince's Street on the night of Thursday, 1 March 1900. At about midnight he passed the *Marlborough Hotel* and heard a man and woman quarrelling inside. The woman said: 'Don't, Tom', twice, and the man said: 'You are a lazy woman',

to which she replied: 'I know I am.' He resumed his beat and passed by again an hour later, but a few minutes later returned with PC Puttick. Standing near the door, Puttick heard raised voices and a man say: 'You ought to be killed', then something indistinct and then: 'You ——, I'll kill you.' A woman's voice twice pleaded: 'Oh, don't!' and then there was a thud and the sound of someone walking about. Puttick knocked at the door but no one responded. As the noise had ceased he walked away. He had heard similar quarrels there before and recognised the voices of Thomas Packham, the landlord, and his wife. What he almost certainly heard on this occasion was Lucy Packham being killed.

At four that morning, Thomas Packham went to the bedroom of his housekeeper, a Mrs Bertha Virgo, and asked to her to go to the bar where his wife was either dead or dying. She found the 33-year-old victim lifeless, her head resting on broken bottles and her feet close to the beer pumps. Mr Packham, 34, clearly drunk, stood over his wife moaning: 'Luce, Luce, do come back.'

The family's doctor, Douglas Ross, was summoned but confirmed the heavily-bruised Mrs Packham was dead. The police were called and Tom Packham was taken to the police station, appearing later that day before the magistrates. Mrs Virgo testified that the couple had been quarrelling continuously since she had worked for them (she had slept in the hotel for seven weeks) and she had frequently had to intervene to prevent Packham from striking his wife. Dr Ross said he could see nothing that could have caused the injuries, although the many bruises on her body were consistent with her having been attacked and beaten. He thought Packham had been drunk and not fit to be left alone, so after he called the police the body was moved to an upstairs room and locked in.

The *Marlborough* itself was the venue for the three-hour inquest on Mrs Packham held two days later. The victim's father, Edward Vigor, a butcher of Southover Street, stated that Packham treated Lucy brutally, had often knocked her about, threatened her with a revolver he kept in their room and had on one occasion tried to cut her throat. Lucy was intemperate but never drunk. Packham frequently was, but after his violent outbursts would be repentant and give Lucy presents. She would not leave him because of their three children.

The coroner's jury found that Mrs Packham had died of a cerebral haemorrhage caused by her husband's violence and returned a verdict of wilful murder by him. Packham was placed in Lewes gaol. On 26 March, he appeared before Brighton magistrates for the fourth time. Evidence was given that the couple had married in 1888 and had lived in Coleman Street and Washington Street before taking the *Marlborough* in 1895. Apart from treating his wife cruelly, he had also beaten the children. Evidence from three former potmen confirmed the succession of physical and verbal abuse. Packham denied striking his wife on the fateful night, claiming he was on the other side of the bar when she fell.

The trial began at Lewes on 30 June 1900 before Mr Justice Mathew. In spite of the overwhelming evidence against his client, the highly persuasive Mr (later Sir) Edward Marshall HALL was able to convince the all-male jury that the tragedy had been mainly due to drink.

The jury took only 22 minutes to decide that the evidence against Tom Packham was insufficient and returned a verdict of manslaughter. The judge looked slightly surprised when they added a recommendation for mercy. But for that, the four-year penal servitude sentence he handed down would have been a great deal longer.

A framed account of the tragedy which unfolded on the premises so long ago is on the wall above the fireplace in one of the ground floor bars – but it takes some years away from the unfortunate Lucy, stating that she met her end in 1897.

Today, the Marlborough *is a flourishing public house. The upstairs room where the inquest was held is now regularly used as a theatre and for private functions.* The author

The **Metropole** – see also ADULTERY
In September 1896, wealthy socialite Reginald Le Gros came to stay. One evening, he left his meal and shouted at the head waiter, Henry Schroeder, 'You spat in my face!', then shot him at point-blank range. The bullet smashed a bone in the stupefied waiter's right foot. A young American sitting nearby grappled with the gunman and Le Gros was soon disarmed.

The assailant was conveyed to the Town Hall police station and there charged with endangering Mr Schroeder's life by shooting at him. Yet he refused to explain what had happened or make a statement and he reserved his defence. Stubbornly silent, Le Gros spent six weeks awaiting trial in Lewis Prison. He defended himself and pleaded Not Guilty. He had merely fired at the floor to frighten Schroeder and had no intention of wounding him. He was sorry about the injury but was rich enough to compensate his victim if terms could be agreed.

A thin and ill Henry Schroeder hobbled into the courtroom to give evidence. He stoutly denied having spat at the prisoner or anyone else.

Le Gros made a suitable (undisclosed) offer of payment acceptable to Schroeder and acknowledged by the Recorder to be reasonable. He did, however, tell Le Gros that if a man fired a revolver at someone, the act was no less criminal because of the lack of intent to injure. Under the circumstance, he sentenced him to just three months' hard labour.

In her book on the hotel, Judy Middleton records that in the 1960s when two men and a girl who had stayed there were leaving, the man who carried their luggage down thought the cases were somewhat heavy. A phone call from the police to the hotel at 1 am alerted the staff to the suitcases having apparently contained the proceeds of a bank robbery in Leeds. The gang were later caught.

North Road boarding houses
Two killings, just over half a century apart, occurred in boarding-houses in North Road in the centre of the town.

The Clifford case, 1914
Percy Evelyn Clifford, described as a half-caste, was aged 32 at the time of his crime in 1914. Initially a theatrical artiste, he went on to become an engineer. He saw military action abroad as a dispatch rider in the Boer War, in the course of which he was wounded. After his return, he was unable to follow any regular employment. He drove a cab, acted as a commission agent and betted on the horses. From 1903 until 1909 he lived in London with one Susan Hughes, who would later testify as to his instability.

His wife, Maud Clifford (née Walton), was particularly attractive. She first met her husband-to-be in 1909, when she was earning her living as a prostitute; she would continue to do so for the next couple of years. On 7 January 1911, the day before her 21st birthday, she married Clifford at St Pancras Registry Office.

The couple then lived at various addresses in London but the relationship was beset by problems, the main one being that Maud still plied her trade. Clifford strongly objected and began beating her. So violent did he become that she even took out a summons against him (although he persuaded her not to proceed with it). The couple split up in October 1912, yet it later emerged that they met on a daily basis. Nevertheless, Maud did not reveal her new address – a furnished flat in Brixton.

She was nonetheless persuaded by her ex-husband to visit Brighton with him for a short break. On Saturday, 4 April 1914, they took rooms at 57 North Road, not far from the station. At about 12.30 on Tuesday morning, two loud reports were heard, which the landlady, Mary Upton, believed to be car tyres bursting. The Cliffords had still not appeared – nor had they by 3 pm. Mrs Upton knocked, but got no answer. On opening the door, she saw them both lying in bed. Percy Clifford, unconscious and with blood on his face, was alive but his wife was dead from a bullet wound to her left temple. There was a large quantity of blood on the bedding.

Clifford, in critical condition, was taken to the Royal Sussex County Hospital, yet recovered nearly ten days later. On his discharge, he was promptly arrested and charged with murder. His trial at the Lewes Assizes on 8 July 1914 lasted only one day. The prisoner, in a clear, steady voice, pleaded Not Guilty. The prosecution described the crime as a cold-blooded and premeditated murder and read letters from Clifford which showed he had planned to commit the crime. In one, addressed to his mother, he had alleged that his wife was seeing three other men. He even wrote to the Coroner, stating, 'Sir, I am putting some work in your way'.

Clifford's mother testified that after her son's return from South Africa he was very excitable and eccentric and had fits. Susan Hughes revealed that around Christmas, 1913, Clifford was thinking of finding Maud, shooting her and then killing himself. The defence's plea of insanity fell on deaf ears, for it took the jury only 25 minutes to find Clifford guilty. In sentencing him to death, Mr Justice Darling told him he agreed that the crime was 'a deliberate murder resolved on long before and perpetrated in circumstances of great treachery'. An appeal heard on 27 July was dismissed and on 11 August 1914, Percy Clifford was hanged.

The death of James Maidment, 1965

A verdict of Murder by a Person or Persons Unknown was returned on 15 December 1965 by a jury at the inquest on James Bender Maidment, aged 36, a van driver of California Road, New Malden, Surrey, who had been found dead with a stab wound in his chest in a rooming house on 25 July.

Det-Supt John ('Jim') MARSHALL said at the time that although 40 police officers had interviewed 40,000 people and made 15,000 visits to commercial premises, taking 600 statements, no charge had been preferred. He recalls today that New Scotland Yard were called in but the crime was never solved.

On 30 July 1965, the *Evening Argus* reported that squads of detectives were hunting the killer and were still interviewing people living in the area. A massive search had been conducted for information about a fair-haired youth in Mod-style white jeans and blue blazer, who was seen with the murdered man near the Clock Tower after midnight on the morning of Sunday 25 July – nine hours before Maidment's body was found. A search was also made for the murder weapon and for two keys which the murderer is believed to have taken away with him after locking the dead man in his bedroom. The murder was the second in the town in nine weeks (32-year-old off-licence manageress Sylvia Taylor had been stabbed and strangled on 22 May on her premises in Prince Albert Street by a youth 'with a Beatles haircut').

27 Dorset Gardens, Brighton

A letter bearing the above address was received on 30 May 1947 by Cyril Martin, licensee of the *Gloucester Arms* in Gloucester Road, Croydon. It read:

Dear Mr Martin

I am sorry to say that your wife Nancy passed peacefully away at the above address. Please get in touch with her mother at Chichester as soon as possible.

The letter ended with a hieroglyphic. The sender was later established to be Albert Frankling, 42, a plumber, of Queen's Avenue, Chichester. Martin had met him occasionally, but did not know him well. Because of business interests, Martin lived in Croydon during the week but would visit his wife regularly every week.

On 13 June 1947, Frankling was charged on remand in Brighton with murdering, on or about 20 May, Mrs Nancy Dorcas Martin, 39, also of Chichester. She had been found dead with head injuries in a locked room of a boarding house at 27 Dorset Gardens where she had been staying with her 2-year-old daughter, Laura Jill – and with Frankling. Little was made in contemporary press reports of the relationship, but one clearly existed. They had taken a twin-bedded room on 24 May. Mrs Clara Macey, the boarding-house keeper, last saw Mrs Martin alive on the 28th. On the following morning, the day before penning the letter, Frankling had told the landlady that his 'wife' would not be requiring breakfast or have anything taken up to her as she was ill. Soon after 11 am, he left the house, accompanied by the child, but apparently returned later in the day, put the child in bed with its mother, locked up the room and disappeared.

Getting no response to her knocking, Mrs Macey summoned a window cleaner, who found Mrs Martin dead in bed with the child, who was unharmed. The woman was wearing only a vest, her lower half being covered by the bedclothes. Death had been caused within the previous 24 hours by a severe blow on the top of the head with a sharp object and would have been instantaneous. There were no signs of a struggle. The victim's head was lying in a pool of congealed blood. A chopper normally kept on top of a meat safe downstairs was found under the mattress on the bed was clearly that object. She was later found to have been about 6½ months pregnant.

Dorset Gardens from the south. No 27 is believed to be the fourth house on the right. For a time after the tragedy, bus conductors would call out 'Murder Street!' when their buses stopped nearby in St James's Street. Chris Horlock collection

Frankling was quickly traced to Chichester, where, with Mrs Frankling's permission, two police officers searched his house. They found him sitting on a bed in a small back bedroom. Nervously, he explained:

> *I have been expecting you, sir. We were skylarking and playing about. She fell down and I fell on top of her. I tried to pick her up but she wouldn't speak to me. Is she alright?*

He then added, when asked to go to the police station, 'Take me away, but don't let my wife see me. She doesn't know I'm here'. On top of a book in a ground floor bedroom, the police found a business-card for 'A. Frankling', on the back of which was written, in indelible pencil: 'Ring up police and tell them to go to 27 Dorset Gardens, Brighton.'

When charged at Brighton, Frankling said: 'I did not kill or murder her.' He was committed for trial at Sussex Assizes on 14 July 1947, but when there was found to be unfit to plead. Two doctors gave evidence that he was insane and unable to instruct counsel. He was ordered to be detained during His Majesty's pleasure.

Today, 27 Dorset Gardens no longer stands. The numbers at the south end of the street end at 24 and the high side wall of a fashion shop extending to St James's Street has supplanted the murder site.

HOUSE OF CORRECTION

Occasional references are made in this volume to sentences to be served in the House of Correction. A larger and better-known establishment of that name stood in Lewes and it

The diminutive former House of Correction on the corner of Market Street and Brighton Place. Once an antique and gun shop, it has for the last fifteen years been in the hands of Donatello's *restaurant. For three years running (1991–93), it was transformed into a Gingerbread House containing 'Santa's Grotto' in aid of The* Argus*'s Christmas Appeal.* The author

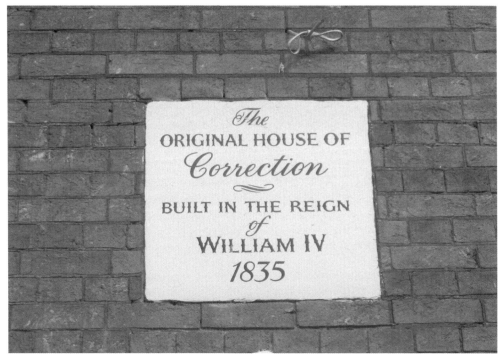

Despite the clear date on this commemorative stone, a careful reading of the Brighton Guardian *for the year 1835 yielded no reference whatsoever to any opening, public or otherwise, of this building.* The author

is possible that was the destination of some of the miscreants. Certainly, the Brighton 'House' could only have accommodated a handful of prisoners at any time, as the photograph illustrates.

Two examples of (somewhat severe) periods of detention are recorded together in the *Brighton Guardian* of 11 October 1837. June Price was committed to the House for 21 days for talking to a sentry at the Pavilion and 'behaving disorderly at improper hours', while Sarah Captin was committed for the same period 'for a like offence'.

I

IMPRESSMENT
A brutal but effective official system of conscripting people to serve as sailors used by the Royal Navy during the eighteenth century and early nineteenth century in time of war as a means of crewing warships.

According to *The Times*, 166 men were required for Sussex in 1795, the burden being distributed among the parishes. Although lists of suitable men were returned to the Petty Session courts and the justices, very few convicted Brighton felons were forced to join. People liable to impressment were eligible men of seafaring habits between the ages of 18 and 55 years, although very rarely non-seamen were impressed as well. The navy had little interest in impressing people without seafaring experience.

Perhaps this is why two Brighton fishermen named Allen and Bishop were impressed at sea by a naval tender on 11 March 1812 and carried into Portsmouth. They were, however, released by order of the Admiralty as a result of representations made on their behalf by the Rev Mr Carr, Vicar, and Mr Edward Blaker. The *Brighton Herald* commented:

We have heard it asserted that if every boat in our fishery were manned, there would be then left a surplus of at least 300, which might well be spared, but the impressing of married men only reduces their families to indigence and increases the already too heavy burthens of the parish.

British impressment ended in practice after 1815, at the end of the Napoleonic Wars. The last law concerning impressment was passed in 1835, and limited the length of service of a pressed man to five years and added the provison that a man could not be pressed twice.

INDECENCY
An outcry against nude bathing, early 1800s
The *Morning Herald* recorded on 28 August 1806 that the greatest novelty of that day was 'a gentleman undressing himself on the beach, for the purpose of a ducking, in front of the town'. Worse, his lady was with him quite unabashed, 'and even assisted him in wiping the humid effects of his exercise from his brawny limbs, as he returned from the water to dress'. Erredge, in his *History of Brighthelmston*, tells us that in the following season the practice of [nude] bathing in front of the town became so general that on Thursday 19 August, a Vestry Meeting was held at the *Old Ship* to devise measures to prevent it. The resolutions that proceedings should be taken against offenders had the desired effect for a while but in 1808 the nuisance recurred, resulting in a prosecution at the Horsham Assizes on 21 March the following year.

In this case (The King v John Crunden), the defendant, a Brighton tailor, was indicted for indecently exposing himself on the beach at Brighton on 26 June and 2 July 1808. He had refused to comply with the stipulations of a committee formed to prevent the nuisance and which, to preserve public decency, had had a hut built on the beach in which anyone might undress under cover. Crunden had persisted in bathing within a few yards of houses. He had frequently been brought to task but had always retorted that the sea was free and he would bathe when and where he pleased. What was worse, he had induced many others to follow his example. As their leader, he was named 'the Captain' and daily exposed himself naked on the beach. The defence's argument was that it had been the custom at all times for persons to bathe where the defendant now bathed and this right ought not to be curtailed by the erection of houses within view.

The Chief Baron deemed this a serious question as an offence against decency and morality was involved. If a town developed, the inhabitants must not have to suffer indecent spectacles so the bather's duty was to retire to remoter situations. Crunden was found guilty, although Erredge does not say what penalty, if any, was imposed.

The historian noted that this verdict was very effective for a time but that up to the time of writing (early 1860s), the nuisance had continued, even though new bye-laws prohibited bathing from the beach in front of the town, except before 6 am or after 9 pm. In addition, all persons bathing from machines were required to wear gowns, drawers, or some such suitable covering.

Women behaving badly

In early June 1835, one Phoebe Harffy, 24, was charged with (unspecified) indecent conduct on the beach between six and seven o'clock on the evening in question. She was sentenced to one month's hard labour.

Two women wearing red turbans were apprehended in March 1860 for 'singing songs of an indecent and disgusting character in the streets'. They were given a warning and ordered to leave town.

Official nude beach, Black Rock

On 9 August 1979, Britain's first nude beach 'opened' in Brighton. A specialist internet site describes this as 'probably the best known, most accessible and most public naturist beach in the UK' – with all the downsides that this implies. It points out that the beach is of shingle and pebbles, with consequent discomfort. 'If you choose to strip off,' it adds, 'you are likely to find yourself playing to an unrestricted audience of binocular-wielding voyeurs – both on the beach and, often, in boats offshore. This might be heaven for some, but it sounds like hell to me.'

INDECENT ASSAULT – see also DNA, RAPE

George O'Callaghan, an old man (on bail) was charged before Brighton Borough Bench on 22 February 1866 with indecently assaulting Susan Cartwright, a little girl living with her parents in Sussex Street. The evidence given by the various witnesses clearly substantiated the case and the Bench committed the prisoner to the HOUSE OF CORRECTION for two months with hard labour.

At the same session, William Ellis, 14, was charged with committing an indecent assault upon Emily Parker, an idiot, thirteen years of age. Evidence having been given supporting the charge and proving the prisoner to have been guilty of 'a most disgusting act of inhumanity', the Bench committed him to prison for three months with hard labour.

In February 1868, a 60-year-old hawker, whom the *Brighton Gazette* described as 'An Old Beast', appeared in court on the charge of indecently assaulting his own 12-year-old daughter. The girl's sister, then aged 19, testified that he had done the same to her when she was 11. He was handed down the then maximum sentence of six months' imprisonment with hard labour. This was the same as that received by a 17-year-old youth on the same day for stealing a small brass ornament from a shop front.

The attack on Florence Lynn, 1886

An immediate Guilty verdict was pronounced, with sentence deferred, on 27-year-old James Gibbs for having indecently assaulted Florence Lynn, 12, of 11 Jubilee Street, on 12 January 1886. He had pleaded Not Guilty.

Gibbs approached the girl in Edward Street and offered her 1½d to go into Dorset Gardens with him. She refused but two or three days later, when she was on an errand in Tichborne Street, she again saw him and ran away. In her fear, she ran into the passage which led to Orange Row and there Gibbs caught and assaulted her. When she screamed, he attempted to put mud in her mouth to silence her then offered her money to be quiet but she continued to scream. A number of people gathered and Gibbs ran away but was later arrested and identified by his victim. The assault had been a serious one, for a neighbour who helped the girl found blood on her underwear and running down her legs.

INFANTICIDE

An odious stepfather, 1901
In a case brought to light by the Society for the Prevention of Cruelty to Children, John Hoskins, 24, was sentenced at the 1901 Winter Assizes to five years' penal servitude. He had been living with a widow and, according to the *Brighton Herald* of 23 November:

> ... *took advantage of his position to commit absolutely indescribable offences upon her four little daughters. One child he had injured seriously by his disgusting practices.*

INFANTICIDE
This is the killing of a child in the earliest period of life, especially before he or she can walk.

No allowance was made by the law in the nineteenth century for women who killed their children when under severe stress or suffering from some birth-related mental disorder. The act was purely and simply ruled to be murder, with conviction carrying a mandatory death sentence. The police accordingly became reluctant to charge women with killing their children and courts held back from convicting mothers in these circumstances.

Under the 1922 Infanticide Act, a partial defence was allowed for a woman who killed her 'new-born child' if she was suffering from a severe mental disorder related to childbirth. She would be convicted of manslaughter rather than murder. In 1938 the Act was amended to remove the death penalty for women who killed their babies in the first year of life and to include 'lactation' as a ground of mental disturbance.

Two 1837 cases
In January 1837, the case came up of Sarah Smith. She was committed for trial on a charge of administering death by poison to an infant, the child of Louisa Mitchener, 'she having sold her syrup of poppies'. The child had died of an overdose of laudanum, obtained from the chemist and druggist shop kept by Mr and Mrs Smith at 120 Edward Street. The case was eventually dismissed on Mrs Smith's payment of expenses and guaranteeing to abstain from dispensing drugs in the future. The Bench agreed that a charge of manslaughter brought by Mrs Mitchener must be dropped and that the child's death was caused by misadventure.

Also in that year, Sarah Deacon, a servant, tried to conceal the birth of an infant; its body was found pushed down a closet.

The Aaron Dellow tragedy, 1993
Aaron Dellow, aged 17 months, died after a savage beating in a flat in Montpelier Road on 3 April 1993. The infant had been battered so fiercely that the pattern of the carpet was imprinted on his head. He was found to have 40 bruises on his face and body and his skull had fractured in two places.

At a trial at Hove Crown Court in July the following year, 16-stone Colin Waters was convicted of murdering the toddler and received a life sentence. Throughout the three-week trial, however, Waters not only denied the killing but blamed the child's mother, Alicia (also known as Lee) Baker for the violent attack which occurred at the flat the couple shared.

Waters has protested his innocence ever since his conviction. He was, however, refused leave to appeal by the Court of Appeal on 6 November 1995.

Lee, who was pregnant throughout the trial, moved to another part of Brighton, where she lives with her daughter, aged 13 at the time of writing. Not only did she suffer acutely through her loss but additionally endured accusations that she had herself killed Aaron.

In January 2006, Waters' case was referred to the Court of Appeal by the Criminal Cases Review Commission, the body which investigates possible miscarriages of justice. His barrister told three judges there were doubts about exactly what time Aaron was fed on the day of his death, challenging the prosecution's claimed time of 6.30 which would only admit of Waters being the killer.

A monstrous couple cleared, 1999

Three babies in the care of a Brighton couple were smothered but the judge at their trial ordered the jury to find the defendants not guilty after ruling there was insufficient evidence to say which of the parents, if either, was responsible for the murders. The prosecution contended that both were in it together, but there had to be evidence that both were there at the time of the deaths, that one committed the deed and the other was there and failed to stop it. The judge stated: 'It is better both be acquitted than one wrongly convicted.' The senior investigating detective in the murder cases, Det Insp Malcolm Bacon, who led Operation Film, joined calls for a change in the law so that a second party with knowledge of a crime and being close to the scene is culpable. In his view, 'the law and common sense have parted company'.

Sussex Police Chief Constable Paul Whitehouse followed the case and also felt a change in the law was needed. A campaign by *The Argus*, backed by MPs, Brighton and Hove Council and concerned residents, fought for that change.

The woman claimed her common-law husband, a 38-year-old caretaker, had used pillows to smother all three infants and after each death threatened to kill his wife if she told anyone. Her first son was eight months old in 1993 when he suffered brain damage from lack of oxygen. It left him blind, deaf and unable to suck and he died the following spring. His mother testified that she saw the child with a pillow over his face after her husband had attended to him. He told her the child would not stop crying and that 'he deserved all he got'.

The couple's five-week-old nephew died while in their care at their home in 1997. The woman said her husband was responsible and had given the same comment. Their six-week-old son died 19 days later, again because he was crying, she said. The father removed the pillow before calling for an ambulance.

All three deaths were originally recorded as cot or natural deaths, but leading paediatricians and forensic experts testified that evidence and circumstances surrounding the deaths suggested the babies had been smothered.

A concerned Brighton mother, 41-year-old Sandra Reed, collected 519 names for a petition calling for a change in the law following the collapse of the murder trial. One of the signatories was the sister of the murderous caretaker and mother of the five-week-old baby boy who had died while in the couple's care in 1997. She went through a second hell following her loss, since she and her partner were driven from their Brighton council house and suffered break-ins and vandalism and abuse from people who blamed her for her son's death.

INNS AND PUBLIC HOUSES – see also DRINK/DRINKING
The early days
By 1800, there were only 1,200 private houses in Brighton but 41 inns and public houses. Many of the town's most famous pubs were already established, including the *The Castle*,

The Dolphin, The Cricketers, The Black Lion (linked to Brighton's oldest brewery of that name), *The Spotted Dog* (now *The Hop Poles*) and *The Greyhound* (now *The Fish Bowl*).

The responsibility of licensed publicans, as opposed to beer shop owners, was underlined in an 1831 judgment of the Court of King's Bench (now a division of the High Court of Justice). A Miss Kent had been staying at a Brighton inn and had 60 shillings' worth of bank notes stolen from her room. She successfully prosecuted the landlord, Shuter. The appeal judges upheld the verdict and declared that the keeper of an inn was 'responsible for the safety of all property'.

Opening hours
Newspapers in both centuries are littered with reports of action being taken against landlords for failing to observe the statutory opening hours of the day.

Some offenders were clearly against the church, notably Thomas Smith, landlord of the *Brighton Arms*, charged in 1831 with keeping an open house during the hours of Divine Service. He was not the only one, for James Stuart, John Chandler and John Best were charged for a similar offence on the same day. All received fines.

George Thomas Harvey, landlord of the *London Arms*, Sussex Street, pleaded guilty in March 1886 at the Borough Police Court to having his house open at 1.40 am on Sunday 28 February. Inspector Howard, who proved the case, stated that he found 11 persons in the house drinking at the time. The Bench imposed a penalty of 40s (£2) and costs, or 14 days' hard labour, and said the license would be endorsed. Seven of the drinkers were fined 2s 6d and costs. One of them had the summons against him withdrawn on his paying the costs – he was the only one who had given the right name and address ...

INSPECTOR HORNLEIGH ON HOLIDAY
Film, 1939
Synopsis
Inspector Hornleigh and his erstwhile assistant, Sergeant Bingham, spend a rain-swept holiday, incognito, in Brighton (Brighthaven). A fellow boarder at *Balmoral Guest House*, a Captain Fraser in the Royal Navy, goes out anxiously one miserable night with his pet terrier after receiving a phone call and is found crushed and burned to death in his wrecked car at the foot of a cliff. The charred body was impossible to identify and the dog was missing. Hornleigh and Bingham, as the last people to see the captain alive, are taken into custody by the local police. Suspecting murder, Hornleigh identifies himself and begins investigating the case. He proves the crash was neither suicide nor accident. What was more, the body was not Fraser's. He soon exposes a murderous scheme to defraud insurance companies by faking the deaths of substantial policyholders and substituting other corpses for those of the victims. Bradfield, the shadowy ringleader, contacts his fellow conspirators by radio. Hornleigh, however, by disguising a reluctant Bingham as a hospital corpse, devises a scheme to ensnare him.

Details and comments
Gordon Harker (as the Inspector) and Alastair Sim (as his assistant) star in this second instalment of the Inspector Hornleigh crime trilogy inspired by the popular BBC radio serial *Monday Night at Eight*. This little-seen comedy thriller was directed by Walter Forde and written by Sidney Gilliat and Frank Launder (who was educated in Brighton). The film script and acting – and the view of the stormy British coastline – have been rated 'excellent'.

J

JIGSAW
Film, 1962
Synopsis
Sgt Wilks (Ronald Lewis) is called to investigate a burglary of property leases from an estate agency. When the agent complains that the police aren't doing enough, Wilks' superior, Inspector Fellows (Jack Warner) joins the enquiry. In the course of their investigation, a woman's headless body is uncovered in an old trunk at an isolated beach house ('1 Bungalow Road, Saltdean', some four miles east of Brighton) leased to a

Jack Warner, Michael Goodliffe and Ronald Lewis in a scene from the film.

man named John Campbell. The local constabulary painstakingly gather the 'jigsaw' of random clues to reconstruct the woman's history and last moments. The police follow various leads – from eyewitnesses, the murder weapon, items found in the beach house and from Campbell's car. After exhaustive enquiries, however, it quickly becomes apparent that John Campbell's name was an assumed one and that the killer has skilfully covered his tracks. A womanising vacuum cleaner salesman, Clyde Burchard (Michael Goodliffe), the owner of a car that fits the police description, is arrested on suspicion. Inspector Fellows calls a great number of key witnesses to the police station in the hope that they will identify the guilty party.

Details and comments

> *A first-rate detective thriller which has the authentic stamp of a documentary in its attention to detail. Plenty of red herrings keep the audience alert and though* [writer, producer and director Val] *Guest resists the temptation to show the murderer at work and his subsequent cutting up of the body, he still provides the audience with plenty of excitement.*
>
> (From *Variety*)

Jigsaw is based on Hilary Waugh's novel *Sleep Long My Love* and set in a seedy Brighton. At 107 minutes, the chilling murder mystery is long but never tiresome. The storyline of Guest's black-and-white pseudo-documentary of police procedure hides nothing from the viewer – the clues are there for the viewer to pick up on them. According to Halliwell's *Guide*, this 'absorbing and entertaining little murder mystery . . . plays as fair as can be with the audience'.

Evidently drawing inspiration from the town's notorious trunk murders, *Jigsaw* was largely shot on location in Brighton and Lewes. Scenes include the then Brighton police headquarters in the Town Hall (Little East Street), an estate agent's in Queen's Road, the seafront, Gardner Street and police cars driving around the streets.

Most interestingly, the local *Evening Argus* features in the film. One of the characters is a reporter from the newspaper who regularly pops up seeking information on the latest developments in the investigation. As many local people as possible were used as extras and many well-known businesses and tradesmen were recruited. JIM MARSHALL advised on how the police should be authentically portrayed.

Prominent among the cast was Jack Warner – at the time most famous as television's *Dixon of Dock Green*. This was to be his last film.

JURIES

Juries in the early days were on occasion tainted by class-consciousness.

The *Brighton Herald* carried an article in 1830 on Justice Tounton's opening address to the jury at the Sussex Winter Assizes in Lewes. The hand-picked 24-man panel was made up entirely of knights of the realm, members of parliament and local magistrates. Addressing them as 'gentlemen of landed estates', he continued 'gentlemen it is of the greatest importance that ignorant men who commit these crimes [burning and destroying property and riotous assembly] learn to pay for their offences with the loss of their lives or with transportation' – a good example of a judge instructing a grand jury on its findings before a trial.

This particular Court List contained 27 cases of rural crime. Among other cases was that of John Virgo of Brighton, who received a 14-year transportation sentence for stealing two handkerchiefs from Lord Gage – a juryman at his trial.

K

KENT, CONSTANCE

This was one of the most notorious murder cases in Victorian England.

In 1860, Constance Kent was 16 and living in Road Hill House, a rambling mansion between Trowbridge and Frome. Her father, Samuel Savill Kent, was an unpleasant character who had five surviving children (including Constance) from his first wife, Mary Ann Windus. In 1840 he had engaged a governess, Mary Drewe Pratt, for his two elder daughters. Pratt soon dominated the household, becoming the mistress of Samuel Kent – then of the house. Kent lived with her openly in one part of the property, his wife being relegated to another. A year after his first wife's death in 1852, Kent married Pratt and proceeded to have five children by her, one being Francis Savill, who in 1860 was nearly four.

At 5 am on Saturday, 30 June in that year, the boy was found to be missing from his cot in the nursery-governess's room. The grounds were searched and his body was found in a large privy near the back door. He had been stabbed in the chest, and his throat cut from ear to ear. Medical evidence later suggested, however, that the cause of death was suffocation, possibly by a blanket, and that the wounds had been inflicted after his death.

Constance Kent – an unlikely murderess. Author's collection

Both Constance – who was known to have no love for her stepmother, and therefore the woman's child – and the nursery-governess, Elizabeth Gough, were brought before the Trowbridge magistrates but released for lack of evidence.

Constance was sent to a finishing school, then a convent at Dinan in Brittany, where she acquired a liking for convent life and began to show an extreme tenderness for young children. In August 1863 she came as a paying guest to St Mary's Home in Brighton, established (initially for ex-prostitutes) by the Rev Arthur Wagner at Nos 1–6 and 10–11 Queen Square. The premises, enlarged to include 1–5 and 8–11 Wykeham Terrace, were run with iron discipline by the nuns of the Community of the Blessed Virgin Mary. The inmates, who included the poor, disabled, infant and aged, came from all over the country. Constance looked after the small children in the orphanage and remained at the Home for 21 months. Her conduct there was later described by Wagner as uniformly good.

The home was attached to the High Church of St Paul's, West Street, and it was there, following her long immersion in a religious atmosphere, that Kent had formed the habit of confessing to Arthur Wagner. In Holy Week 1865, she made her specific confession to him that she had murdered her half-brother, her motive being revenge on Mary Pratt for her treatment of Constance's mother. She added that she had determined to give herself up to the authorities.

When this confession was later made public, both Wagner and Catherine Ann Gream, Lady Superior of the Home, were reviled in a Protestant furore for allegedly having pressurised the girl into surrendering to the law. Wagner repeatedly denied either influencing her to confess to him in the first place or to surrender to justice – although he had not opposed this. At Bow Street, on 25 April 1865, Constance handed the Chief Magistrate a written confession.

She was sent back to Wiltshire for trial, during which Wagner refused to disclose any information about what passed between them during her confessions. This caused a fresh outburst of ultra-Protestant fury. A police guard had to be placed on the Vicarage in Brighton and on St Mary's Home. Paul Foskett, Chairman of the Central Protestant Association, arranged a public meeting in Brighton's Town Hall to protest against confessional practices. A lone dissenter was not only refused a hearing but was set upon, his clothes torn and his hat destroyed. Two days later, Wagner was attacked in North Street by two drunken sweeps. Luckily he was assisted by a passer-by, Sir Thomas Barrett Lennard. The vicar was on another occasion allegedly shot at, while two unruly girls, ex-inmates of St Mary's, shouted insults at the occupants and threw fruit through the open windows.

On 21 July 1865, Constance Kent took her trial at the Salisbury Assizes and pleaded guilty. Sentence of death was duly passed. Following representations made (including by Wagner) this was commuted to life imprisonment. During her 20 years of incarceration, Wagner kept in touch with her. He fetched her upon her release and took her to Buxted, where she could be looked after by the Sisters of St Mary's Home, Brighton, at their country retreat known as St Margaret's Cottage.

The following year, Constance, by now 42, went to Australia with her brother, William, who had come to fetch her. There she adopted the name of Ruth Emilie Kaye and took up nursing, qualifying in 1892. She became a matron and in 1910 acquired her own nursing-home at Maitland, New South Wales. She did not retire from this until she was 88 and died there in 1944 at the age of 100, having given 42 years of her life to nursing service.

KEPPLE, WILLIAM

It has never been resolved at what exact time 7-year-old Maria Ann Colwell's death took place but it was at 10.35 am on Sunday, 7 January 1973 that her body was delivered to the Casualty Unit of the Royal Sussex County Hospital, Brighton. It was brought in a white pram, covered in coal dust, by Pauline Violet Kepple, the child's mother, and William Kepple, her husband.

The doctor who first examined the child found severe bruising on the body and shocking bruising of the head, particularly the eyes. Both Kepple and his wife explained the injuries away by saying the child had fallen down the stairs in an epileptic fit. The body was in such a state that the Hospital Authority contacted Brighton police, and it was then examined by Dr Hilary Jarvis, the Police Surgeon for Brighton. He pronounced that the child had been dead for a number of hours.

The girl weighed only 36 pounds (the average for that age was 50). Professor James M Cameron carried out the post-mortem examination at Brighton Mortuary and reported that such a loss of weight from the norm could not have occurred during the space of a few days. It would take several months. The bruising he found on the child's body was not all new. Some was several days' old (bruising normally takes ten days to disappear completely). The child must have been unconscious for some hours before death. To anyone who had seen her during the 48 hours prior to her death, it must have been obvious that she had suffered serious injuries. 'It was,' he recorded, 'the worst bruising I have seen in the whole of my experience with battered children.' The cause of death was multiple injuries.

Maria's death was not so much a local scandal as a national one. Solo Syndication/Mirrorpix

William Kepple, whose brutality led to murder.
Solo Syndication/Mirrorpix

Maria Colwell, the youngest of five children, had been born in Hove to Pauline Violet Colwell in March 1965. At that time, the future Mrs Kepple was married to Raymond Leslie Colwell, who died four months after the birth. In August of that year Maria was taken to Mrs Doris Cooper, the sister of the dead man. The baby was in poor condition, unable to retain food, extremely thin and generally neglected. With proper care she thrived, and Mrs Cooper and her husband were prepared to bring her up as their own child. Eighteen months later, however, the child's mother took her away. Only a week afterwards Mrs Cooper was taken by the Child Welfare Authority to an address in Hove where Maria was found in a filthy condition, with no shoes or socks. A magistrate placed the youngster in the care of the East Sussex County Council in October 1966. Mrs Cooper became a foster-mother and continued to look after Maria, who moved with her foster-carers to Brighton in 1968.

In October 1971, Maria's mother successfully applied for her to be returned to her. At that time she and William Kepple were living together at Maresfield Road, Whitehawk, Brighton, and had had three children. They were married the following year.

Following the delivery of the dead girl to the hospital, the Kepples were taken to Brighton police station and detained. Mrs Kepple, who was obviously terrified of her husband, told lies in several statements. Eventually, however, she told the police that it was her husband who had hit the child and, in the end, he admitted striking Maria around the chest and stomach.

Kepple, aged 42, a builder's labourer, was charged with the murder of Maria Ann Colwell. At Lewes Assizes that charge was reduced to manslaughter and he was sentenced to eight years' imprisonment. This was reduced to four years on appeal.

The case so shocked the nation that there was an immediate public inquiry at which more than a hundred people gave evidence. What emerged was a story of muddle, and sometimes incompetence, by a series of public bodies. There had been 50 official visits to the family, including from social workers, health visitors, police and housing officers, and 30 complaints from neighbours. The parents' explanations for Maria's bruises, tiredness at school, weight losses, etc were accepted.

All the agencies involved in the case were criticised. The inquiry censured two welfare departments and the National Society for the Prevention of Cruelty to Children and, in a 60,000-word report, it was stated that many of the mistakes made by individuals were either the result of, or contributed to, by inefficient systems operating in several different fields, notably training, administration, planning, liaison and supervision.

In 1974, HARVEY HOLFORD set up the Maria Colwell Memorial Fund to fight for legislation to protect children from abuse.

L

LAWRENCE, JOHN

I know I have done it, I hope I have killed him, and I hope I shall be hung for it.

(John Lawrence, March 1844)

On the evening of Wednesday, 13 March 1844, the path of John Lawrence (spelt in some accounts 'Lawrance') fatefully crossed that of Henry Solomon, Brighton's Chief of Police.

Lawrence had come to Brighton the previous autumn. Aged 23, he had been apprenticed in his native Tonbridge to his father as a plasterer but did not serve his time. After working for his stepfather for a while on a farm at Speldhurst, he left home, drifting into a dissolute life, although he was employed for a time as a labourer on the railways. His petty thefts including robbing his own parents of £25.

His victim, Henry Solomon, was originally a watchmaker but had been in the service of the town's Commissioners since 1821. After holding various municipal positions, he was made Joint Chief Officer of Police in 1832. On the resignation of his co-equal, William Pilbeam, through ill health in 1836, Solomon was given sole responsibility as Chief Constable.

In Brighton, Lawrence consorted with a gang of thieves and prostitutes and committed a great many petty thefts. He lived in Cavendish Street (see William WILTON), supported by a prostitute known as 'Hastings Bet'. Before his attack on Henry Solomon, he had been drinking hard for several days but was not drunk. He was,

indeed, clear-headed enough to attempt the theft, with a companion, of a roll of carpet from the shop door of a draper's in St James's Street. Lawrence was followed up a side-street, Chapel Street, where he dropped the carpet and was taken back to the shop. Constable John Barnden then took Lawrence to the police offices in the Town Hall.

In the course of questioning, Lawrence suddenly rose from his chair, seized a poker and for no reason whatsoever struck Solomon on the head with it. The victim was carried to his home in nearby Princes Street, behind Pavilion Parade but, despite medical attention, died from his injury the following morning.

The inquest jury, almost without hesitation, returned a verdict of 'Wilful Murder' against Lawrence. The prisoner, utterly dejected, burst into tears when boarding the conveyance to take him to Lewes Gaol.

No fewer than 10,000 townsfolk joined Solomon's funeral procession to the Jewish

John Lawrence, an impulsive and infamous killer.
Author's collection

burial ground off Ditchling Road. A subscription was raised for his widow and nine children, to which the Commissioners subscribed £500. The trial jury, and all the witnesses, donated their fees, while other contributions included £30 from the Royal Bounty and £50 from Queen Victoria. The total sum received exceeded £1,000 and was invested to bring in £2 a week for Solomon's widow.

The assailant's trial was held one week after the crime. It only lasted three hours, as there were three eye-witnesses to the murder and no witnesses for the defence. Counsel for the defence could only allege that the crime was committed in a momentary fit of insanity. But the Lord Chief Justice had little difficulty in showing that the circumstances did not come within the scope of the recently-formulated McNaughton rules. The jury did not even retire and took just 12 minutes to arrive at a Guilty verdict. The next day, Lawrence was taken from Lewes to Horsham Gaol, where the death sentence was carried out.

Like HOLLOWAY and BURT before him, Lawrence became deeply penitent. He spent much of his time writing to nearly all his old abandoned associates, earnestly entreating them to renounce their present course of life and refrain from the conduct that had led to his own destruction.

On Holy Saturday 1844, a crowd estimated at between 1,000 to 2,000 people, observing the strictest order and decorum, witnessed John Lawrence's execution. The following year, Horsham Gaol (see PRISONS), which had been deliberately 'run down' prior to ceding its place to the Houses of Correction of Lewes and Petworth, was sold by public tender for demolition, salvage and disposal. The body of John Lawrence – Horsham's last executed murderer – was exhumed and for a short time exhibited to the morbidly curious in the stable of the nearby *Queen's Head* at 2d per head. Finally, it was transferred to the south-west corner of the old churchyard.

LEFROY, PERCY MAPLETON

Like George GRIFFITH, 60-year-old Frederick Isaac Gold, a former stockbroker, of 13 Clermont Terrace, Preston, Brighton, was a worthy citizen who met his end while travelling in another part of the county. Although retired, he still travelled to London weekly to attend to some investments.

On the sweltering afternoon of 27 June 1881, seated in the Brighton-bound train at East Croydon station, he was selected as a suitable victim for robbery by Lefroy, 22, a failed author, journalist and actor from Wallington, Carshalton, Surrey. Ambitious, vain and greedy, a petty thief, prone to mood swings, and quite brazen and plausible when the occasion demanded, he was physically no match for his heavier-built victim.

There was, however, great pressure on him to get money. His pretentious socialising, during which he announced plans to write for the stage, had almost bankrupted him. His cousin and landlord, Mr TG Clayton, and Mr Seale, another cousin, were pressing for the repayment of loans and pledges.

Armed with a small-calibre revolver and a first-class single ticket from London Bridge to Brighton, Lefroy left his carriage at East Croydon in search of a solitary first-class passenger on the same train – someone he could shoot in a noisy place like Merstham Tunnel. This is precisely what he did. The shots, heard by a number of passengers, were inexplicable and therefore ignored.

Yet Lefroy had not killed Gold. A violent and protracted struggle ensued, with the intended victim trying to throttle his assailant. Finally, in Balcombe Tunnel, many miles down the line from Merstham, Lefroy opened the door and forced Gold out of the compartment to his death.

The victim's purse yielded barely half a sovereign. Lefroy hurled his revolver and other incriminating items out of the window and slipped his victim's watch into his shoe. When he alighted at Preston Park Station, the last before Brighton, he asked the staff if he could see a doctor, explaining that he had been attacked by two fellow passengers in Merstham Tunnel who had vanished by the time he regained consciousness.

Lefroy was duly sent to Brighton for a medical examination and police questioning. His insistence on being taken back home to Surrey was – curiously – unchallenged but his escort, Detective Sergeant George Holmes would later fail to keep adequate guard on his charge, who escaped. After wandering round London (where he threw Gold's watch over the middle arch of Blackfriars Bridge) and environs for a couple of days, the killer took up lodgings in Stepney under the name of 'Clark'.

Gold's body, a dreadful sight, had meanwhile been found by two gangers in the mile-long Balcombe Tunnel.

Early in the afternoon following the killer's escape, 'Wanted for Murder' police notices giving a concise description of the man and details of the watch began appearing at virtually every public location. A week later, on 4 July, Scotland Yard issued a new notice, this time offering a substantial reward of £200 for information. The *Daily Telegraph* made newspaper history by obtaining and publishing Lefroy's picture.

Writing from 32 Smith Street, Stepney, Lefroy broke cover by having a telegram sent to his workplace requesting his wages be brought to him. On 8 July, two CID inspectors descended on his lodgings and arrested him on the charge of murdering Frederick Gold. Lefroy denied any guilt. At the same time, he said he was glad he had been found for he was 'sick and tired of it all'.

Taken initially by rail to Lewes Gaol, he stood trial before Lord Chief Justice Coleridge at Maidstone Assizes on 4 November 1881. Defending Lefroy was the noted barrister, Mr Montagu Williams (see BIGAMY), who made a courageous, but ultimately unsuccessful, plea on his client's behalf. The case against Lefroy grew inexorably, strengthened by the many contradictions in his statements. Influenced no doubt by the judge setting himself against the accused in his lengthy summing-up, the jury took only ten minutes to reach their Guilty verdict.

Just under three weeks later, on 29 November, Percy Mapleton Lefroy was hanged at Lewes Gaol – but not before recording his appreciation of Mrs Gold's charitable and free forgiveness for the wrong done her. 'I can,' he added, 'only humbly confess my fault and ask forgiveness of Almighty God.'

LEIGH, JOHN

John William Leigh was dubbed 'Mad' with good reason. His behaviour was un-predictable and frequently violent, culminating in murder in a Brighton public house in February 1866.

He was born in the town in 1840, the result of the seduction of one Emma Leigh by an American with the surname Farren who held the post of American Consul at Pernambuco, NE Brazil. Both parents married others; Emma became Mrs Mottley while Mrs Farren, having no child of her own, generously adopted the boy in 1846. It was doubtless a gesture she would regret, for John was uncontrollable. He ran away from school and from her and for some weeks, aged eight, lived rough in Brighton. More wild schooldays followed his recapture, with a relatively settled period at a boarding school.

Bowing to the 13-year-old's determination to go to sea, the kindly stepmother even assisted him in his ambition, putting him initially aboard a collier, after having him taught navigation privately and purchasing an apprenticeship for him with a shipowning firm. Leigh nearly drowned when the *Tyrone*, taking troops to the Crimea, was wrecked in 1854. He went on to make many voyages and was made a chief officer before he was 20. Yet his violence was never far below the surface: he stood trial in Calcutta for the savagery with which he quelled what he considered to be a mutiny, but got off with only a fine.

In the Indies he married a Spanish girl in a Catholic church, but deserted her after nine months. To escape from her, he went to China, where he traded in human cargo, seizing seamen from naval ships and selling them to crew-hungry merchant owners. He then made his way to Singapore, where he looked after a sailors' boarding house, then, with a band of English followers, fought for the rebels during the so-called Taiping Rebellion (1851–64). Days of piracy in south-east China followed, during which the 21-year-old Leigh preyed on all who were loyal to the Emperor. When the British took the ruler's side, he and his companions had to flee to avoid arrest, but his piracy was soon resumed, together with gun-running activities. In one of his many courageous fights on land and sea, his skull was smashed open when a cannon-ball crashed into a bulkhead above him. A protective silver plate was fitted in his head to cover the wound.

A large reward for him, dead or alive, was put up so he pulled out of China with his companions. There were now eight left out of his original band of eleven – the other three had been taken and executed.

On his return to England in 1863, still only 23, Leigh – now dubbed 'Captain' – took the *Oddfellows Arms* public house in Queens Road. He was a bad landlord, neglecting the business and giving himself over to his great love – drink. Despite his downing raw spirits by the pint, no one ever saw him drunk. Attention-seeking antics and foolish wagers were his hallmark and there is no doubt that he kept the regulars entertained. Despite his unprepossessing appearance, he was able to attract one Jane Stringer, whom he bigamously married. They lived at 3 St Anne's Terrace in her home town of Lewes. His flamboyance, generosity and story-telling soon made him a popular figure at the *Pelham Arms*, his favourite inn in that town.

In March 1865, Leigh went to Brentford with his new wife and took a public house there called the *George and Dragon* (still in business and located at 29 London Rd). Fatherhood and apparent devotion to his wife did not, however, make him change his behaviour, which became increasingly eccentric.

One day, without telling his wife, he sold all his possessions at the *George and Dragon* and threw all the proceeds to a crowd from the balcony. He then wrecked the pub building, smashing more than 100 panes of glass and trashing the interior before fleeing with his wife and child. The furious landlord naturally sent for the police, who soon caught up with him at his mother's house in Birdcage Walk. Leigh was sentenced to three months with hard labour at Coldbath Fields.

Jane Leigh, now destitute and understandably terrified of her husband, went with their child to live with her sister, Mrs Harriet Harton, wife of the landlord of the *Jolly Fisherman* in Market Street, Brighton. Leigh, deprived of his brandy, was more violent than ever in prison, where for much of the time he was held in a padded room, restrained and manacled. On his release, he wrote to Jane asking her to join him in London but she refused. He tried again two or three times without success, his wife's resolve doubtless being strengthened by her sister. Certainly Mrs Harton flatly rejected Leigh's proposal that he should come down and live in the pub.

Inn of death: the Jolly Fisherman *in Market Street, long since demolished.* Author's collection

He did come to Brighton, however, to try and see his wife. He was unsuccessful on three occasions in gaining entry into the *Jolly Fisherman* but after finally meeting Jane for a drink at *Payne's Hotel*, he made his way on to the pub at 10 pm – alone. The date was 1 February 1866. Entering via the tap room with a revolver in his hand, he shot Mrs Harton directly he saw her. The bullet went through her body from her back and was followed by another, fired at point blank range, which lodged in her left armpit. Her sick husband – who Leigh claimed owed him £50 – came downstairs and tried to seize his brother-in-law, but the mad captain escaped and ran out of the front door. A crowd gathered and hemmed him in. He could probably have got away but leant calmly against the wall of *Harrison's Hotel*, eyeing the mob with contempt. Three constables arrived in the company of Superintendent Barnden. Despite being warned that Leigh was armed, Barnden courageously tackled him. He was lucky – a shot from the murderer went through his clothing without wounding him. Leigh was overpowered and taken to the nearby Town Hall.

Despite prompt medical assistance, Mrs Harton lost too much blood and died the next day.

John William Leigh was hanged at Lewes Gaol on 10 April 1866 before a 2,000–3,000 crowd, his colourful and bizarre life snuffed out almost instantaneously and without a struggle.

LYON, KEITH (victim)

Happy Valley, Woodingdean, in the eastern part of greater Brighton is a downland area popular with walkers but has, tragically, lent its name to a shocking murder which remains unsolved after 40 years.

On the afternoon of 6 May 1967, 12-year-old Keith Lyon set off from home, a 100-year-old converted farmhouse in the nearby suburb of Ovingdean, for a walk before music practice. His father, Ken, a well-known Brighton bandleader, had given him his pocket money of two shillings, with which the boy wanted to buy a compass for his geometry set. He was attacked about 45 minutes later, as he neared the end of the bridle path leading to Warren Road, Woodingdean, just over a mile away. He was stabbed 11 times in the chest, back and abdomen and his body was left lying a few feet from the side of the path. A teenage girl out walking came across it a short time later. Keith, a very promising pupil at Brighton and Hove Grammar School, was smartly dressed in a white shirt, school tie, blue pullover and grey flannels, when he was attacked. One theory is that he was targeted because of the way he was dressed.

The crime scene was sealed off and a temporary murder HQ set up in the head-master's study at Woodingdean Primary School. Scotland Yard was called in to head the investigation. Hard evidence proved difficult to come by. Some schoolboys did find a white-handled steak knife, which tests confirmed was probably the murder weapon, in a sports field at the rear of nearby Fitzherbert School. Detectives became convinced that the perpetrator(s) had scaled a flint wall behind the school immediately after the stabbing. Two youths had reportedly been seen running from the direction of the murder scene and there were other reports of boys scuffling near the spot where the victim's body was found. Bloodstains discovered in a lavatory at the neighbouring Lawns Memorial Gardens pointed to someone having washed blood from their hands and clothes there.

Intensive investigations were undertaken. Large numbers of people were interviewed, from rough sleepers in the area to the girls of Roedean School. At the end of the month, a massive fingerprinting operation was announced. Special centres were set up to allow no

The downland track along which Keith Lyon (inset) was walking when he was attacked. To the right is the suburb of Woodingdean. The author

fewer than 4,000 Brighton boys to be fingerprinted. The exercise was then extended all over the town. In addition, 75,000 house calls were made and 17 schools visited, with nearly 1,900 schoolchildren being interviewed. Forensic work was carried out in tandem with these enquiries. A special magnetic mine detector with 260 magnets and capable of pulling metal objects out of the ground was borrowed from Aldermaston to search for the murder weapon.

The jury at Keith's inquest returned a verdict of Murder by a Person or Persons Unknown.

On the anniversary of Keith's death, his father offered a £1,000 reward for information leading to the killer's arrest and conviction, but no one came forward. Ken Lyon died in 1991 without knowing who killed his son. He had never got over his death.

In 2000, Peter, Keith's musician brother, urged detectives to use new DNA techniques to reinvestigate the case. The following year, the murder was featured on the BBC's *Crimewatch* programme and a £10,000 reward put up to find the killer. An emotional plea for help in solving the mystery was made by Keith's mother Valda, who was by then in her 80s. She died in October 2005. The case featured on the programme again the following year.

In November 2002, workmen uncovered a trove of evidence in the basement of Brighton Police Station which lent new forensic hope to the enquiry. Inside one of the boxes was the probable murder weapon, the white-handled steak knife, still stained with Keith Lyon's blood, and that of another person – possibly his killer. Other items

The search for clues to Keith's killer(s) could not have been more thorough. Solo Syndication/Mirrorpix

discovered included a cigarette butt found at the murder scene, clothing, and a blood-stained tissue, all of which could carry incriminating DNA. The evidence had probably been put in the room more than 20 years previously. It was locked and forgotten about until the workmen stumbled across it.

In a startling new development, there were hopes of a breakthrough in the case following the arrests, on 27 July 2006, of a 56-year-old man from Brighton and a 55-year-old man living in Manchester. Both men were DNA-tested and released on police bail until 14 November. Two days later, however, *The Argus* reported they were no longer considered as suspects.

Peter Lyon, who lives in Kemp Town, Brighton, was seven at the time of the murder, an event which has overshadowed his life ever since. He was naturally disappointed that there had been no outcome from the latest line of enquiry by the police but remains hopeful of 'future developments that may eventually result in the long-awaited justice we all wish for Keith'.

M

MAGISTRATES – see also COURTS

Mercer records that magistrates were elected periodically and were usually eminent, well-educated gentlemen with time to give to public service. Some favoured particular punishments (the harsh Sir David Scott, for example, was all for transportation). Some basked in the public eye as supporters of the poor and the church: to the latter, William Seymour and George Basevi donated £20, and W Borrer £100, clearly thinking that ecclesiastical efforts to reduce crime were a more worthwhile investment than helping the poor, who were the subjects of a concurrent appeal.

David Scott, who qualified for service in 1821, was still very active in, for example, 1835 when his name appeared in the *Brighton Guardian* with unfailing regularity. An editorial in the issue of 26 August expressed the view that he had overreached himself in one case, however, having betrayed 'great want of tact'. It was hoped that as he got older he would get wiser, but the writer did concede that he 'had many good parts', adding that 'but for the occasional excesses into which he is led by an unfortunate irritability of temper, he certainly is the best Magistrate on the Bench'.

Leniency in 1950

An editorial well over a century later, this time in the *Brighton and Hove Herald* (7 January 1950) asked 'Are Magistrates Too Lenient?' It focused on two cases of ASSAULT and one of threatening behaviour. All the perpetrators had previous convictions.

In one case a Brighton man was struck in the face repeatedly with a broken milk bottle as he was going to his garage. He had to have 22 stitches in his face and six in his right hand. The magistrates sent his assailant to prison for six months, the maximum sentence they could give. The writer suggested that better justice would have been done if he had been sent before a higher court where a more appropriate penalty could have been imposed.

In another ASSAULT, a Scottish street trader attacked a barmaid in a public house. He threw a pint glass at her and broke her nose. His sentence was just four months' imprisonment.

In the third case, a strapping young Irishman so intimidated people from whom he was begging in a quieter part of the town that three 999 calls were received by police in the space of a few minutes. He was removed in a patrol car, brandishing a pair of scissors. He was sentenced to one month in prison for BEGGING.

The editorial emphasised that there should be sterner treatment for such vicious men, who were a danger to the general public. Indeed, the severity should be such as to 'discourage these evil-doers from coming here at all'.

MANCINI, TONI – see also TRUNK CRIME No. 1

Why did he do it? There hasn't been a word. There has been no word, no question, no hint, no suggestion of any kind, as to that vital matter as to why he should do it, and upon that vital question, the answer is complete and impenetrable silence.

(Norman Birkett, defending Mancini at the Sussex Assizes, December 1934)

A couple calling themselves Watson took up lodgings in the basement flat of 44 Park Crescent, off the Lewes Road, in March 1934. 'Mrs Watson' was a former music hall dancer named Violet Saunders, who preferred to be known as Violette Kaye. One of 16 children, with a failed marriage behind her, she had turned to prostitution when work in shows became more difficult to obtain. Now 41, faded and into drink and morphine, she would continue to ply her trade from the flat. The couple, from London, had been in the Brighton area for six months and moved around a lot – this was their thirteenth home in the district.

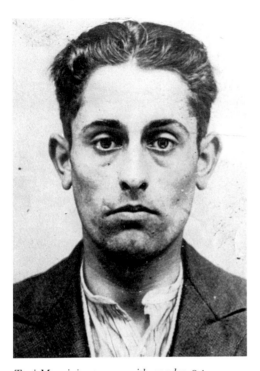

Toni Mancini got away with murder. Solo Syndication/Mirrorpix

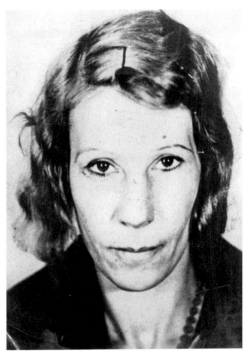

Violette Kaye, a trunk murder victim stored intact. Solo Syndication/Mirrorpix

'Mr Watson' was a thuggish small-time crook and former lightweight fairground boxer named Toni Mancini (other aliases were Luigi Mancini, Antoni Pirille, Hyman Gold and Jack Notyre). Swarthy in appearance and ruthless by temperament, he had been born Cecil Lois England in 1908. While still in his teens he had deserted from the RAF. He very soon became a member of London's underworld, working as a strong-arm man for a gangster named 'Harry Boy' Sabini (see RACECOURSE/ RACES).

In early May, Mancini got a job as a cook, waiter and general handyman at the *Skylark Café*, between the piers. Somewhat worse for drink, Violette turned up unexpectedly in the middle of the afternoon on Thursday the 10th. When she saw Mancini hand a young waitress, Florence Attrell, some tea, saying: 'Here you are, mate', her suspicions were aroused. She said, in a loud voice: 'I won't have it. Don't call her mate!' The café went quiet and Mancini told her to pull herself together. An ugly scene was averted when she walked out. Some hours later, following a fearful row at the flat, Violette was killed by head injuries inflicted by Mancini. Her body, wrapped in bedclothes, was placed in a cupboard in the basement flat. Mancini turned up for work as usual the following morning, and told the other staff that Violette had left him and gone away to Paris. To other people he gave similar reasons for her absence. The ice-cool waiter even gave Attrell some of Violette's clothes at the flat – and took her out dancing twice.

It was time to find new lodgings. In order to move the body, Mancini bought a large strapped trunk, paying a man to help him push it on a handcart to his new address, 52 Kemp Street, quite close to Brighton Station. For two months, the killer lived there with the increasingly odorous trunk. Outwardly unconcerned, he must have been in turmoil by a discovery made at the station's left luggage office on 17 June. This was a locked trunk containing the torso of a young woman, which had been deposited there 11 days previously (see TRUNK CRIME No. 1). Efforts were made by police on a mammoth scale to identify the victim. Of over 800 women reported missing, 730 were traced. Ultimately all efforts were unavailing, and the mystery remains unsolved to this day.

However, the reports of missing females did result in responses from friends of Violette Kaye who had not seen her for a while. The police homed in on Mancini. On 14 July 1934, he went willingly to the police station under the Town Hall and made a detailed statement, following which he was allowed to leave. With the heat on him, however, he was close to panic and left Kemp Street for London. In his absence, Violette Kaye's body was discovered in his lodgings and a post-mortem examination was conducted on the same day by eminent pathologist Sir Bernard Spilsbury.

Mancini only remained at large for 48 hours, being picked up on the road to Sidcup in the early hours of 17 July. He was charged, under the name of Jack Notyre, with wilful murder and taken back down to Brighton to face the accusation. Following an appearance at the Magistrates' Court, his trial at Lewes Assizes was set for the 10 December 1934 and he spent much of the intervening period in Brixton Prison. Despite a very powerful prosecution case against him, he was acquitted through the brilliant advocacy of his defence counsel, Norman Birkett, later Lord Birkett of Ulverston.

After hearing the Not Guilty verdict, an incredulous Mancini, a free man, staggered down the steps of the dock to be released after having been a prisoner since 18 July.

In the following summer, he toured fairgrounds. Billed as 'Toni Mancini, the Infamous Brighton Trunk Murder Man', he used a mock guillotine with which he pretended to chop off the head of a pretty girl. In September, he received a three-month prison sentence with hard labour on a charge of stealing a watch from a jeweller's in Tonbridge.

Later years were spent roaming the world and there were two broken marriages, although he found happiness in a third – and a new life in the north of England.

Over 40 years after the trial, at the age of 69, he gave an interview to *News of the World* reporter Alan Hart. The edition of 28 November 1976 contained a startling confession and appeared with the headline I'VE GOT AWAY WITH MURDER. In it, Mancini gave a vivid account of what happened to Violette Kaye on that fateful day in May 1934. As for the trial itself, he confessed: 'When I gave evidence I had carefully rehearsed my lines like an actor. I had practised how I should hold my hands and when I should let the tears run down my cheeks.'

Two years after this confession, Mancini gave a considerably different account of the quarrel and what led up to it in an interview to journalist Stephen Knight. As a result of these revelations, the case was reopened but the DPP ruled that independent corroboration of Mancini's claim was essential and because of the years elapsed between 1934 and 1976 this would not now be forthcoming. He therefore closed the Mancini case by stating there was insufficient evidence available, or likely to become available, to prosecute the suspect for perjury.

At the end of July 1986, in a further twist, *Evening Argus* reporter Carolyn Robertson tracked Mancini down to an address in South London, where he was living under an assumed name. In the interview, the frail 78-year-old protested his innocence in respect of both trunk killings and vowed to fight the 'lies' until the day he died.

MARSHALL, JOHN JAMES ('JIM'), MBE QPM (1916–) – see also POLICE

Jim Marshall, Britain's longest-serving CID Chief, joined the County Borough Police in Barnsley, South Yorkshire, in 1937 and was transferred to the CID there in 1939. After war service in South Africa, India and Burma, he returned to Barnsley CID and was immediately promoted to Sergeant, then Detective Inspector.

In early 1959, a vacancy arose for the post of Head of the CID in Brighton – believed to be the first time such a position had ever been advertised nationally – in a shake-up following an investigation by New Scotland Yard officers (see POLICE – CORRUPTION). Marshall was offered the appointment and almost immediately rose two ranks to Detective Superintendent, Class 1. 'The officers I took over in Brighton,' he told me, 'were some of the best I'd come across in the whole of my police career – and many of them are friends of mine today [2006].'

The Department was, he recalled, housed in a separate building in Bartholomews, just across the road from the entrance to the Town Hall and near the Surveyor's Department. He was consulted about the location of the new Brighton Police Headquarters in John Street (to which the CID would also relocate) and visited the site at the outset with the Chief Constable.

On 1 January 1968, when the five Sussex forces (East and West Sussex, Brighton, Eastbourne and Hastings) were amalgamated, Marshall was promoted to Detective Chief Superintendent in overall charge of the CID across East and West Sussex. The Department's work was not confined to investigation – there were, he recalls, about 17 different sections, including the Criminal Record Office and the Criminal Intelligence Office. There were a score of dog handlers for which Marshall was responsible.

The CID building near the Town Hall was vacated when the new police headquarters opened in John Street. Chris Horlock collection

At that time, detectives were working from 20-odd stations throughout Sussex. 'Anything connected with investigations was down to me. I went out to almost every murder that happened, often being called out in the middle of the night.' Such an instance was the hospital bedside interview of HARVEY HOLFORD or the post-mortem on the murder victim, BARBARA GAUL (he remembers pieces of shot extracted from her body falling onto the floor).

Before his retirement in 1976, he was responsible for clearing up virtually all of the serious crimes committed in his extensive area. The only murder case he recalls being connected with but which remains unsolved is that of KEITH LYON. New Scotland Yard assisted with the investigation (it was the practice at that time to call them in) but all efforts to trace the perpetrator(s) were unavailing.

The case of MARIA COLWELL, which Marshall was able to clear up within 24 hours, is the saddest he remembers. Later, in his capacity as Vice-Chairman of East Sussex Social Services Committee, he was able, with his experience of the case, to influence the way children in care were supervised. He also served on the Adoption Committee and was governor of seven schools, five of them 'special'. For many years he served on East Sussex County Council and Hove Borough Council.

Jim Marshall was awarded the MBE by HM The Queen in the year 2000 for community services in Hove and has been made a Freeman of the City of London; he also holds the Queen's Police Medal for Distinguished Service.

He is the author of *The True Story of the Ollie Murder* (1986) and lives in Hove.

MASON, NICHOLAS

Nicholas Mason, 24, a printer, went on a random stabbing spree in Brighton on 27 November 1999, wounding two men and killing a third. He stabbed one man in the eye, a second in the back and the third fatally in the heart. Mason, of no fixed address, pleaded guilty to two counts of wounding but denied murder, admitting instead manslaughter on the grounds of diminished responsibility.

His first victim was caterer Ruan Ali Malkovich, 35. He was in his flat above Buxton's furniture shop in London Road when Mason banged at the door, asking for a girl named Suzy. Malkovich explained he was the only person living there and shut the door. Seconds later Mason kicked it open and stabbed him just below his left eyeball and at the bottom of his rib cage.

The assailant, who worked at New England House in New England Street, then went to the headquarters of the Farside advertising agency in Providence Place. The employees were winding down after the day's work when Mason marched in at around 9.30 pm and asked: 'Is there a party going on? Why have I not been invited?' He was ushered outside but returned. Justin El Korashy, 19, of Saltdean, stepped in to make Mason leave again and as he followed him through a doorway was stabbed through the heart. Mason's third victim, Justin's colleague, Thomas Meakin, 20, from Hove, ran to escape an attack. He was stabbed in the back and was treated later in hospital. His attacker left and returned to his nearby place of work. With dried blood caked on his hands, he persuaded a frightened workmate to drive him to Brighton station.

Police, meanwhile, cordoned off a huge area of the town. Teams searched the streets while the force helicopter flew numerous sorties in the hope of spotting someone running or trying to hide.

Mason threw his combat knife out of the train window before reaching Gatwick, where he caught a plane to Amsterdam. He was there when Justin lost his fight for life in hospital, five days after being stabbed.

Descriptions of the knifeman were circulated but there were still no clues to the killer's identity until Mason's mother telephoned. Press reports, the youth's history of violence and his sudden disappearance made her come forward and she provided police with a photograph. His details were circulated throughout the country and abroad through Interpol. Police were waiting when he returned to Britain by ferry at Harwich.

Mason was apprehended and his criminal past was revealed. He had been convicted of theft in 1992 and of violence the following year. He had been arrested for murder after a gang fight during the Finsbury Frolics fair in London, a charge later reduced to manslaughter, of which the jury in any case found him not guilty. He was cleared of the murder of Justin El Korashy but convicted of manslaughter on the grounds of diminished responsibility and committed to Broadmoor Mental Hospital.

MEYRICK, KATE, 1875–1933

> *I discovered that men will pay anything to be amused. Pleasure and amusement are the only things in the world where the buyer rarely counts the cost. A man buying life's necessities is clever and calculating; a penny more on his pound of sugar will drive him frantic. But there are few who, on pleasure bent, will not empty their pockets quite light-heartedly.*
>
> (Kate Meyrick, *Secrets of the* 43 Club, 1933)

It should be said at the outset that the more colourful days of the life of Kate Evelyn Meyrick (née Nason) did not begin until after she had left Brighton. Her years of residence in the town cannot, however, be ignored, particularly on account of their sharp contrast with her subsequent career.

With her husband, Dr Ferdinand Richard Holmes Meyrick (d. 1941), and their eight children, she moved in 1914 to Sylvan Hall, Brighton, described by them as 'a lovely old-world house', where they stayed until 1918. Here the doctor, whose surgery was at 34 Wakefield Road, ran the establishment as a home for the mentally ill. These included badly shell-shocked soldiers. Kate, herself the daughter of a doctor, assisted him and, following lessons in hypnotism and suggestive therapeutics, was able to do useful work with chronic nerve cases.

The family remained in Brighton all through the First World War (her daughters attended Roedean School) and frequently gave entertainments in the grounds, sometimes for the soldiers themselves and sometimes to raise funds for them.

In 1918, she left her husband for good on the grounds of his cruelty (there had been a year's separation prior to the move to Brighton). Kate's overriding motivation in all her subsequent dealings was to provide for her children rather than create wealth for herself (they did well – three of her daughters married into the aristocracy).

By the following year, she had opened her first London business venture, *Dalton's Club* in Leicester Square, which would often be targeted by the police on account of its reputation as a pick-up point for prostitutes.

'Ma Meyrick', as she became known, appeared in a lightly disguised form in Evelyn Waugh's *Brideshead Revisited*. She went on to open many more establishments, most famously the *43 Club* in Gerrard Street, which was noted for attracting a mix of bohemians, writers, aristocrats and gangsters – particularly members of the Sabini gang and their racetrack rivals (see RACECOURSE/RACES). Today the premises are home to a Chinese restaurant and supermarket.

The clubs were frequently raided, since DORA (the Defence of the Realm Act, which prohibited the sale of alcohol after 10 pm) was still in force. Fines were followed by periods of imprisonment on other charges. In January 1929, she achieved notoriety when she was tried at the Old Bailey as a co-defendant in the 'Goddard Case', one of the most important police corruption trials of the century. Convicted of bribing the police, she was sentenced to 15 months' hard labour in Holloway Gaol.

This and the other jail sentences which the 'Queen of the London Clubs' served at various times and which totalled three years three months took their toll on her health, even though she always returned to her night club career. She died of broncho-pneumonia in January 1933 at the early age of 57.

By her own estimate, Kate Meyrick saw the phenomenal sum of £500,000 pass through her hands in the course of her nightclub career. Her estate on her death amounted to a mere £58.

MILITIA – see also ASSAULT, COURTS-MARTIAL, RAPE, UNREST (CIVIL)
By 1810, as many as 10,000 troops were stationed in Brighton following the feverish anti-invasion measures adopted when war between England and France had been officially declared in 1793. With such a large contingent in and around the town, problems in co-existing peacefully with the residents would inevitably arise from time to time. That said, the *Brighton Herald* of 7 November 1807 revealed another side to the soldiers, referring to the 'usual benevolence in all cases of distress' displayed by officers of the Royal South Gloucester Regiment; they each gave up one day's pay in support of the widow and orphans of Nathaniel Harman, who had drowned in a dreadful storm on the 22nd of the previous month.

Clashes with civilians – and each other
What the *Sussex Weekly Advertiser* described as 'a most unpleasant disturbance' took place on 10 April 1811 in North Street. Some 200 soldiers of the Royal South Gloucester Militia and a very large proportion of 'the lower orders of the people of the town' were involved. There were numerous and contradictory accounts of the causes of the trouble, although the newspaper did not feel the military were the aggressors or that there was any premeditation – on the soldiers' part at least. The forces of civil order, such as they were at that period, were quite unable to cope and the high constable and his headboroughs (petty constables) were very severely treated in the heat of the moment. The town beadle nearly lost his life and there were many black eyes and bloody noses. The regiment's picket guard finally restored order, but not without difficulty.

Less than a week later, a second disturbance took place between some of the South Gloucesters and a group of the town's lowest rabble. The picket guard was again called out to restore order and one of the townspeople was taken to the guard room for the night pending his appearance before the magistrates at Lewes later that week.

So strong was the resulting prejudice against the militia that a meeting of the Town Commissioners was held at the Town Hall the next day. Many witnesses were examined and a memorial to Sir David Dundas, the Commander-in-Chief, was drawn up, accompanied by a request to remove the South Gloucester Regiment from the town.

That April continued to be a black month indeed for disturbance involving soldiers, for on Saturday the 29th a major clash took place in Church Street (the location of the barracks) between a party of the 10th Hussars and a party of the South Gloucesters, some of whom reportedly received several severe wounds.

Caricature of Lord Henry Paget, Marquess of Anglesey, 7th Hussars, with his false leg over his shoulder. Etching by 'Paul Pry' (William Heath), 1829. National Army Museum

At 2.30 in the morning of 11 August 1823, officers of the 7th Hussars created a disturbance in Grand Parade. When remonstrated with, 'they both began with all the abusive language possible to the watchman, calling not only him and the rest of the watchmen every ill-name possible but told him that both the watchmen and the magistrates should be thrown into the sea'. However, these officers escaped arrest. Later in the year, the same army officers were involved in another disturbance when leaving the *York Hotel* in the Steine between 2 am and 3 am. Finding an empty carriage known as a 'fly', belonging to a man named Vaughan, they shoved it over and broke the glass frame and assaulted the man with sticks. They got away but Vaughan followed them and, having met a watchman, gave them in charge. When they reached Church Street, however, 'Captain Molineux and his party ran away and effected their escape, the watchman being unfortunately unprovided with a rattle'.

Confrontations with the Police

The militia came into conflict with the POLICE in August 1842 and again a year later. The 1842 incident involved only one soldier – Sergeant Simpson of the 19th Regiment of Foot, then doing duty at Brighton, who lost £5 at the Racecourse. Although he had been playing at the pea and thimble table (contrary to military regulations against betting), he later swore that he had been robbed of the amount.

Writing on the matter the following year in a pamphlet published from Bond Street and whose main title was *Extraordinary Disclosures of the Conduct of the Brighton Police*, one ER Hearn recorded that on the following day, the soldier, accompanied by two or three comrades, went up to the racecourse and succeeded in apprehending the culprit, handing him over on a charge of felony to the custody of Superintendent Elmes in the police booth.

Elmes heard the man's defence and actually discharged him by a back door. Laughing at the soldier, he told him he had 'fairly' lost his money. In *Brighton Town and Brighton People*, however, Antony Dale writes that Elme [sic] recommended him to settle the matter by accepting two sovereigns. Either way, Elmes was out of line and the magistrates were indignant at his conduct. Dale adds that, with the assistance of the barracks adjutant, the truth was established and the superintendent cleared. Hearn did not follow the case through but railed against the behaviour of Elmes and the confused state of authority over the police. He earnestly hoped that 'means will be taken by the magistrates to prevent hereafter the disgraceful scenes enacted annually at our Race Course, and which in time will be the ruin of the races'.

There is no apparent reference in Dale to the serious affray the following year involving the 7th Hussars. Hearn relates how, on 4 August, a corporal standing at a gaming table

Preparing to start for the Brighton Stakes, 6 August 1851. The brand new stand is full to capacity.
Author's collection

with a female companion was surrounded, robbed and shamefully maltreated by a gang of thieves. They cut off his stripes and otherwise defaced his jacket. On returning to barracks he got into trouble, and was ordered into confinement.

Determined to avenge the insult, a hundred or so of his comrades met on the course the next day, armed with sticks, etc. They vented their spleen on the keepers of the gaming tables, smashing every table on the course, and their paraphernalia, to pieces. The thimble riggers put up no resistance, but scattered in all directions, trying to save their roulette boards and other items.

When the soldiers had completely cleared the course and were going away, the police mustered all their force, and rushed down the hill after them. Serjeant [sic] Major Nutt, who was greatly thought of by his soldiers, was on the course with his wife and daughter; seeing a clash between the two forces seemed likely, he intervened and assured the police he would call off all his men if they would retire.

Scarcely had he uttered these words than he was savagely struck on the skull by one of the policemen and fell unconscious to the ground. Two or three of his comrades picked him up, and immediately conveyed him to the Military Hospital. Furious at the conduct of the police towards their Serjeant Major, the soldiers fell on them. A violent conflict ensued, with the faces of many of the fighters streaming with blood. The mob did not interfere in the slightest, except in cheering on the soldiers. Finally the parties appeared to separate by mutual consent, each conveying their wounded away. The police took one soldier prisoner. Amongst their number, the officer who received the most serious injury was Inspector Crawhurst of 'A' Division, whose skull was fractured.

Information of the riot reached the Lewes Road barracks and a strong guard was immediately turned out, proceeding, under the Adjutant's command, to the scene of action. The returning soldiers mistook them for a reinforcement of comrades coming to their assistance and immediately went back to the fray, but on discovering their mistake again retired. The guard then examined every booth, and ordered home their few remaining men. Order was soon completely restored. The next morning, Frank North, a private in the regiment, was called before magistrates in a packed courtroom and charged with assaulting Inspector Crawhurst. He was found guilty and fined £3 plus costs. On payment being made, North was discharged – amidst a burst of applause.

Hearn had a lot more to say against Brighton's police in his pamphlet, and especially their chief, Henry Solomon (see LAWRENCE, JOHN), on matters connected with both Brighton and Goodwood racecourse.

Murder at Church Street Barracks

The Infantry Barracks in Church Street were originally intended to provide temporary accommodation for the duration of the Napoleonic Wars, yet continued in use for nearly 74 years (1796–January 1869). Living conditions were atrocious, and the soldiers quartered there were often stressed and subject to depression. The unmaintained buildings had become an eyesore as early as 1818, when C Wright expressed the view in *The Brighton Ambulator* that 'this cumbrous pile of bricks and mortar ... [should] ... be condemned and another building erected in a more conspicuous and agreeable spot'. In Wallis's *Brighton as it is* (1836), the barracks are described as offering 'accommodations for about 400 men', although 320 had been quoted as the figure in a guide book of 1813.

On 20 November 1819, the funeral took place of a Sergeant of the 90th Foot. He had been shot three days previously by a private of the regiment, who was executed at Horsham for the offence.

In 1858, Trooper John Flood and his comrade, John O'Dea, aged 17 and 19 respectively, enlisted together in Limerick in the 18th Hussars. When the regiment moved to Brighton, the pair were allocated to the infamous barracks. Here a primitive and unofficial system of courts-martial was in operation which was contrary to army regulations and involved weaker men like Flood being illegally tried by their comrades for petty offences and having severe punishments inflicted on them.

O'Dea, a notorious barrack room bully, applied this system with the help of two other troopers named Filburn and Gassett. On one occasion, they stripped Flood and lashed him so brutally with an army belt that he told other soldiers that he wished he were dead. The breaking-point came on 1 June 1862 when he was placed on sentry duty. O'Dea complained about the condition of his saddle and when Flood answered that it had been left clean, the bully said: 'You are a liar and I will have you tried by one of our courts martial when you come off guard!' When relieved at seven, Flood, who had all the

time been brooding about a further beating, returned to the guardroom and, instead of eating, drank several pints of beer and two large glasses of rum.

By nine o'clock he had resolved what he would do. He placed a cartridge into the breech of his weapon and a short time later, when O'Dea was seen crossing the barrack square towards the guardroom, he stepped out from within the shadow of his sentry box and asked: 'Is that you O'Dea?' When the unsuspecting O'Dea identified himself, Flood shot him in the stomach. He made no effort to escape when the sergeant and the soldiers of the guard ran towards him,

The only known depiction of the entrance to the Church Street barracks. Chris Horlock collection

A barrack room can on occasion simmer with discontent. Author's collection

simply asking whether O'Dea was dead. On hearing he was still alive, he desperately tried to reach the sergeant's sword but was rapidly pinned down by the others before he could do so. O'Dea, after lingering for several minutes, did die, despite efforts by the barrack surgeon to revive him. Flood was handed over to the civil authorities who charged him with wilful murder and sent him for trial at the Sussex Summer Assizes in Lewes.

Despite being given good character references by many of his former comrades, including the regimental Adjutant, and notwithstanding the plea of provocation, Flood was found guilty of murder by the jury after only 30 minutes. Sobbing, he responded: 'I was greatly excited at the time. I did not know what I was doing and I am very sorry for it.'

After the trial, many appeals were made to persons of influence and eventually to the Secretary of State, Sir George Grey, who expressed the view that 'This unhappy culprit [had been] goaded into an act by continuous and irritating provocation, from which he could not escape.' The Queen agreed to extend her Royal Mercy to the soldier, although notice of the reprieve only arrived at Lewes Gaol a few hours before the execution. Flood's coffin had already been made, with the metal plate recording his name and the date affixed to it. Despite being told by the Governor that he was condemned to a lifetime of penal servitude in the harsh confines of the prison, Flood knelt down on the cold stone floor and thanked God for his deliverance.

Robbery

On 18 June 1800, Luke Newman and James Piercy, late privates in the Hampshire Fencible Cavalry, were committed to Horsham Gaol charged with feloniously breaking into the dwelling house of Mrs Sarah May of Brighthelmston and stealing sundry articles of children's apparel, two mahogany tea chests, a family bible, a common prayer book and other items belonging to Mrs May. The robbers were traced to a wheatfield, where they were caught sorting and dividing out their booty.

No. 4 Marine Parade, occupied by one Edward Lewis, was burgled in the early hours of 6 June 1807 and 12 silver tablespoons and eight teaspoons were stolen. A few days later, a private of the First Dragoon Guards named John Spiller offered three tablespoons and seven teaspoons for sale to, coincidentally, a Mr Lewis, pawnbroker, of Ship Street Lane. As they were damaged, the shopkeeper's suspicions were aroused. Spiller told him that another private by the name of Carr had found them in a livery stable in North Street. Lewis secretly sought help from the constables and Spiller was taken into custody. His commanding officer, Colonel Sergison, examined him and sent him to Lewes Gaol for further examination later. Carr deserted and Lewis was thanked for his public-spiritedness. A soldier, subsequently passing his shop, loudly remarked that Spiller had used the wrong shop – he could have told him one to use where no questions would have been asked. *The Herald*, shocked, commented: 'We hope this man did not speak the truth.'

MODS AND ROCKERS – see also QUADROPHENIA, RIOTS

In the wake of pitched battles between Mods and Rockers at Clacton and Hastings at Easter 1964, Brighton police leave was cancelled in case of a possible invasion of troublesome youngsters. Whit Sunday, 17 May, marked the beginning of a spectacular, and sometimes bloody, two-day running battle between the two factions along the promenades, in the streets and on the beaches, which did not end until late on the Bank Holiday Monday. The police were prepared for the violence but residents and family visitors were not.

The Rockers, leather-clad biking descendants of the 1950s' teddy boys, arrived first and by midday were in possession of the seafront. Then the Mods, in their trademark parkas, started arriving in swarms on their multi-mirrored scooters. Fighting started following an incident on the beach when 30 jostling youths clashed. Two Rockers attempting to ride off on a motor cycle were dragged to the ground and set upon. The Mods chanted 'Down with the Rockers!' while the Rockers shouted 'We want blood!' Soon bottles, stones and even deckchairs were hurtling through the air in the battle for possession of the seafront. Other weapons included knives, iron bars and leather belts. Innocent bystanders were caught up in the violence and while some trippers and families ran for safety, others watched the youngsters fight it out, especially around the Palace Pier and Aquarium. There were, surprisingly, no serious injuries.

The weather was bright and sunny, with well over 2,000 cars an hour arriving in the town and visitors in their hundreds streaming down Queen's Road from Brighton Station. Down by the Palace Pier, hundreds of stone-throwing youths dashed across the road, halting traffic, to break the windows of the ABC cinema in East Street.

Although the police, reinforced from other towns in Sussex and as far away as Hampshire, endeavoured to keep the rioters on the move, the disturbances continued until midnight, with small groups of youngsters cornering, intimidating or beating up others. Youths in their hundreds slept out on the beaches, or under the piers and upturned boats that night. Many had brought sleeping bags. When there were no Rockers to fight, the Mods threw one another into the sea or bathed nude. Others rode further afield on their scooters. At the *Devil's Dyke Hotel*, the manageress, Mrs Norah King,

A dramatic clash near the beach. Royal Pavilion, Libraries and Museums, Brighton and Hove

was threatened by a gang of 20 invading Mods who stole food. She was rescued by 10 Territorial soldiers who called in for an early morning cup of tea and cleared the youths off.

Soon after 9.30 on the morning of Bank Holiday Monday, the battles were resumed, with deckchairs, stones and wastebins being hurled around in a violent clash at the Aquarium. Hundreds of shouting Mods streamed down to Madeira Drive from the West Pier. On the way, 200 of them, roughly jostling elderly holidaymakers and families, chased a 13-year-old boy across the beach, hurling stones at him until the police, under a fusilade of pebbles, managed to rescue him. He was sent to hospital by ambulance with a leg injury.

Between 2,000 and 3,000 people, mostly sightseers, crowded into the Madeira Drive area at the height of the battle, watching large numbers of teenagers fighting, scuffling and running on the terraces and promenade. The crowds made the job of the overstretched police – who were trying not to provoke the youngsters – more difficult. Officers vainly appealed for visitors to keep moving and residents to go home. The Rockers, outnumbered 10 to 1, were cornered by hordes of Mods at the Aquarium but most escaped by jumping 20 feet over the railings into the arms of the police below.

Police reinforcements arrived in vans and managed to split up the rival factions, although shortly before 1 pm the mobs regrouped near the Palace Pier. The police horse Kim, and officers with dogs, just about managed to keep the crowds moving, while boys chanted and jeered at one another and verbally abused the officers. Hundreds of them, some only 13 or 14, started an afternoon of stone-throwing at the pier entrance.

Business was of course seriously affected, with most of the beach kiosks, shops and amusement arcades closed and boarded up and many thousands of visitors left the town early by car or train. The decorative lights were not switched on that night. 40,000 deckchairs were hired out, but this was nearly 10,000 less than at Whitsun the year before. On the promenade, 140 seats were broken and 123 were stolen, burned, or hurled into the sea, the bill for chair damage alone being £400.

As the sun set, further police reinforcements arrived from Crawley, Eastbourne, Hastings, Lewes and Worthing. A massive uniformed force started rounding up the gangs, and youths with motorcycles or scooters started moving homewards. At the central station, police trapped groups of youngsters by barring all the exits. Plain clothes detectives mixed with the crowds, searching youths for weapons. At 8.30 the AA reported a line of hitchhikers, mostly Mods, stretching 20 miles along the main road from Brighton to Bolney.

The magistrates' court was kept busy on Monday, Tuesday and Wednesday, hearing cases concerning police assault, the carrying of offensive weapons, obstruction, discharging missiles, threatening behaviour, the theft of milk bottles, window-breaking, stone-throwing and wilful damage. The 26 youngsters who appeared in court received very harsh sentences – two jail sentences, 17 fines and six remands in the adult court. An 18-year-old Hackney boy who was said to have waved a cricket bat overhead and shouted 'I'm going to get me a Rocker's head' was jailed for three months. The same sentence was handed down to a 19-year-old Hove boy who admitted insulting behaviour in Whitehawk Road. Nine youths of between 17 and 19, mostly from Brighton, were sent to detention centres for three months.

At Easter 1966, there were more Mods/Rockers disturbances. Gangs of youths beat up a man near the Clock Tower, hitting a honeymooner who protected his wife. Cafés were forced to close. On Easter Sunday, a Rocker and his pillion passenger riding along Madeira Drive were surrounded by 20 or so umbrella-waving Mods chanting 'Kill these Rockers!' One of the pair was struck.

Although nothing ever again compared with the 1964 weekend battle, smaller numbers of Mods and Rockers returned again at Easter 1969, 1970, 1974, 1977 and May 1980. Under various disguises and different names, they arrived as Bovver Boys, Hell's Angels, Mad Dogs, Skinheads, Greasers, Punks, Freedom Riders and football fans. One 15-year-old juvenile mobster boasted he had been expelled from five schools and beaten up a teacher. 'The trouble wiv teachers,' he argued, 'is they teach you things, don't they?'

N

NEGLECT
The cruelty of James Greenfield, 1807

One of the most interesting and well-attended cases before the Sessions for the Eastern Division of Sussex which began at Lewes on 16 January 1807 was that of James Greenfield of Brighthelmston.

He had married in 1782 at the age of 25 when a journeyman carpenter. His wife, the widow of an innkeeper, was 56 years of age. She twice had a paralytic stroke after their marriage and was so cruelly neglected by her husband that she became a pitiful sight, having no bed and only rags to cover her. She developed ulcers on her legs and back, from which maggots bred. Details about the case were passed to some medical men and she was removed to the workhouse, where she died about a fortnight later.

The defence argued that Greenfield did not marry for money, since all he got was the furniture from the inn and some reversionary property, the combined value of which did not exceed £380. He had lived with his wife for two decades and provided her with every comfort; she also had a female servant to attend to her and he himself did the same, despite being on parish relief. Witnesses called following the long and powerful speech testified that Mrs Greenfield had never complained of any neglect or cruel treatment from her husband and had always stated that she did not want for anything. This testimony covered the period up to her removal to New Steine Street – six weeks before her transfer to the poorhouse.

The heartfelt plea in Greenfield's defence counted for little. The jury returned a verdict of 'Guilty of Neglect and Cruelty' and the prisoner was sentenced to twelve months' incarceration in Lewes's House of Correction.

Ernest Sinden's heart of stone, 1900

Your conduct appears to me to have been as bad as it possibly could be. There is no doubt that your neglect of your wife drove her to drink, and was the primary cause of her death.

(JE Bush, coroner, 13 June 1900)

The Sinden case of 1900, in which a brutal husband made no effort to save his wife from death, scandalised Brighton. Ernest Walter Sinden, his 29-year-old wife Hannah and their small child had arrived from South Africa the previous year to live at *Indwe House*, 306 Ditchling Road, Brighton. Within just over a year, Hannah was dead – from neglect. She had been ill ever since leaving Johannesburg, and became seriously sick early in June 1900.

She became an alcoholic. Although she had never previously drunk spirits, she now relied on gin and whisky to keep going, and ate little. Her alcoholism was caused by her husband's neglect, abuse and unkindness.

When she died, the peculiar circumstances of her death led to a coroner's inquest at the *Stanmer Park Hotel* further along Ditchling Road.

Throughout most of the proceedings, Ernest Sinden appeared indifferent to what was said and the coroner had great difficulty in extracting information from him. He 'didn't remember' whether, on the Saturday night before Hannah's death and when she was lying seriously ill, he brought home a woman who stayed all night in the house with him.

Eliza Dore, the servant, testified that Sinden had also bullied the couple's child, who was locked out in the back yard when it cried for its mother. When she was asked who had laid out the body, she gave the names of two men, both friends of Mr Sinden, whom he had called to the house. At this, the jury, already disgusted by Sinden's past behaviour and present nonchalance, showed renewed indignation (in those days it was considered unseemly for a man, particularly a stranger, to lay out a woman's body).

When Dr Fitzgerald Fraser, who had been attending Hannah for about a month before her death, found she had pneumonia, he sent round a qualified nurse. Sinden did not let her in. Had the doctor been called in earlier, Mrs Sinden might just possibly have been saved. The jury told the coroner that they thought Sinden had been guilty of gross neglect and cruelty. A formal verdict of death from pneumonia, aggravated by alcoholic excesses, was then returned. Sinden was recalled and told by the coroner that he was lucky there was no evidence to show that death was accelerated by his brutal behaviour. He had thoroughly earned the contempt of every man in the room and was not worthy to be called a man himself – comments which were applauded by the jury. Yet Sinden left the *Stanmer Park Hotel* a free man.

Infant abandoned in St James's Street, 1963

Jean Rose Smith, 23, of no fixed address, was placed on two years' probation at the end of June 1963 for abandoning her two-year-old daughter, Jane, in the blazing sun outside a St James's Street store for two hours in a manner likely to cause her unnecessary suffering. She pleaded guilty. When found, the infant was weak from lack of food and drink. Smith had been living with a man who was now in prison. Her parents, who were very concerned about her, agreed to support her and take her back into the family.

NEWLAND, CHARLES

Gladstone Place lies off the Lewes Road, between the town's borough cemeteries.

At the foot of the area steps of number 47, Mrs Kate Loula Newland, aged 44, was brutally murdered at about midday on 1 August 1899. Her throat was cut from ear to ear. The killer was her husband, Charles Newland, 45, who was promptly arrested.

The couple had three sons, aged seven, nine and 12. The sixth member of the household was Newland's niece, Nancy Martin. It was Albert, the eldest boy, who summoned the police. PC Groves found Newland and a Mr Ernest Grenville, a house painter, standing by the woman, who was then still alive. Grenville had been working at a property opposite and had run into the house, into which Newland had dragged his blood-drenched wife. He was holding her head up with one hand and patting her face with the other. Two women arrived within three/four minutes and one gave Grenville her apron, which he put round the victim's neck. Newland kissed his wife's hand, went to get some water and washed her face and hands. He then tried to give the painter, whom he knew, a knife from his pocket, saying (pointing to the small blade): 'This is the blade she done it with.' Yet when PC Groves questioned him, Newland said: 'I did it but I didn't mean to do it.'

Mrs Newland died a few minutes later, before the doctor arrived, having been unable to speak. When Dr Cousens, of Islingword Road, reached the scene, he saw there was a cut five inches long across the victim's throat and that the body was smothered in blood; there was also a superficial stab wound on the right side of the woman's back.

The inquest was held on the following day at the nearby *Alexandra Hotel*. The jury was escorted to the house to see the body and view the scene of crime. On the way, small groups of whispering neighbours watched their progress. Bloodstains were still visible on the basement steps and there were smears of red on the walls of the passage and scullery. Most of the reluctant visitors hurried past the waxen figure lying in the coffin, giving it only a hasty glance.

On returning to the hotel, the jury heard testimony from Nancy Martin. She described her uncle as a bricklayer's assistant in the town's Sanitary Department and reported how, on the night before the tragedy, he had been very restless and roamed about the house. At lunchtime the next day, she witnessed her aunt run out of the scullery with her uncle holding onto her. She caught hold of her uncle's jacket and tried to pull him away. On reaching the area door, she heard her aunt cry out: 'I am stabbed! For God's sake, Nan; run and cry murder!' At this moment, she saw the sunlight glistening on a knife in her uncle's hand. Then she looked down and saw the victim lying in a pool of blood at the foot of the area steps.

Miss Martin added that nine weeks earlier, her uncle had complained of severe attacks of neuralgia. Her aunt had told her he was behaving strangely. However, she had never known him to strike his wife. He had been temperate until two months earlier. On several occasions during the previous two months he had been roaming about the house at night, and for three weeks had not taken his food.

47 Gladstone Place. The author

The most vivid evidence came from a neighbour, Mrs Ellen Pollard, of 34 Gladstone Place. She told how she had seen Mrs Newland run up the steps to the street. Her sleeves were rolled up and her arms were stained with blood. She was shouting something that sounded like: 'For God's sake, Bertie, Bertie!' (the name of one of her children). Newland was close behind her and as she reached the top of the steps, he caught her and dragged her down again. Mrs Newland was screaming loudly. Mrs Pollard looked over into the area and saw Newland kneeling by his wife, blood pouring from her throat. He got up and then stood and looked over her and said: 'You ——. I meant to do it and I've done it.' He then went inside via the area door and Mrs Pollard ran away, intending to get a policeman.

On the same day as the inquest, Charles Newland appeared before the magistrates at the Church Street courthouse. His niece testified that during the year she had lived in the house there had only been slight quarrels between her uncle and aunt, the last one having taken place weeks earlier.

Evidence emerged at the hearing of marked insanity in Newland's family. His grandfather had died in Bethnal Green asylum after being an inmate there for 35 years, while his father had also been insane and spent the last years of his life confined at home.

At Lewes Assizes several months later, the defence plea was that the prisoner had been insane at the time of the murder and was therefore not responsible for his actions. The only new witnesses were three medical experts. The first two, produced by the prosecution, claimed that Newland was sane. Dr Saunders, medical superintendent at Haywards Heath asylum, with 35 years' experience, was unable to agree. The jury, reminded by the judge of the undoubted taint of insanity in Newland's family, conferred briefly without even retiring. They found Charles Newland guilty of the crime, but 'temporarily insane when he committed it'. The judge ordered him to be detained under proper care at Her Majesty's pleasure, which in those days meant for the term of his natural life.

NOLAN, NIGEL

The sheets looked as if they had been arranged quite carefully – almost mummified. I lifted up one sheet and another one under it and I saw a head and a pool of blood.

(Brian Cox, landlord)

Unemployed Nigel Patrick Nolan, 36, of no fixed address, was charged on 7 December 1998 with murdering out-of-work electrical engineer Brendan Byrne, 51, in his basement flat in Chichester Place (near Brighton seafront) between November 24 and 30 that year. He denied the charge. At first there was erroneously believed to be a possible link between this killing and that of Michael Furnival, whose body was discovered under a mile away and less than 48 hours earlier (see WHITTAKER, MARK).

When police received an emergency call from Brian Cox, the owner of the building, officers found that Byrne had sustained a brutal attack and died from head injuries. Cox had used a master key to enter the flat on receiving no reply from within. The room was in darkness and the curtains closed. When the light was put on, some bedding with a person underneath could be seen on the floor around the bed. He had suffered multiple fractures, bruising and cuts to his face and body and white strips of cloth were found in his groin area where somebody had tried to set fire to his body. He had been dead for three or four days.

Forensic experts moved into the sealed off four-storey Edwardian block and 15 police officers were assigned to the case. An incident room was set up at Brighton police station. Two days later, two grey dustbin bags containing jeans with blood on them, dentures, a sheet, an inhaler and a pair of boots covered with the victim's blood and hair were found in a nearby skip. A third bag discovered by a binman contained more clothes and also documents belonging to Nolan, who by that time had fled to Ireland.

The prosecution told how, on the previous Saturday, Nolan – who had moved in with Byrne after losing his job as a cook – had met a friend on Brighton Pier and asked to borrow £100. He confessed to him that he had got into trouble and had to get away. Days later, he cashed Byrne's disability allowance cheque at a post office in Paddington and went to Galloway City, in Ireland. There he told his brother Patrick he had killed someone and Patrick told the police.

Nolan was convicted by a jury and received a life sentence on 12 November 1999.

P

PANTRY, JOSEPH

I felt lonely for her and for myself. After her husband died she always said she wanted to die to be with him. That is why I killed her.

On 10 January 1958, Joseph Leonard Charles Pantry, 27, a trainee nurse of Upper Lewes Road, Brighton, was charged with the murder, on the previous day, of Mrs Sarah Louisa Hewlett, 88, whose husband had died a year previously. She was found dead at her flat after a telephone call to police that same morning. Detectives led by Det Spt William Cavey got no response to their knocks on the door and broke in. Mrs Hewlett's body was found beneath a bed. A scarf and wire flex were round her throat. Pantry and his wife had lived in the same house as their landlady for about 18 months.

Pantry, who worked at Cuckfield Hospital, had the day off on 9 January. The following day he reported for duty there as usual, handing the ward sister, Miss Margaret Sorrell, a note which read:

I know what I am saying and I know how things will turn out for me. I am so tired of hearing her say I want to die. Now I have helped her. God rest her and keep them both.

Asked by the sister what it meant, Pantry added: 'I have strangled the old girl in the flat upstairs.' He asked her to telephone the police, but Miss Sorrell said she must report it to the matron. Pantry later told police:

It was about six o'clock last night I made up my mind to do it. I got near to her twice before but just did not do it. Finally, as she came along the passage I grabbed her by the throat and she fell on the floor. I got her in the bedroom and tied round her throat a piece of electric wire and the scarf I was wearing.

That same evening, he joined his wife at the home of her sister, Mrs Margaret Howarth, in Rudyard Road, Woodingdean. He was quiet when he arrived and complained of a headache. Otherwise, Mrs Howarth found him normal.

In the Assize Court, the killer, wearing heavy-rimmed glasses, made his Not Guilty plea in a whisper. Dr F Brisby, principal medical officer at Brixton Prison, testified that Pantry had 'an air of detachment from the world of reality' while Dr David Rice, Medical Superintendent at Hellingly Hospital, had found him a pleasant, cooperative person, and a gentle man. He had, however, had a deplorable home background. His father had been a prisoner-of-war (Pantry had been eight when the war started) and his mother brought home men. Indeed, as a child he was turned out of bed and sent downstairs while his mother took her 'visitors' upstairs. A number of children were born to her but died young. A brother was born in the same bed and Joseph was sent out for the nurse. His relationship with his mother was never satisfactory and he ran away from home on a number of occasions. Partly due to evacuation, he had attended school irregularly. At 18, he joined the Army and went absent without leave. He joined the Merchant Navy for a year, but was troubled by the overt homosexuality he witnessed and did not wish to participate. He nevertheless had homosexual inclinations and in 1950 made his first attempt at suicide because he felt he was losing the attachment of a man friend who had got engaged. Two further attempts followed, one by gas and another by wrist-slashing. In 1953, he got engaged but was plagued by feelings of sexual inadequacy. His marriage was never consummated.

The defence argued that Pantry knew that in general it was wrong to kill but felt it was reasonable because he felt he was doing Mrs Hewlett a kindness.

Found guilty of manslaughter by the jury, which did not retire, Pantry was jailed for life at Lewes Assizes on 24 March 1958. Mr Justice Gorman commented that the verdict clearly showed the jury had found the prisoner to be someone suffering from an abnormality of mind.

PEAKE, ARTHUR

Arthur Cyril Jefferson Peake was a colourful character – a sports promoter, playwright, producer and art collector. In 1934, after going bankrupt as a showman and boxing promoter, the 44-year-old ex-army officer opened a small flower shop in Brighton's romantic, narrow and devious passages known as the Lanes.

His prices were too high for local tastes but he was cushioned by a handsome allowance from his ex-wife, the beautiful, talented daughter of a rich Londoner from whom she had inherited nearly a million. Peake had left her soon after their marriage but found a new interest in the young man assisting him in the shop. Arthur Geoffrey Noyce was a handsome, athletic 21-year-old, uneducated and unused to luxury, towards whom Peake had a strange, possessive attitude. He described him as his 'son', further fostering suspicions of a homosexual relationship.

The shop failed but Peake was able to live comfortably on his allowance in a two-bedroomed flat at 33 Brunswick Terrace, Hove. Noyce continued to be employed as

The Lanes, popular with shoppers and sightseers.
Author's collection

chauffeur/companion although he lived with his mother, who also ran a shop in the Lanes. When Peake sometimes went away from Brighton on business, Noyce would occasionally go with him.

On 8 October 1936, the young man went to visit Peake at his home. They dined together that evening by candlelight (because, Peake later testified, the electricity had failed) and at 9 o'clock next morning the maid took breakfast up and saw both men in bed, apparently asleep. Later that morning, Noyce's mother went to the house to find out why her son had not returned home. Noyce, either drunk or drugged, told her that Arthur had left him at about ten the previous evening. Dissatisfied, Mrs Noyce went to report the matter to the police. Later, an unconscious Peake, with small slashes on his throat and wrist, was found lying on the floor in the gas-filled bathroom with his head close to a gas fire. A cord was tied around the gas tap to prevent it being turned off. Noyce's body, with a sash cord tied around his neck, lay under a blanket on the bed.

When Peake appeared before the magistrates, he was charged with Noyce's murder. Medical opinion showed that the young man had been throttled with the sash cord and had evidently also received blows, apparently from a fist. Peake, who had been receiving treatment for mental distress and insomnia, declared that he had left Noyce in the bedroom while he went out to telephone his sister. On returning he found the young man foaming at the mouth. He had put him to bed. It was suggested that while Peake was away the youth had committed suicide by hanging or throttling himself with a cord. However, Hove doctor JH Crawford felt all the signs indicated that the cord had been tightly drawn from behind – not by the victim's own hands in front. The prosecution also pointed out that it was strange that Peake had not summoned assistance and instead shared his bed with the body for the whole night.

Peake pleaded not guilty at Lewes Assizes. Mrs Noyce told the court that he became distressed whenever her son threatened to leave him. He had talked of getting married to a girl in Staffordshire and this had upset Peake. He denied being jealous of the girl but agreed that he had told the young man that he could not go to her.

Sir Bernard Spilsbury, the eminent Home Office pathologist, categorically stated Noyce's death was due to strangulation by someone else. He had carried out an experiment with a police officer to prove it.

Peake had left a suicide note blaming his wife for Noyce's death; she had stopped his allowance in December because he 'would not give up the Noyces'. He said that when he found Noyce dead he knew he would be accused of murder, and decided to kill himself. The jury took nearly two hours to return their 'Guilty' verdict. Before sentence of death was passed, he exclaimed: 'Before Almighty God I am not guilty!'

Mrs Peake took on the cost of her husband's appeal and retained the services of Norman Birkett. She told Brighton journalist Leonard Knowles: 'I have never for one moment altered in my unswerving, unchanging love for my husband.' The appeal was heard in late January 1937 at the Court of Criminal Appeal. Birkett pointed out that there was no motive for murder and claimed Peake had a genuine affection for Noyce, with every reason to wish him to live. Winding the piece of cord around his own neck, he demonstrated that suicide was possible. Yet even he failed to win over the judges, who dismissed the appeal. Leave to appeal to the House of Lords (for Mrs Peake was determined to save her husband) was refused by the Attorney-General. There seemed no hope for Arthur Peake and the execution was fixed for 11 February.

Whether because of the growing national feeling against capital punishment, fostered by the eccentric, wealthy Mrs Van der Elst (see ANDERSON), or because the Home Secretary had been impressed by Birkett's dramatic pleading, he reprieved Peake – just three days before the execution. Announcing his decision, he said he had investigated the prisoner's long history of instability and the medical evidence of severe nervous breakdowns. The man who killed Arthur Noyce but had failed to kill himself cheated the hangman and was sent to Broadmoor, there to be detained during His Majesty's pleasure.

PERRIN, GEORGE

Spa Street, Brighton, no longer exists. Neither do Leicester Street or Egremont Street which stood on either side of it. All of them were off Edward Street, but today that eastern section of it lies in Eastern Road. In place of the varied shops and tenements which once lined the north side of the thoroughfare are a car showroom and blocks of flats. For many years in the 1800s, 84 Edward Street – close to the corner of Spa Street – was a baker's shop with accommodation above it run by the Hall family.

On Friday, 19 June 1896, the police were summoned to the address. There they found the proprietor, Mrs Charlotte Hall, lying dead in a pool of blood. She had seven severe wounds to her head. A local doctor confirmed these could not have been self-inflicted. The 53-year-old widow was found fully dressed in a hay loft used for storing flour and yeast.

Although Mrs Hall lived alone, the 11-year-old daughter of her baker and delivery man, George Perrin, had been going to the house each evening to stay with her. When questioned, Perrin told the police that a tall, dark stranger had been visiting Mrs Hall. He was quite specific in his description of him (dark moustache, plaid suit, black Oxford hat) and claimed she had arrived back with the man at nearly nine on the night of the tragedy. He himself had been left minding the shop when she had gone out at around 4 pm.

When, later on, he sent his daughter to stay with Mrs Hall as usual, the house was in darkness and there was no reply to constant knocking, so the girl returned home. She tried again later but there was still no reply. Perrin said he went to open up the shop next morning at 5.40 but found the door locked and bolted from the inside. He feared something was wrong, so fetched a policeman. While PC James remained outside the front of the shop, Perrin entered the house from the yard at the back. He found it empty and the bed not slept in. It was in the hayloft that he made the grim discovery.

The constable fetched a doctor and searched the house. He found no sign of a struggle or a weapon and no money had been taken (there was 27s in cash on the property).

The post-mortem revealed that the wounds were the cause of death and had been inflicted by a blunt instrument like a hammer or iron bar. Death would have been almost instantaneous.

At the coroner's inquest at Freshfield Road Police Station on the following day, everyone was surprised to note that George Perrin, who was due to give evidence, was absent from the court. The proceedings were adjourned but other witnesses were heard. PC James had found no sign of a weapon but did tell of having found bloodstains on the landing and stairs and finger marks on the walls. There had also been blood on the water tap in the kitchen and in the sink. An old sack cloth had apparently been used to wipe bloodstained hands.

On the afternoon of the adjourned inquest, a groom, Alfred Hards, of 34 High Street, was walking on the beach just east of the Paston Place concrete groyne. There he saw a man lying face-down on the beach, whom he recognised by his clothes as being Perrin. He did not disturb him, believing him to be asleep. When Perrin began to cough and groan, however, he ran over to him. Turning him on to his side, he saw blood on his hands and on the pebbles.

Hards ran off to find a policeman. They saw that Perrin had cut his throat, having clearly used a sixpenny pocket knife which was partly buried in the stones. It had been bought in St George's Road, Kemp Town, at about eleven that morning.

Summoned to the beach, the Chief Constable, Thomas Carter, found Perrin on his back, still alive. He said: 'Hullo, Perrin, what's the matter? What's the meaning of this?' Perrin replied: 'Do you know me, Mr Carter?' The officer could see from the severe gash on Perrin's throat that his windpipe must be nearly severed. Carter and the others fetched some boards out of a boat, improvised a stretcher, and carried the injured man to a cab which took him to the County Hospital nearby.

Carter sat by his bedside hoping to obtain a statement, but Perrin died only a few minutes after being put to bed.

At a coroner's court investigating this second death, the jury returned a verdict that the dead man had killed himself while of unsound mind. Subsequent inquiries revealed that Mrs Hall had been afraid of Perrin, who had been a more passionate and excitable man than people thought. At the resumed inquest into her death, the jury announced after about 15 minutes' deliberation that George Perrin had been guilty of murdering Mrs Hall.

No one, however, has ever been able to explain exactly why he should have killed his employer. He may have had a few small debts, but paying those off could hardly have been a motive. It was possible, but unlikely, that he was in love with her or jealous of her or he may have harboured some deeply-hidden grudge. We will never know.

PICKPOCKETING

In 1824, the presence of two organised gangs of pickpockets in Brighton was acknowledged. They were reported as being 'numerous, active and successful'.

On Saturday, 12 September 1885, 15-year-old Henry Smith appeared before the magistrates charged with stealing a purse and money from Sophia Simmons, of 5 Victoria Street, Brighton, at the railway station. He had been observed going up to her – and to two other ladies – in a suspicious manner and was seen to have a companion acting with him. On the alarm being raised, Smith was chased and subsequently identified by the station witness at the Town Hall where he was being held by the police. He was remanded until the following Monday.

Pickpocketing naturally flourished at crowded venues such as the RACECOURSE. Shirley Jameson, 54 (a man) got caught red-handed when attempting to pick the pocket of Thomas Hallett, a visitor from Tunbridge Wells, on the Race Hill on 27 June 1901. PC Charles Forward was on the racecourse in plain clothes with PC Sinden when he saw Jameson go and stand close to Hallett just as the horses were going round the course. As the horses got to where the victim was standing, Jameson placed his right hand in his waistcoat pocket. In answer to the charge at the police station, the culprit simply said: 'Ah, well!' The sum of 4s 2d was found on him but Hallett did not know if it had come out of his pocket. Jameson was sent to prison for a month with hard labour.

Two years later, Brighton's Chief Constable was congratulated by the magistrates for the fact that 'the races should have passed off with such an utter absence of crime that only one pickpocket was brought to justice'. They commented that this was 'an almost incredible state of affairs'.

PILLORY

JA Erredge, in his *History of Brighthelmston* (1862), refers to the stocks 'in Brighton's Market place and the parish pound at the back of the Old Church'.

John Fuller, a huckster, was very publicly reminded of his wrongdoing. He had induced an illiterate countryman to give him 40s change for a '2d' note and had actually got off with the money. When apprehended, a '5d' note was found on him. The week before being pilloried, he had obtained from another countryman, in return for a '2d' note, no less than 32s-worth of potatoes and apples, and 8s change.

He will always be associated with the *King and Queen* public house in Marlborough Place, for he was located there on 28 March 1811 prior to being pilloried at the bottom of North Street. Ahead of the event, the *Sussex Weekly Advertiser* announced that he would be parading 'on a *Wooden Horse* [. . .] for the space of one hour, with his head in *a peculiar situation*. This *Machine* is constructed so as to revolve, like the *Earth*, on its own *axis*, and therefore, the Spectators who are expected to be extremely numerous, will have an opportunity of witnessing his *Speed*'. Bishop adds that the pillory was fixed upon a platform about 10 or 12 feet from the ground.

A vast crowd assembled outside the inn to see him escorted to his place of 'exhibition'. The *Advertiser* reported that a little before noon, the offender, attended by the Keeper of the Lewes House of Correction, and Mr Eager, his assistant, made his appearance and mounted the platform. With his head and hands having been placed in the proper positions, he traversed round it for the mandatory hour. The novelty of the exhibition attracted an estimated 5,000-plus spectators, a good few of whom were 'apparently of rank and fashion'; most of the windows in the neighbourhood were used as vantage points. Every shop in the vicinity was closed.

No 'pelting' took place since there had been a public warning that it was illegal and would be punished with imprisonment. There was, of course, much excitement (Fuller became almost black in the face before his hour had expired) but no serious disturbance occurred, thanks to the judicious arrangements made by the Under-Sheriff, G Palmer, who was present with his officers, as were the High Constable of Brighton (Mr Hargreaves), the headboroughs, and others, not forgetting old 'Billy' Catlin, who administered Fuller's punishment. According to the report, there was a prevalence of:

> *order, regularity, and good humour; not the least harm, or even insult, was offered to the culprit, who would have done well had he felt half as much from his disgraceful situation as the spectators appeared to feel for the safety of his person.*

On being released, Fuller respectfully bowed to the populace and, after being refreshed, was taken back to Lewes to complete his term of imprisonment, which was understood to be ending by the following June. The multitude dispersed in orderly fashion, 'and thereby stamped credit on the town'.

PINK STRING AND SEALING WAX
Film, 1945

> *DAVID: Arsenic, digitalis, belladonna, strychnine; there's enough in that one to kill half Brighton.*
>
> *PEARL: Just imagine that.*

Synopsis
Pink String and Sealing Wax tells of a scheming and frustrated pub landlady (Googie Withers) who befriends an innocent chemist's assistant (a 22-year-old Gordon Jackson) in order to get hold of poison to do away with her brutal, alcoholic husband (Garry Marsh). Mervyn Johns plays the respected chemist and public analyst.

Details and comments

This Ealing production was based on a play by Roland Pertwee, the father of Jon ('Dr Who') Pertwee and directed by Robert Hamer. It was released almost simultaneously with *THE BRIGHTON STRANGLER.*

In Chibnall's view, the film explores the sexual tensions and repression of Victorian England: the God-fearing gentility of the respectable chemist's household in Regency Square contrasts sharply with the gin-fuelled permissiveness of the *Dolphin* pub. This use of the town's symbol links Brighton and crime, a link brought out by *Evening Standard* reviewer Patrick Kirwan in his piece entitled 'There's murder in the seaside air', in which he commented that the film did full justice both to the Brighton backgrounds and its tradition of fictional crime. Yet topographical inaccuracies abound – an anonymous *News Chronicle* critic felt that 'golden opportunities of projecting the adorable and unphotographed glories' of Brighton had been missed.

The film has been described as fascinating but uneven, with a hurried and unsatisfying denouement.

POLICE – see also CORRUPTION, FRAUD; LAWRENCE, JOHN; MARSHALL, JIM; MILITIA (clash with); TOWN HALL

Pre-Victorian development of the force

A committee was appointed in Brighton on 12 January 1807 to consider the measures necessary for the establishment of a police force and for the recovery of small debts. There was strong local feeling from the townspeople for a vigilant force, if the extract reproduced below from a letter sent on 18 April to the *Brighton Herald*'s editor is anything to go by:

> *When houses are said to be broken into and robbed three or four nights in one week and that too with impunity, what can the town in which such premises are situated, be considered in want of so much as a viligant police?*
>
> *When individuals are said to be nightly knocked down in the streets, and that too often during the hours of business, what can be more required by the industrious merchants and the prudent part of society than a vigilant police?*
>
> *When the evils to which a town may be subject are said to be daily growing and their consequences more menacing to the peaceable inhabitants, what do the interests of the peaceable inhabitants of such a town more require than a vigilant police?*

Five years later, eight night watchmen were appointed, supplemented by a further 16 (given the title 'Constable') in 1814. This force was stiffened by local residents and special constables. George Richardson became the Chief Constable of Brighton in 1816 and he was succeeded two years later by Richard Bodle.

The uniform comprised a top hat, black tail coat and white trousers and the officers carried a baton and a rattle. They were controlled by two superintendents based at the old Town Hall. For the next eight years, they had to call out the hours and the weather to inform the public. Then came the formation of a 'day and night' paid police force. Two head constables, James Feldwicke and Samuel Simes, took command at the Town Hall on alternate nights, overseeing the eight watchmen on duty in their individual district each night (during the day, the policing of the town was in the hands of beadles). The districts, or beats, were doubled following the appointment, by the Night Watch Committtee, of a further eight watchmen in 1823. Nine new watch boxes were made and the Night Constable was provided with a staff.

Among the resolutions passed by the Committee was one whereby the reward of one guinea was given to watchmen on the conviction of any robbers they had apprehended, and another requiring that all vagrants be brought before the magistrates.

Henry Solomon, the first Chief Constable of Brighton.
Author's collection

The new police force and its development

In 1829, Sir Robert Peel's Metropolitan Police was set up and Brighton's new force, consisting of 25 Watchmen under the direction of a Mr Pilbeam, followed on 3 March the following year. The post of Chief Officer (or Chief Constable) soon fell to Henry Solomon (see LAWRENCE), who had held a number of offices in the town before joining the force in 1832. By May 1838, his force comprised two Superintendents, one Night Constable, three Inspectors and 24 Watchmen. There were three Divisions, made up of one Inspector and eight men, and the town was divided into 16 beats for night duty and six beats for day duty. For protection, the men were provided with a baton, and when on night duty, with a rattle.

In 1855, the uniform was changed from dress coats to frock coats and eleven years later, the Corporation decided to supply the police with helmets instead of hats. A police surgeon was appointed and, on a detective officer being provided with a suit of plain clothes, the CID came into being.

In February 1860, one of the 'old school', James Thoburn, who had been in the service for some 36 years, died aged 82. He had joined as one of the old Brighton watchmen, subsequently being made parish beadle. A subscription started by the Mayor for his impecunious widow met with liberal support.

The town continued to expand and by 1871, with a population of over 92,000, the force had a strength of 108 men. Preston was incorporated with Brighton in 1873, adding further to the population. In 1881, the post of Chief Constable was filled by Superintendent James Terry, who had joined the Brighton force on 4 October 1843 and had thus served for most of the time the force had been in existence. On his retirement, he had served in the force for over fifty years.

At the end of the century, the Town Hall was enlarged and remodelled and the basement converted into the central police station and offices which were occupied for much of the twentieth century. *Kelly's Directory of Sussex* for 1899 informs us that the police force of Brighton and Hove included a chief constable, three superintendents, a fire superintendent, one clerk, a superintendent of hackney carriages, a detective inspector, with four detective officers, four divisional inspectors, twelve sergeants and 148 constables.

Five additional police stations had been opened over the years at Freshfield Road (opened in 1885 to replace disused premises at the top of Grafton Street), Preston Circus, Preston Village, Westhill Road and The Level, but the latter two would close in 1919 and the others later in the century. All the emergency services were the responsibility of the police; fire-fighting equipment was kept at the police stations and a proportion of the force was trained and employed as firemen.

Into the twentieth century

By 1901, a population of over 123,000 was served by a force of 150 men. This was divided into territorial divisions operating from the six police stations – which by 1912 had each been provided with a pedal cycle. At this period a fire engine and motor ambulance were acquired. A different sort of ambulance was a hand-barrow, and later a stretcher on wheels, on which a drunken or violent prisoner was trundled through the streets to the station. PC William Scales (see page 165) recalled the stretcher attached to Freshfield Road Police Station being used for 'bad ladies who got drunk'.

During the First World War, 101 members of the force joined up; 11 were killed or died through injuries received in action. This period saw the first policewomen appointed due to the force being below strength.

Between two wars

Growing discontent over pay and conditions of service culminated elsewhere in the police strikes of 1918 and 1919. Following the report in 1919 of the Desborough Committee, the Police Act of that year introduced standard rates of pay and conditions of service, with a common code of discipline for all forces.

By 1920, the 200-strong force was based at the Town Hall, Preston Circus and Freshfield Road. It became increasingly involved in traffic control and eleven roads previously used as trading grounds were placed out of bounds to costermongers and hawkers.

By 1922 the Fire Brigade had ceased to be a police responsibility and had become a separate entity with its own personnel and accommodation. Mr Griffin informed the Watch Committee in that year that he had provided himself with a motor car 'the better to supervise the police on duty'. The year 1926 brought the General Strike and, locally, 'The Battle of Lewes Road' (see UNREST, CIVIL).

In 1928 the police telephone box system of beat working was introduced and proved an immediate success. Beat constables booked on and off duty at their beat boxes, so there was therefore no longer a need for police stations to be located at strategic points in the town. The force thus reverted to the original station at the Town Hall, although rooms were retained at Preston Circus for training and recreational purposes until 1937, when they were closed due to the building of the new fire station.

When the town boundaries were extended to take in a number of suburbs in 1928, the need for increased mobility was met by the introduction of motor vehicles for general police use. In January 1931 three motor cycles were purchased.

With crime on the increase, a fingerprint bureau was established in that year as part of the expansion of the CID. By 1934 the Department had increased to one Inspector, four Sergeants and 12 Constables, and that year saw the provision of the first car for their exclusive use.

On 14 September 1933, following experiments over a lengthy period, a wireless transmitter was set up on the top of the Town Hall and 30 wireless receivers were issued to patrols. Brighton was the first police force in the world to use wireless in this way and it greatly increased efficiency.

The year 1938 marked the centenary of the force as established under Solomon and this was celebrated by a ceremonial parade and a celebration dinner.

The Second World War

When war broke out in 1939, 17 reservists in the force were re-called to the colours and an additional wartime strength of 44 First Police Reserves (retired policemen) and 130 War Reserves was approved by the Home Office. The basement of a new police building in Market Street had been completed just before the outbreak of war, and the basement rooms were converted into a 'Battle Headquarters' for the force.

Many officers joined up and served in all three services in all parts of the world (by 1943, 61 of the force were on active service). The Special Constabulary again helped to plug the gap at home – no fewer than 248 of them were regularly employed in 1942. Three of Brighton's policemen were killed by enemy action during the war.

The postwar period

In 1946, the '999' emergency service was set up in the town and an information room to receive these calls was established at the Town Hall, with wireless equipment capable of one-way speech to wireless-equipped cars.

On 1 October 1948 the emergency ambulance service ceased to be a police responsibility and the police ambulances were handed over to the Borough ambulance service.

The old training school at Wellington Road was converted into a police station in 1949 and the force was divided into two Divisions, with headquarters and 'A' Division being based at the Town Hall and 'B' Division at Wellington Road (to where the traffic offices, information room, criminal records office and the social club were also moved from the Town Hall). At this period, two-way wireless was introduced in police vehicles, enabling officers in the cars to transmit information back to the information room.

The 1950s – Progress and crisis

On 15 February 1951, a 'Beat the Burglar' exhibition, the first of a number of a similar kind, was opened at the Corn Exchange and attended by no fewer than 18,000 people in nine days.

In 1958, police dogs – initially two alsatians – were added to the force's resources. Working hours were reduced to an 88-hour fortnight. By the following year, the force totalled 277 men and six women and the fleet of vehicles numbered 20, including five motor cycles.

On 1 July 1956, CFW Ridge took over as Chief Constable but the following year a cloud hung over the force as he and two Brighton CID members were arrested on conspiracy charges (see POLICE – CORRUPTION). Ridge left the force.

The sub-divisional station opened at Rottingdean in 1959 has long been closed at the time of writing.

The 1960s – A pivotal decade

Early in the decade, approval was obtained for the long-awaited new headquarters for the force. WT Cavey was the thirteenth – and was to be the last – Chief Constable of the Brighton force. In 1964, a regional crime squad was based at Brighton.

The new headquarters, with every conceivable facility, were completed in 1965 and opened on 27 September by the Home Secretary, the Right Honourable Sir Frank Soskice, QC, MP. The following year, the Sussex Fingerprint Bureau was established there and personal radios were (again) obtained and issued to all patrolling officers. Facilities were provided, too, for the Special Constabulary.

The last year of the Brighton police as a separate entity was 1967, following the Home Secretary's announcement in 1966 of the Government's plans for the amalgamation of police forces. The new force established by the scheme was known as the Sussex Constabulary and combined the police areas consisting of the counties of East Sussex and West Sussex and the county boroughs of Brighton, Eastbourne and Hastings. The first Chief Constable of the combined force was TC Williams and the force headquarters were the former HQ of the East Sussex Constabulary at Lewes. The new combined police authority was to be known as the Sussex Police Authority.

Brighton County Borough Police therefore ceased to exist as from 1 January 1968. By then its strength was 424, with a CID complement of 47. The enhanced facilities and accommodation were timely, for in the previous decade the number of crimes had risen

Brighton Police Station, John Street, is adjacent to the court complex, here shown under construction.
Chris Horlock collection

from 1,924 to 5,242, while the number of persons prosecuted for indictable offences had increased from 698 to 1,518 and for non-indictable offences from 3,709 to 14,141.

In 1974 the Sussex Constabulary was renamed Sussex Police.

On 4 May 2005, Brighton's Police Museum was opened in the Town Hall and has since attracted large numbers of visitors.

The Brighton police force and the town's population, 1841–1967

	Strength of force	Population
1841	31	46,661
1851	61	65,569
1861	81	77,693
1871	108	92,471
1881	130	107,546
1891	140	115,873
1901	150	123,478
1911	156	131,237
1921	200	142,430
1931	216	147,427
1941	228	151,500
1951	256	156,440
1961	327	162,650
1967	424	169,000

(From Gerald, W Baines, *History of the Brighton Police, 1838–1967*, c.1967)

POLICE – CORRUPTION

Brighton has the finest police force money can buy! (popular quip)

This case, which opened at the Old Bailey on 3 February 1958, was described by its judge, Mr Justice Donovan, as 'one of the most serious tried in this or any other criminal court for a long time'.

The five accused included three Brighton police officers – one of them the Chief Constable himself – arraigned there after months of meticulous investigation by their Scotland Yard colleagues. They were accused of lining their own pockets through favours to crooks, or promises to 'help' lawbreakers. The officers were Charles Feild Williams Ridge, 58, Chief Constable; Detective-Inspector John Richard Hammersley, 40, second-in-command Criminal Investigation Department; and Detective-Sergeant Trevor Ernest Heath, 36, plus the civilians Anthony John Lyons, 59, licensee, of Marine Gate, Brighton; and Samuel Bellson, 42, bookmaker, of The Drive, Hove.

Each of the policemen pleaded Not Guilty to the charge that between 1 January 1949 and 18 October 1957 they conspired together, and with other persons unknown, to obstruct the course of public justice in that they acted contrary to their public duty as police officers in relation to the administration of the law.

The prosecution case was based to a great extent on evidence from persons who, at one time or another, had flouted the law and paid the penalty. One was a 41-year-old wholesale fish merchant who claimed that Det Insp Hammersley and Det Sgt Heath had asked him for £250 to drop a charge against him of receiving stolen property. It was claimed that Bellson, the bookmaker, and Lyons, the licensee, had acted as go-betweens in the collection of 'fees' for the police.

The Crown produced its star witness on the third day. He was Alan Roy Bennett, a 40-year-old company director who had started the whole case off by going to Scotland Yard with information that prompted a small team of investigators, led by Detective-Superintendent Ian Forbes-Leith, to probe into the state of affairs in the Brighton police force. Bennett had once accepted police demands for bribes but had begun feeling uncomfortable about the whole situation. Nine months previously he had changed his name by deed poll from Brown (although he had had a host of aliases) and until 1949 he had been in quite a lot of criminal trouble, serving 10 terms of imprisonment for offences including housebreaking. Soon after his last release from prison he went to Brighton as a chef, opening a club in Brighton in 1954 he had called the *Astor*, better known, on account of the violent scenes enacted there, as the 'Bucket of Blood'. Yet the premises had never attracted adverse police attention – and this was the whole basis of the Crown's case.

58-year-old Charles Ridge was found Not Guilty but soon stepped down from the post of Chief Constable. Popperfoto

153

Lyons, said Bennett, had introduced Ridge to him at the *Astor* and from that day he had paid Ridge a 'retainer' of £20 a week. The money was at first personally collected by Ridge, and then by Sergeant Heath who also occasionally received a £5 'present' from Bennett. In return for the payments, Bennett was allowed to keep the club open without interference until any hour he chose. 'I had the freedom of the city,' he said.

Asked where he got all his money from, Bennett's answer was to produce £500 in notes from his back trouser pocket. Under cross-examination, he startled the court by loudly declaring: 'It was known that the Brighton police had been crooked all their lives!' He had been told that by many people. He did, however, modify his assertion to 'some of them, not all'. He also told how he had bought neckties for Sergeant Heath in the fashionable Burlington Arcade, off London's Piccadilly, and given him cast-off clothing. Far from being unwelcome in Brighton, he was welcomed with open arms by the police ('I was providing them with money'). He did what he wanted. This included house-breaking and cracking open the safe at Woolworth's – at Heath's suggestion.

Bennett's Norwegian-born wife confirmed there was an arrangement about the club between her husband and Ridge, but she was unhappy about it and told him not to give any money to policemen. Ridge, she testified, came to collect money which she saw her husband give him in a newspaper. It was in £5 notes. Later, Sgt Heath was the collector; if her husband was absent the notes were left in an envelope on a shelf below the bar. She even gave money to him herself on several occasions and thought other people did too. When uncorrupt officers were planning to raid the club, the owners were warned by Heath not to open that night.

In the trial's second week a Mrs Alice Brabiner appeared in court saying she had been involved in an illegal abortion and that Sergeant Heath had taken a total of £68 from her to 'do what he could to help me'. The last 'instalment' of £25 was paid to him on the day her trial for the illegal operation opened.

Ernest Waite, a Brighton greengrocer, who admitted dealing in stolen property, claimed he had a 'gentleman's agreement' with Inspector Hammersley whereby Waite would not receive goods in Brighton, 'but I was given a sort of freedom of the town with regards to things outside Brighton. If any goods came to the town and I was suspect, Hammersley would give me the tip-off to get rid of them.' As a result Mr Waite's 'business' flourished, and Hammersley benefited to the tune of £200 for his 'help', quite apart from regular supplies of produce from Waite's shop. The procedure there, Waite explained, was that Hammersley would 'pay' for the produce with a £1 note and be given several pounds in 'change'.

Numerous witnesses, most with convictions to their names, told how the police had made their lives bearable by 'a consideration'. The officers then appeared in court.

Sergeant Heath had joined the CID in February 1948 and had first teamed up with Hammersley in CID work the following August. He had made more arrests in 1955 than any other detective constable on the Brighton force, and had received 11 commendations. He completely denied all the charges. Inspector Hammersley, who had joined Brighton police in 1937, was also able to boast of a good past record and denied involvement in any 'disgraceful crime'. Finally, Chief Constable Charles Ridge declared that he himself had always been careful of the honour of the force and warned young officers of the perils of accepting bribes. He even produced charts and graphs to show just how well the war against crime had gone in Brighton since he took command.

On 27 February, more than three weeks after the trial had started, Hammersley, Heath and Bellson were found guilty. Bellson was sentenced to three years' imprisonment and

They may look unconcerned, but Hammersley and Heath seriously tarnished their previous good records – and the name of Brighton police. Sport and General Press Agency Ltd

the officers to five. Had Ridge given them the professional and moral leadership they had been entitled to expect, their sentence, declared the judge, would have been harsher.

Lyons and Ridge were found not guilty.

PRENDERGAST, BEATRICE (victim)

Beatrice Prendergast, 56, who had lodged in Cavendish Street (described in *The Times* as a 'slum area') for two years, was found in the early hours of 8 June 1930 stabbed to death in a little side-street a few yards from St James's Street. She had sustained three wounds in the left breast, two of which led directly to the heart and the third, which broke a rib, to the left lung. The attack was thought to have been made just before midnight. A man in an adjoining garden had heard a woman scream three times but took no notice. The body was found at about 12.30 am by a Mr John W Nye, a stock-jobber's clerk of St James's Street Mews, when the headlights of his car shone on the woman, who was lying face down on the ground. Thinking she was drunk, he fetched a policemen and then they both discovered she was dead. One hand was clasping a handbag and as her body was being lifted, five shillings fell from her right hand. Her hat was about five yards away.

The inquest on the victim (who, it was learned, was well-educated but seldom spoke about herself and had few friends), was opened then adjourned until 4 July to allow further enquiries to be made about her. Dr HJ Pulling, the police surgeon, had been called to the scene of the crime at about 1 am on Whit Sunday the 8th and found the woman lying against the right-hand wall about 40 yards from the street. The jury's verdict was that she had been murdered by a person or persons unknown. A police search for a tall Irishman who Prendergast was known to have been with on that fateful Saturday night was unsuccessful.

On 24 August the previous year, there had been an attempt to murder one Alice O'Grady. She had been stabbed twice in the back in Cannon Lane, Brighton. It was natural to believe the two cases were linked. Charles Gasson, a married 46-year-old carpenter from Haywards Heath, was arrested on suspicion of attempting to murder O'Grady. When confronted by Det Sgt Wells in Haywards Heath, Gasson said: 'I know what you are after, it's that Brighton affair but I know nothing of the murder.' He consistently pleaded Not Guilty, and judgment to that effect was pronounced at Lewes Assizes on 7 July 1930. The only mention of Prendergast during the trial, however, was when Wells testified that Gasson had denied knowing her. He had likewise denied knowing O'Grady, although he had been for a walk on the night in question with one May Murray, in whose company O'Grady had been (confusingly, a *Times* report prior to the Assizes stated O'Grady's companion had been Beatrice Prendergast).

PRICE, RICHARD and SUMNER, RICHARD

Police and prison officers jumped into the dock at Lewes Crown Court to separate Richard Lyn Price, 25, and Richard Sumner, 35, after a jury found them guilty on 5 April 2002 of killing a 63-year-old hotel worker. They had kicked and stamped William John Carmichael (known as 'Billy') to death after a row, put him to bed and left him to die in his blood-splattered flat. Both denied murder. They were alcoholics who mixed with drinkers in Brighton and had befriended the victim. The body of the 64-year-old Irishman was discovered in his top floor flat in Lower Rock Gardens, Kemp Town, on 14 November 2000. His fully-clothed body was discovered slumped on his bloodstained bed when entry was forced into his flat after he had gone missing.

Carmichael, who was gay, was well known in Brighton where he had lived for about 20 years. He had connections with the theatre world and artists and much of his own artwork was in his flat. He was a very mild and sociable individual who would sometimes invite people back to his flat. The ex-waiter had formerly run a bar in Ireland but had left in the 1970s and spent some time in London before moving to Brighton.

PRISONS/IMPRISONMENT – *Horsham and Lewes*

The Sussex County Gaol was established at **Horsham** as early as the time of Henry VIII, and was in continuous use until 1845. For three centuries, therefore, all those crimes and misdemeanours dealt with at the Sussex Assizes, from Hastings in the east to Chichester

Horsham Gaol. Sussex County Magazine

in the west, and from Brighton in between, were focused at Horsham. There was scarcely a parish that did not contribute an inmate, be it a man, woman or child.

The prison wound down during the last decade of its existence and lay nine-tenths empty, almost derelict. Following demolition, it was invaded on its western side by the new railway line from Horsham to Portsmouth, and today hundreds of trains cross and re-cross the very spot of the 'Horsham drop'. The remainder of the land stood as waste ground for 30 years before being developed.

Lewes Prison was built in 1853, when the House of Correction put up 60 years earlier was sold to the Admiralty and became the Naval Prison.

On 11 August 1914, the hanging of PERCY CLIFFORD was the tenth and last to take place at the Gaol.

The establishment houses trial/remand and sentenced adults and also a small number of Young Offenders committed from local courts in the East and West Sussex area. In the early 1970s, it became a training prison (with one wing devoted to 'lifers'), whilst retaining its remand function for the Sussex courts. This function continued until 1990 when the prison once more became a 'local' establishment, housing mainly short-term prisoners and remands.

The prison's population as at 30 June 2000 was 455 (but was reported in June 2006 to be 533 – 75 more than the 458 it was meant to hold).

In recent years, the prison has acquired a poor reputation on account of over-crowding and the number of suicides. But things are improving. An insight into life within it and the efforts made to better conditions all round has been provided in a number of interesting features in the local press (e.g. *The Jail where life begins*, in *The Argus* of 28–29 January 2006, and *Life is not easy inside – but some prisoners find a way*, in the *Sussex Express* of 3 February 2006).

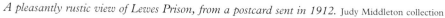

A pleasantly rustic view of Lewes Prison, from a postcard sent in 1912. Judy Middleton collection

PROSTITUTION

Prostitution was, and is, not itself illegal. In the past, poverty would have obliged many a young girl to sell her body. The age of consent was low – 12 until 1875, although over ensuing decades various Acts would raise it to 13, then to 14 and 16. Incredibly, there was opposition to the moves on the grounds that the children should be allowed to choose how to make their money.

Prostitution became, in the eyes of the law, a health issue as much as anything else. Laws such as the notorious Contagious Diseases Acts of 1864, 1866, 1869 were introduced in order to protect members of the home forces from sexually transmitted diseases. In their final form, they provided that where a woman was believed to be acting as a 'common prostitute' (a term not defined in the Act) within 10 miles of one of 18 specified naval and garrison towns, she could be reported to a magistrate and be obliged to attend for inspection at hospitals created for the purpose. If found to be diseased, she could be detained for up to nine months for treatment; refusal to attend could be met with forcible examination (labelled 'instrumental rape' by opponents of the Acts) or by imprisonment. The Acts were repealed in 1886, following a campaign led by Josephine Butler.

Later legislative milestones include the 1959 Street Offences Act, based on the Wolfenden Report. The Act dealt with the entire problem of prostitution and other forms of sexual conduct between consenting adults. It forbade open solicitation by prostitutes but permitted prostitutes to ply their trade in their own homes. For those wishing to give up prostitution, the teaching of commercial or technical skills at rehabilitation centres was provided for. The Act also removed voluntary sexual acts between adults from the category of a punishable crime.

More recent legislation governing prostitution in England and Wales comprises the 1964 Licensing Act, the 1985 Sexual Offences Act, the 2001 Criminal Justice and Police Act and the 2003 Sexual Offences Act.

Pre-Victorian Brighton whores and brothel-keeping

In October 1796, the local *Gazette* revealed, that 'The Cyprian [prostitute] corps stationed in this town is now estimated to amount to over 300, exclusive of those at Brighton Camp' and remarked that the fact that those 'good-natured but unfortunate creatures could be supported by the wages of prostitution cast a melancholy reflection on the increasing depravity of the age'.

Kezian Furner found herself before the bench in 1810 (twice), 1811, 1812 and 1813 for vagrancy and stealing and finally received a 4-month sentence for prostitution. Another unfortunate, Maria Bishop, was committed for two months on a similar single charge of prostitution in 1812, while Charlotte Brown was committed for only 14 days.

In 1823 a shoemaker named Jonus Tettersell was given a 12-month custodial sentence by magistrate Sir David Scott for keeping a brothel. Scott said: 'it offended his morals'. For a similar offence five years later, Mary Altenacher (alias Burchall) was given only six months for her 'lucre and gain'. In 1831, also at the Quarter Sessions, a man applied for a £10 reward for informing the police that Altenacher was running a brothel, saying 'he had only just realised he could claim a reward'. The magistrates responded that they 'wanted time to consider it'.

Mercer refers to a sample of cases heard at the Brighton Quarter Sessions covering the years 1820 to 1839, in which four men and eight women were variously charged for keeping bawdy houses over that period.

The 1850s

To help fallen women, Reverend George Wagner founded St Mary's Home for Female Penitents in Queen Square in 1855. Women and girls were often sent there by the police, by doctors and from the hospitals, and by the Wagners and their clergy, who carried out mission work amongst the poor and degraded occupants of the mean streets in the vicinity of their churches. George Wagner himself was claimed to have persuaded five women to give up keeping brothels and to turn to a better way of life. The Home was originally established in two small houses capable of receiving twelve penitents and eventually came to consist, in addition to the 'home for fallen women', of a lying-in hospital, housing about 40 occupants, plus a Nursery for Orphan Children, an Industrial School for training young girls for domestic service, an Infirmary for aged and disabled women and a Dispensary for the poor of the district (see also CONSTANCE KENT).

Musgrave quotes the Judicial Statistics for 1859 recording 325 prostitutes in Brighton. This figure excluded the large annual influx of their sisters from London. There were, it was reported, 'good grounds for believing that double that number would be nearer the truth'. Twenty-five of them were under 16. The number of public brothels was stated to be 97, although these were far from being the only places where prostitution was carried on. At night the scenes on the beach in front of the King's Road, on The Level and 'opposite the Theatre Royal' were said to beggar all description.

The New Road area, 1860

The 'Graduate' (see DRINK/DRINKING – Beer Shops) wrote in his rather unusual guide book:

> There is the Theatre [Royal] in the New Road, conducted as theatres usually are, and attended with all those evils which experience has proved to be incidental to amusements of this kind. Close by there is a gin-palace with the usual appendages of plate-glass and flaring gas-lights, where prostitutes resort, in order to ply their sinful calling when the Theatre dismisses. The colonnade, after 1 o'clock, presents a very animated appearance, being then

The Colonnades, extending along both North Street (left) and New Road (right) were the notorious haunt of prostitutes. Chris Horlock collection

used principally as a promenade by the 'women of the town', who are either there for the purpose of entrapping the unwary or of keeping some previous appointment. The women for the most part observe the outward rules of propriety, although, on some occasions, we have witnessed scenes of drunken lewdness.

Church Street, Edward Street and environs

The lowest prostitutes infested the neighbourhood of Church Street and Edward Street. In one of the lanes leading from the former there was, Musgrave recorded, 'a whole block of houses, too notorious to be required to be named, entirely garrisoned by females of the most depraved and abandoned class'. Many of them lived under appallingly servile and wretched conditions of servitude and were not even allowed by their exploiters to possess their own clothing.

In connection with a case against a woman brothel-keeper named Read, which is quoted by Wojtczak (undated but stated to be from the 1860s), a revealing insight into prostitution in the Edward Street area of Brighton was provided:

Several of the streets leading from Edward-street towards the Downs are crowded with brothels, where scenes of the greatest depravity are enacted, and it is deplorable to observe the number of girls, mere children, from 12 to 18 years of age, who are nurtured in these hot beds of vice and immorality, and who infest our streets in the evening to the great annoyance of the respectable portion of the community.

Read herself kept a notorious brothel at 46 Edward Street and was charged with being drunk and disorderly and creating a great disturbance at about two o'clock in the morning, to the great annoyance of the neighbourhood. PC Knight's endeavours to quieten her were unavailing and she was taken into custody.

There had evidently been several complaints against this woman and it was felt the parish officers and High Constable should take up the matter. A document signed by the owners and occupiers of several houses in the vicinity complaining of the repeated annoyances they had had to endure during the two months of Read's occupation of the property (including the house being the resort of 'improper characters' and the drunken conduct of Read herself) had been handed to the High Constable. The magistrates ordered the prisoner to enter into her own recognizance of £30 (a large sum in those days), to find sureties in a like amount for her appearance at the Sessions and to answer any indictment that might be preferred against her.

Another brothel-keeper, Hannah Fry, a 55-year-old widow, had to enter into recognizances of £50 with two sureties of £25 each, to be of good behaviour for 12 months.

It was not always native Englishwomen who appeared before Brighton's magistrates under prostitution-related offences. A Frenchwoman, Emily Chapardarze, served 10 days with hard labour in 1865 for 'importuning and annoying gentlemen' in North Street.

Streetwalkers often fought amongst themselves. Wojtczak records that many cases of violence between streetwalkers were brought before the town's magistrates. Elizabeth Turner, quaintly styled a 'nymph of the pavé' in the press report, was fined 5s plus costs for blacking the eye of 'a fair sister of iniquity'.

How girls fall

Writing in 1870, one William Acton saw poverty as the root of prostitution:

. . . many women stray from the paths of virtue and ultimately swell the ranks of prostitution through being by their position peculiarly exposed to temptation. The women to whom this remark applies are chiefly actresses, milliners, shop girls, domestic servants and women

employed in factories or working in agricultural gangs. Of these many, no doubt, fall through vanity and idleness, love of dress, love of excitement, love of drink, but by far the larger proportion are driven to evil courses by cruel, biting poverty.
(*Prostitution, considered in its Moral, Social and Sanitary Aspects*)

A brothel boss run to ground, 2001
Wealthy Stephen O'Callaghan, 47, of Maresfield Road, Brighton, was jailed for 20 months on 15 June 2001 for raking in thousands of pounds from Brighton brothels. He employed a string of call girls at back-to-back properties in Waterloo Street and Lower Market Street and boasted they could earn up to £1,500 a week. His lucrative business of charging customers between £30 and £45 and offering a 'full unhurried personal service' ended when an attractive undercover police officer infiltrated his activities and gathered vital evidence against him. She got a job as a receptionist at one of his two massage parlours which were a front for prostitution in the houses and watched as O'Callaghan answered the phones and gave details of the girls available to punters. She would then take the money from the girls, fill in a ledger, ensure clients did not run over the allotted time and cash up at the end of the shift. O'Callaghan even tried to persuade her to become a working girl herself, claiming she could earn £500–£1,500 per week.

His girlfriend of 12 years, Deborah Hughes, 42, had been responsible for banking the girls' takings and helped to move money out of the country to avoid it being confiscated. He would give her bundles of cash in exchange for blank cheques which he would cash in Spain. She used the proceeds from *Top to Toe* and *Angels Delight* to renovate his Spanish villa on the Costa Blanca. A police raid on Hughes' address revealed a bag of 588 condoms, Spanish bank details and, hidden in her bread bin, a list of girls. Hughes was given a nine-month sentence suspended for two years.

O'Callaghan, who drove a Rolls Royce, admitted living off immoral earnings between 1997 and 1999 and was convicted by a jury of removing the proceeds from the country, which he denied. He had received a police caution in 1995 and from that point on knew it was a criminal offence. Judge Charles Kemp said: '. . . you played a risky game for high stakes and you lost.'

Sergeant Richard Siggs, in charge of the crackdown, said the 20 or so brothels in the city were not causing problems but it was the CARDING that was upsetting people.

An unhappy juxtaposition
A sex service establishment called 'Dimensions' in Elm Grove, Brighton, which has been operating on the site since 1981, was the focus in March 2006 of an item in *The Argus* highlighting its undesirable position opposite Elm Grove Primary School, attended by 431 pupils aged 5 to 11. The police have not received any complaints but the newspaper found at least eight women working on the premises. The law allows prostitutes working alone in flats to offer sex but any premises with more than one sex worker is illegal and can be shut down by police.

Working girls today
Government plans to change the law to allow two prostitutes and a receptionist to work together in brothels, on the basis that working in groups would be safer for women, are still in their early stages.

The Brighton Oasis project is a service for women substance misusers and their children which also provides a specialist service for women sex workers.

PUBLIC HOUSES – see INNS AND PUBLIC HOUSES

Q

QUADROPHENIA
Film, 1979 – see also MODS AND ROCKERS

Synopsis
The year is 1964 and battles between the rival Mods and Rockers are at their height. The clash is seen through the eyes of Jimmy Cooper (Phil Daniels), a smouldering youngster with a hatred of authority and conformity and a passion for rhythm and blues music. When the rival factions both arrive in Brighton on holiday, a riot breaks out. Jimmy is arrested, held and tried with a large group which includes the Mods' idolised leader, Ace (Sting in his acting debut). When Jimmy returns to London, his parents kick him out, his scooter is smashed in an accident and he loses his job – and also the girlfriend with whom he shared moments of passion in an alley off Brighton's East Street. Drawn back to Brighton as the only place with any meaning in his life, he discovers Ace is working as a bootlicking bellboy at the *Grand Hotel*. Enraged, his disillusion with life now complete, Jimmy steals his fallen idol's scooter and rides to the clifftops at Beachy Head. At the last second he jumps off, and the scooter crashes onto the rocks below.

Details and comments
A number of reviews refer to Franc Roddam's directing debut capturing the 'amphetamine-fuelled narcissism' of 1960s' youth culture perfectly. The film's raw energy makes up for the frankly hideous idea of adapting The Who's rock album to screen, yet Roddam keeps a firm hand on the riotous proceedings. There are good individual performances, too, with Daniels in particular excelling as a youth chasing dreams whose world collapses around him platform by platform.

On the Brighton road. A gang of Rockers taunt a lone Mod in the film. Chris Horlock collection

What is to some an underrated classic has to others become something of a cult. *Halliwell's Guide*, however, assigned the film no merit at all, its verdict being that 'what passed for a successful musical at the end of the Seventies is typified by this violent, screaming and wholly unattractive amalgam of noise, violence, sex and profanity'. Yet in 2004, the magazine *Total Film* named *Quadrophenia* as the 35th greatest British film of all time.

R

RACECOURSE/RACES – see also GAMBLING, MILITIA, PICKPOCKETING, WELSHING

History
The first Brighton Races were organised on 26–27 July 1783. In the following year, when the Prince of Wales visited the second meeting, the venue became very fashionable. Three years later, the first stand was erected by subscription. Although it burnt down in 1803, it was replaced the same year. In 1822, the area known as the Race Ground was granted to the town. Unsavoury elements visited the races in greater numbers in the 1840s after the opening of the rail link with London. By 1898, the whole course and ground were in the hands of Brighton Corporation.

Crime and gambling
Although the popular perception is that racecourses were a hotbed of petty crime, they could also be associated with more serious offences, for in 1831 the mother of JOHN HOLLOWAY was convinced that the body of a girl which had been found when Celia Holloway went missing was that of a woman who had disappeared after going to the races.

On 17 July 1835, the following letter from 'F.C.S.', Regency Square, Brighton, was sent to the editor of the *Brighton Guardian*:

> *Sir – Have the goodness to spare the space for a few lines, to call the attention of your Brighton Magistracy to the peremptory necessity of suppressing* all *gambling, both refined*

The Racecourse and Stand, 1790. The first ever meeting was held seven years earlier. The stand burned down in 1803. Author's collection

and vulgar, at the ensuing [upcoming] *Brighton races. As by far the best means of preventing crime, let them remove temptation, and let the Police have the most positive instructions to order away all gaming booths and tables of every sort of description;* [I am] ... *most anxious thus publicly to implore the Brighton Magistrates to interfere in time, to save the young, the thoughtless, and the ignorant from the inevitable consequences of gambling; or, failing to do their duty, let the* onus *of the sin and the suffering rest on their own heads!*

Of course, the plea went unheeded.

The racecourse was described by the *Brighton Herald* in 1836 as a 'magnet of attraction for a host of swindlers and other blacklegs who prey upon the incautious and inexperienced'. Following several cases before the local magistrates, the headboroughs were reminded that unless they cooperated with the High Constable to keep order, they were liable to prosecution themselves. Not long afterwards, a man died in a prize fight near the course. Although the High Constable had known the fight was going to be held, he had been unable to intervene, since the location lay just outside the boundary of the area he policed. Quite apart from that, his men would have been well outnumbered by a crowd which wanted blood.

William Tayler was a Brighton footman who had the unusual distinction of keeping a diary for the year 1837. On 10 August, the town was full and he spent the very hot afternoon at the races, where he noted that 'There were whores and rogues in abundance and gambleing tables plenty and everything elce that is jeneraly at races.'

The tables he was referring to were no doubt used for thimblerig, a swindling sleight-of-hand game in which the victim guesses which of three thimble-shaped cups a pea is

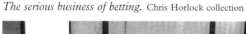

The serious business of betting. Chris Horlock collection

under – see MILITIA/Confrontations with the Police (in 1828, one Michael Rose had been charged with decoying the unwary into a game of thimblerig).

In the summer months, criminals had a well-established pattern of following fairs and races around. Railways facilitated travel to specific locations further afield, such as Goodwood and Lewes, where rich pickings were to be had during the Sussex Fortnight, which had been established by the 1860s. Favourite targets of the pickpockets were wallets, watches on chains and tiepins, when the victim's attention was distracted by a race (see PICKPOCKETING) or a disturbance created by accomplices. Local crooks often avoided Brighton races during the Fortnight as they would be recognised there by the local police. Instead they 'worked' in the town and environs.

Passing counterfeit notes and coins was an activity for which the Racecourse was a favourable location. As bookmakers increased in number during the nineteenth century, so did the practice of WELSHING.

Bookmaker protection

In *Mad Frank's Diary*, Frankie Fraser, the notorious henchman for the Krays and, formerly, for South London's Richardson gang, remembers there were 'a great number of bookies' pitches' at Brighton, where the East End Jewish gangster Jack Spot 'used to try to organise who stood where and who paid what. Just like the Sabinis did twenty and thirty years earlier.' He adds that there were 'some good fights at Brighton'.

Fraser worked as a bucket boy for the Sabinis. They:

ran the bookmakers on the courses in the south of England. If the bookmaker wanted a pitch he had to pay the Sabinis. They sold him the tissues on which he put up the names of the runners, they sold him the chalk to write the odds, and they had little bucket boys who brought a sponge round to wipe off the odds.

Darby Sabini and his five elder brothers were the core of a gang which dominated racecourses in the south of England. London-based, they had additional business interests in slot machines and Soho clubs. At Brighton races, the Sabinis could expect to make as much as £4–5,000. But gang warfare led to the demise of the Italian mob.

Police Constable 8137, William David Scales, was a member of Brighton Borough Police from 1913 to 1938. He recalled, in a video made by Sussex Police's TV Unit to mark his 90th birthday, the happenings up at the Race Hill on race days:

In three days in August, crowds came from all over the country. There was lots of trouble with the 'Birmingham Boys' and the 'razor slashers'. They used to demand money from the different bookmakers up on the hill and if they didn't pay, they paid at night... They used to go down to Sherry's and all these different places where the racing fraternity used to meet and slashed them with razors – not only in Brighton but in other places too. We used to have a lot of it here.

The villains had on one occasion earmarked a victim for treatment but PC Scales and another officer looked after him well, so nothing happened.

A cutthroat attack was made on a member of a rival north London gang, the Whites, at Liverpool Street station in 1936. On 8 June, 30 members of White's mob went in search of their rivals at Lewes Racecourse and took revenge on one of their bookmakers, Arthur Solomons, and his clerk. Some of the avengers received long prison sentences for their part in the clash – which would inspire the racecourse battle in *BRIGHTON ROCK*. It also marked the beginning of the end for the Sabinis.

By the late 1930s, Jack Spot was prepared to defy both the Whites and the Sabinis. He developed a system powerful enough to prevent displays of violence at race meetings which he described as 'an association'. He allied himself with the notorious robber and racketeer Billy Hill and by the summer of 1947 they acquired control of Brighton Racecourse just before location filming for *BRIGHTON ROCK* moved there.

Darby Sabini was in fact the model for Colleoni in Greene's novel. With much of his power already eroded, he 'retired' to a penthouse in Brighton's *Grand Hotel* and died in Hove in 1950. He had never got over the death of his son, who was killed in action with the RAF. Darby left hardly any money – despite his years of control over a large part of London's underworld.

RAPE – see also DNA, INDECENT ASSAULT and WOOD, GEORGE

Rape and the law

In the eighteenth century, rape was considered a crime against property – a man's property.

For much of the period covered by this book, the subordinate position of women in society and their own anxiety not to have their loss of virginity publicised meant that, in those cases which actually did reach the courts, a just verdict was by no means guaranteed. Another perennial problem was the lack of witnesses – it was often the woman's word against the man's. Conviction rates were therefore dismally low. Attempted rape, a misdemeanour, was easier to prove, and was more often prosecuted, even when the facts might suggest that the rape had been completed. In 1841, the penalty for rape was reduced from death to transportation, a penalty in turn replaced by imprisonment under later statutes. Several nineteenth century cases made it clear that the essence of rape was lack of consent, rather than force; hence sex with a woman who was asleep or too drunk to consent could be rape.

Radical legal changes took place in the last century. The marital rape exemption, which had previously meant that a husband could not be convicted of raping his wife, was abolished by court decision and statute in the early 1990s. Even so, perhaps as a result of the difficulties involved in proving lack of consent in acquaintance and other non-stranger rape, the conviction rate (convictions as a percentage of offences reported to the police) plummeted from 25% in 1985 to only 7% in 2000.

A gang rape by militia, 1800

A Sussex case in 1800 – although it took place outside Brighton – is of interest

Miss Catherine Wade, daughter of the Master of Ceremonies at Brighthelmstone, being carried off from St Nicholas' Churchyard by John Motherill in 1786. Henry Smith collection

from a number of viewpoints. It was a multiple rape; there were – unusually – witnesses; and punishment was inflicted at both military and civil level. The *Sussex Weekly Advertiser* reported that in June, four men (Patrick Shee, Michael Donellen, John Cullen and Robert White), privates in the 13th Foot, who had not long before marched through Lewes, were committed from Chichester to the county gaol at Horsham. They were charged with raping, in a field near Westbourne, one Miriam Bennet, a 'decent servant girl living at Emsworth'. The assault was witnessed by some seafarers ('Mariners'), who had just put off in a boat. They hastened ashore and ran to the girl's aid, arriving just in time to rescue her from the brutal attack of the fourth assailant, who immediately fled together with his associates. Two of them, however, were shortly afterwards apprehended on parade and identified by the victim. They were promptly court-martialled, found guilty and each sentenced to receive 700 lashes. After about 150 strokes in both cases, the remainder was remitted provided they confessed and divulged who their associates had been. This they did and the other two guilty parties were likewise punished. They were all also committed to take their trials at the hands of the civil power at the next Assizes. The victim had initially been reported as having died but this was established to be untrue.

A subsequent report names only three of the men (all except Robert White) as having been capitally convicted at the Assizes and duly executed at Horsham in the presence of over 1,000 spectators. One of them observed to Jack Ketch, as he was placing the halter round his neck, that *he* was trembling more than he was himself.

Miscellaneous cases, 1807–1850

On 10 February 1807, Thomas Pope, 24, the servant of a gentleman who had recently arrived in Brighton, was taken before a magistrate at Lewes charged with raping Elizabeth Gallup, spinster, in a house in Brighthelmston on 8 February. Gallup was employed to clean up the house for the reception of the gentleman's family. After a short examination, Pope was committed to Horsham Gaol to take his trial at the next Assizes. These ended on 17 March. Pope was acquitted together with eight other offenders charged with various misdemeanours. All were discharged by proclamation.

The Sessional Offenders Lists record four cases of attempted rape between 1822 and 1835.

In Brighton, one Thomas Welfare, aged 70, was charged with making a girl of 13 drunk before raping her. As there were no witnesses, the case was dismissed.

In 1850, a Brighton bricklayer, Henry Toule, was sentenced to 12 months with hard labour for raping a 6-year-old girl, while in 1857 a married Irishwoman, lodging for the night in a low-class Brighton beer-shop, was required to share the same bed as the landlord's daughter. During the night, the landlord, who was sleeping in the same room, dragged her into his bed and raped her. Sceptical of his claim that she had entered his bed willingly, the magistrates gaoled him for two months.

A servant girl violated, 1857

In January 1857, Louisa Abinett, a 15-year-old servant girl, was raped by her master, James Bowtell, a shoemaker. A married man with four children, he had made advances to her two days previously but she had shunned them. On the night in question, she had gone downstairs for some bread and butter. She was about to go back upstairs to bed when Bowtell entered the room. He grabbed her round the waist and said: 'You are very fond of a cuddle.' He offered her some gin and water, which she refused. Then he started to rape her. She told him he was hurting her and to stop immediately. He replied: 'Be quiet, or you will have your mistress down.' Some 10–15 minutes later she went to bed and found she was bleeding. The next day she went and told her aunt who lived nearby. Bowtell was arrested later the same day. The magistrates decided that, 'in consideration for the prisoner's position and the feelings of his wife', not to imprison him and to release him on payment of a £10 fine. The case illustrates clearly the lack of status in the eyes of the law for women of a lowly position, for Louisa Abinett was an orphan under the care of the Brighton Guardians. She had been living in the town's workhouse at Church Hill and had been placed out to service by the Guardians. After Bowtell's release, she was returned to their 'care'.

Rape has sometimes gone hand-in-hand with murder. The most shocking local case, involving a 5-year-old child, was that of GEORGE HENRY WOOD in 1891.

RESURRECTIONISTS

Erredge writes, in his *History of Brighthelmston*, of Resurrectionists, or graveyard robbers, being the dread of surviving relatives. In the autumn of 1820, these 'desecrators of the silent tomb' paid the Old Churchyard a visit and conveyed away at least one body. The chief culprit was one Williams, who, in 1831, was executed at Newgate with a man called Bishop, for 'Burking' an Italian boy. The theft of the body greatly alarmed the inhabitants, and for many years afterwards it was the constant practice to have watchers, accommodated in a makeshift tent, on guard night after night for months at a time following a decease to prevent the body from being carried away. At one period, however, the system of watching had become such a nuisance that persons were afraid to venture through the burial ground after dusk, when the watchers went on duty. These individuals made their vigils more agreeable by taking creature comforts with them in the form of beer, spirits, and tobacco. In addition, they armed themselves with pistols, guns, and swords. Predictably, matters often got out of hand after a few drinks, prompting the churchwardens to intervene and prevent the men from bearing any arms other than stout sticks.

St Nicholas' Churchyard, drawn and published by R Havell in 1824. Author's collection

ROBBERY – see also HIGHWAY ROBBERY, THEFT, TRAIN ROBBERIES

When a robbery is committed there has to be both violence, or the threat of violence, and a theft. Robbery can take many forms, ranging from a street mugging to an armed robbery of a bank or a night security guard of a warehouse being tied up while its contents are stolen.

What we would now refer to in slang as 'casing a joint' was evidently carried out in the early days under the guise of hawking. A local press report of 29 April 1839 tells us that the Royal Commission on Police had been informed that Brighton contained numerous lodging houses whose keepers furnished matches, songs, lace and many petty articles hawked about as an excuse of vagrancy. This gave them 'opportunities of greater consequence', whereby fastenings and other circumstances could be observed which could lead to robbery. The main robberies were 'concocted in vagrant lodging houses and rendered effectual through the agencies of the Keepers. Intelligence is given and received by clients'.

The Preston Manor raid, 1968

We went in the van to Preston Park. Scrase and I took the gear and went over to the manor. I climbed up the scaffolding and Young opened the skylight. We knew the nightwatchman would come in and we just waited for him. After five minutes he came in and we tied him up. He was not hurt at all. No violence was used and we filled both sacks with silver.

(Patrick Cullen)

Preston Manor. This reputedly haunted house was originally built about 1600, rebuilt in 1738 and subsequently added to and altered in 1905. The Stanford family occupied it from 1794 until 1932, when the building and contents were left to Brighton Corporation. Chris Horlock collection

SABOTAGE

Five men were jailed at Sussex Assizes at Lewes in December 1968 for their part in a £15,000 silver robbery at Preston Manor Museum, Brighton. The offence was described by Mr Justice Chapman as 'a shocking outrage', depriving the general public of the enjoyment and privilege of seeing some of those beautiful old pieces of silver. Alan Joseph Scrase, 19, a general dealer, of West Hill Street; Trevor Whitley, 25, a painter and decorator, of Carlyle Street; Ian Duncan Cameron, 28, a hairdresser, of Laughton Road; and 19-year-old Michael Ian Young, an apprentice electrician, of Hertford Road, Brighton, all denied robbing nightwatchman Edward Thomas of the silver with violence. After a 21-hour retirement the jury found Scrase, Whitley and Young guilty of robbery with violence. It was Young who hid in the manor and opened the window to let the others in. They were sent to prison for four, four and a half and three years respectively. Cameron was found guilty of simple robbery and jailed for five years. Another associate, Patrick Joseph Cullen, aged 21, of no fixed address admitted simple robbery and was jailed for three and a half years. All had previous convictions. The jury added a rider that they did not think there was premeditation in the violence.

During the four-day trial, the jury were told the nightwatchman was hit over the head with 'something like a poker'. The men then bound and gagged him and escaped with the silver. Scrase and Young were arrested the following day, when they went to Preston Park to retrieve a sackful of silver hidden in some bushes. A police officer then posed as a 'fence' and bargained for the stolen silver with Cameron and Whitley in a Brighton hotel. When the officer eventually agreed to 'pay' £500 for the silver, Cameron was arrested on the way to a bank in North Street. Whitley was arrested shortly afterwards.

S

SABOTAGE
In July 1837, the Secretary to the Board of the Brighton General Gas Light and Coke Company offered a £50 reward for information, 'it having been ascertained that some evil disposed person or persons have at different times caused obstruction in gas pipes and tubings of the above Company by wilfully installing cork and other substances therein'.

SHERWOOD, CAROLINE
On 10 March 1853, the *Brighton Gazette* reported 'considerable excitement has been caused among the inhabitants of this town and Hove in consequence of the occurrence of one of those dreadful events, human murder, from which this town and neighbourhood had so long been exempt'. On the 6th, a brickmaker called Joseph Anderson, walking up Hove Drove (Sackville Road), had looked over a briar hedge and seen the body of a 4-year-old girl. She had been strangled with a small plaid silk neckerchief. Although she was fully clothed, her bonnet would later be found by a labourer opposite Mr Rigden's farmhouse, close to the footpath leading through the fields to Hove Church. She was quite an attractive child but the upper part of her face was much pitted by smallpox scars. The cleanliness of her skin and the good quality of her garments and footwear showed she had been well cared for.

A constable, William Willmer from Preston, was summoned and the body was conveyed to the *Ship Inn*, Hove Street, where the coroner, Francis Harding Gell, presided

Marlborough House, 54 Old Steine, where Sherwood worked. The Grade 1 listed building was erected as a red brick structure in around 1765 and later altered to a Georgian design by Robert Adam.
The author

over the inquest. The illegitimate child's mother, 22-year-old Miss Caroline Sherwood, was quickly traced – and accused of the murder. A native of Brighton with three brothers, she was employed as a cook to Judge Furner at 54 Old Steine (better known as *Marlborough House*), Brighton. Her unfortunate daughter, also called Caroline, had been boarded with a woman called Hannah Delves at a cost of 2/6d a week. Removed to the Town Hall, the accused unsuccessfully attempted to strangle herself with a shoelace on the night of the first day of the inquest.

One of her brothers was in Australia and Sherwood had a number of papers already signed so that she could emigrate there herself. Her daughter, it was alleged, stood in the way of her starting a new life. Indeed, so detached was the mother from her crime that she even attended a Railway Ball on the evening the body was discovered.

The coroner returned a verdict of wilful murder ('Wilful murder by her mother' is actually stated on the child's death certificate – ahead of the trial) and Sherwood was tried at Lewes Assizes in July 1853. She suffered from hysterical fits throughout the proceedings and restoratives had to be given. Found guilty and sentenced to be publicly executed at Lewes on 9 August, she was reprieved by Queen Victoria only six days before the scheduled event. She did finally get to Australia – on a transportation vessel.

SHOPLIFTING
Two 1800 cases
On 5 November 1800, a woman named Davey, the wife of a journeyman stonemason in Brighton, was committed to Horsham Gaol charged with stealing, in the shop of a Mr Burfield, a linen-draper in North Street, a calico-muslin gown-piece. The offence had been committed some time earlier. The item was traced to Davey through Mrs Burfield chancing to see the stolen property being made up at a mantua-maker's (a mantua was a loose gown worn over a petticoat and open down the front) with whom she had business dealings.

On the same evening, at about 6 pm, two watches were taken from the shop window of a Mr Greenfield, a watchmaker and silversmith on The Cliffe, Brighton, by some thieves who broke a pane of glass to get into the premises and got clean away.

Shopkeepers unite, 1963
Shoplifters were in August 1963 reported to be costing Brighton shops, and especially supermarkets, hundreds of pounds a week. There was a regular parade of offenders, the majority middle-aged housewives, before the magistrates. Their story was nearly always the same: 'I don't know why I did it.' Uncomprehending husbands would plead in mitigation. One supermarket manager caught 12 shoplifters in one week, although for various reasons it was not always possible to prosecute them. It was felt in some cases that the low value of the goods taken did not justify the time wasted on proceedings. Nevertheless, then as now, many shopkeepers were banding together to blacklist known shoplifters. The offender's name and address were taken and he – or it seems more likely she – was banned from purchasing anything in the shop in question.

According to one manager, culprits fell into three broad categories: the down-and-out who steals the odd item and later sells it at the local pub for a few bob; the professionals (he was sure a ring was operating in the town); and, lastly, women aged between 50 and 70. For some reason, females in this age bracket (many of them respectable) were the worst offenders.

In July 1967, a mother of three was jailed for nine months for shoplifting.

SMOKESCREEN
Film, 1964
Synopsis
Tight-fisted insurance investigator Roper (Peter Vaughan) travels to Brighton to investigate a claim related to a blazing car that was driven over Beachy Head. The opening sequence in fact shows the burning vehicle being pushed over the cliffs. The accident is seen by onlookers but because no body is recovered from the scene, the Australian Life insurance company suspects it could be fraud.

In Brighton, Roper conducts himself like a dogged bloodhound and pieces together information from the scene, the police, and acquaintances of the supposedly dead man. Meanwhile, in a brief pause from the investigation, we get an insight into Roper's private life and the reasons for his fanatical thriftiness.

Details and comments
This above-average B-movie written and directed by Jim O'Connolly, is a mildly diverting story. Its passable plot, involving a little bit of skulduggery in suburban Brighton,

is kept moving swiftly and painlessly. Adultery, embezzlement and murder are all taken in his stride by Peter Vaughan as the fastidious insurance claims inspector who suspects there is more to a blazing car wreck than meets the eye.

SMUGGLING

Mary Waugh, in *Smuggling in Kent and Sussex*, relates that contraband goods were certainly landed on the beach at Brighton and sometimes taken directly into inns and shops within the Lanes, although a much better landing place was at the seaward end of Hove Street in Hove, a site now submerged under blocks of flats and a dual carriageway section of King's Esplanade.

Early illegal imports

Passenger vessels were also a vehicle for smuggling goods into the town (Brighton had a cross-channel service to Dieppe from 1761) and the presence of the royal court in Brighton created a brisk demand for luxuries, such as lace, which could be met in this manner. When one French gentleman landed from the ferry, lace was discovered under fruit in chests belonging to him. In 1816 a young man was caught using stone bottles with false bottoms filled with spirits to try and smuggle cotton stockings and thread. Discovery came when he overdid the weight with one bottle and the bottom fell out. Excise men would occasionally stop a packet in the English Channel and find contraband when they searched it.

The ultimate price

A notorious local smuggler was Daniel Skayles. On the night of 7 November 1796, while making his way, heavily laden, over the hill to Patcham in company with many of his fellows, he was overtaken by excise officers and soldiers. The smugglers dispersed in all directions. A riding officer rode after Skayles, who was likewise on horseback, and called on him to surrender his booty. This he refused to do. Knowing from the experience of fellow officers that the smuggler was too good a man for him, he shot him through the head.

In Patcham churchyard, a monument was erected to his memory which included the lines:

> Alas! swift flew the fatal lead,
> Which pierced through the young man's head
> He instant fell, resigned his breath,
> And closed his languid eyes in death,
> All you who to this stone draw near,
> Oh! pray let fall the pitying tear:
> From this sad instance may we all
> Prepare to meet Jehovah's call.

Fights at sea and vessel detentions

On 10 January 1800, several of the Brighton fishing boats, alarmed at the appearance of a lugger which was thought to be a French privateer, ran ashore opposite the town. The commander of the Sea Fencibles immediately put to sea in a rowing-boat with a dozen of his men, suitably armed. On boarding the lugger, they found she was clearly used for illicit traffic in gin but since there was none on board, she was permitted to pursue her course.

A smuggler, drawn by William Heath. From 'Smuggling in Kent and Sussex' by Mary Waugh

On 24 April 1806, an encounter took place off Brighton between the revenue cutter, *Leopard*, and a smuggler. Aldridge, the commander of the contraband vessel, was killed in the action, and one of his crew, named Morris, was so severely wounded in the chest that he died a few days afterwards.

Boats captured from smugglers might be seen from time to time in the early part of the nineteenth century on the beach in the area opposite Regency Square. In the 1820s and even later, contraband ventures were, according to Erredge, of very common occurrence.

Beaches strewn with liquor

In June 1800, at Rottingdean, a few miles east of Brighton, smugglers suffered a serious loss because their signal lights were not properly attended to. A boat containing 150 tubs of contraband spirits was seized by waiting Revenue Officers as it was being rowed ashore. A larger boat, laden with 450 tubs and packages, had to jettison its cargo in order to make good its escape. Most of the booty was recovered later by boats from Shoreham Custom House.

Hufton & Baird record that Brighton witnessed more than elegant holidaymakers strolling on the Steyne in 1803:

> ... *fishermen picked up at sea and brought to shore upwards of 500 casks of contraband spirits, of which the Revenue soon got scent and proceeded very actively to unburden the fishermen. This landing and seizing continued with little intermission from six to ten, to the great amusement of upwards of 2,000 people who had become spectators of the scene. When the officers had loaded themselves with as many tubs as they could carry, the fishermen, in spite of their assiduity, found means to convey away as many more, and by that means seemed to make a pretty equal division.*

They quote another incident which resulted in excess – and tragedy:

> ... *some soldiers stationed in Brighton, hearing a 'bustle' on the beach, fetched some comrades and dispersed the smugglers and seized the tubs. However, the two soldiers who were first supposed to have discovered the above mentioned tubs took such immoderate draughts of the baleful spirit as rendered them incapable of getting far from the spot where the casks were deposited. They were both found early the next morning lying dead drunk below high water mark. One of them, belonging to the artillery, never survived the shameful fit of intoxication in which he was taken up – he was generally estimated to be a sober man, and was to have been married the day he died.*

A coast road seizure

On 10 August 1811, one Cruttenden, riding-officer of customs, seized at Pevensey, where he was stationed, the stagecoach and horses that ran to and from Brighton and Hastings. It was on its way to the former place, carrying contraband goods intended for persons in that town and elsewhere. The goods were all taken to the Custom House at Eastbourne.

Caught in possession

In 1819, a husband, his wife and another man were apprehended in the Apollo Gardens with three gallons of foreign brandy and no explanation. The wife claimed that she was acting on instructions of her husband and was dismissed; he, however, was fined £100, but was unable to pay or go into the navy so he spent three years in jail instead. In another case in the same week, Martin Clack also received a three-year sentence for being in possession of a tub of 'foreign geneva' in Lavender Street.

Daylight runs

A successful run in broad daylight took place at about 3pm on 19 July 1821 at the bottom of Ship Street, while the Custom House Officers were away at the Level watching the Coronation sports. The gang had assembled in the Old Ship Yard and, on the signal being given, 300 kegs of Hollands (Dutch gin) were slung by way of the Gap and removed before the few bystanders realised what was going on. As usual, most of the cargo was conveyed inland for concealment and disposal.

Smugglers who were captured were, at that time, put on board the *Hound* revenue cutter which was stationed off Brighton. A smuggler chase by her was very exciting to witness from the shore. Quite often, smugglers went missing – either they were killed or captured and shipped off on foreign service in the Royal Navy.

Another incident, quoted by Hufton & Baird as occurring at the dawn of the Victorian age, took place in Kemp Town:

> ... *many successful runs have been made, and one no longer ago than daylight on Saturday morning, when a boat came on shore on the beach opposite Burlington Street and ran a hundred and fifty tubs up a tunnel which passes under the Marine Parade from the sea, to the western corner house of that street. The policeman on duty there was surprised to see men emerge from the area of that house with half ankers on their shoulders, and gave notice of the event to the Coastguards men of the Black-Rock station. They ran over the Downs just as fast as they were able in pursuit of some light carts which were promptly laden with the crop ... among the places examined was a barn at The Bear near the Barracks, on the Lewes Road, where a swift horse was found harnessed to a light cart, bearing the name of 'Stephen Heather, Butcher, Brighton' and upon searching among the hay in the building, thirteen tubs were found, which with the horse and cart were seized by the officers, and three men who were there cutting potatoes were detained on suspicion of knowing how the hay became the positum of so foreign an article.*

In connection with this occurrence, two policemen who had been on duty changed into plain clothes and were then seen carrying baskets. Their houses were searched and 'Eight glass and three stone bottles of spirits of brandy were found.' This dereliction of duty was suitably dealt with by Henry Solomon, Brighton's new Police Chief.

A shopkeeper pays his way

In *A Peep into the Past* (1892), JG Bishop tells of the singular detection of smuggled goods in the shop of one Spencer Weston, a tradesman of North Street. Weston, formerly of Seddlescombe, near Hastings, traded as a silk-mercer and lace-man in a shop where Nos 18 and 19 stood in Bishop's day. Excise officers discovered goods on which no duty had been paid. Weston was fined £120. However, that was nothing compared with the penalty he received when, probably by a charwoman, the whereabouts of a secret chamber was made known to the Excise. Weston's kitchen extended the whole width of the premises at the rear, and the fire-range was so contrived as to draw out and in on hidden wheels. Behind the range was the little room in which the smuggled stock was kept snug and dry. This time the Excise thought they would finish the miscreant off by imposing a fine of no less than £10,000! Weston had, however, saved a few 'pieces' – and had recently been the lucky winner of the Grand Prize in a lottery. He paid up. Supplementing Bishop's reference to Weston are notes from family member Jay Glanville, from which we learn that the trader was based for some time in Hackney, had retired by 1871 and died in early 1874, his death being registered at Epsom.

Such offences as Weston's were regarded by the public in those days as very minor. The goods were 'run' for him by what was then the fastest cutter on the coast, owned by 'Master Wren' of Brighton. They were taken from where they were landed by cart to a pre-arranged place in the vicinity of the shop, to await the signal that the way was clear.

The death and rebirth of smuggling

More effective anti-contraband vigilance helped to reduce smuggling substantially in the first decades of the nineteenth century.

The Coast Blockade was a deterrent, although with the Sussex line being 98 miles long and only two men per mile keeping watch, bribery became a problem.

In *Brighton As It Is* (1836), visitors were informed:

> Among the many improvements of Brighton may be mentioned the New Custom-house, which was commenced on the demolition of the old one in 1830. The plan is one which is capable of affording every convenience requisite in such a building. It is situated at the south end of West street.
>
> The regulations of the revenue are in every respect closely attended to, and the searches, as well personal as of boxes and luggage, are very strict.

Another nail in the coffin was the reduction of customs duties after 1840, which took much of the profit out of contraband trading.

Today, the smuggling of alcohol and cigarettes via the cross-Channel ferry services between Newhaven and Dieppe has severely affected retailers in Brighton. According to a survey, smuggling beer across the Channel became one of the fastest-growing retail businesses in the UK during 1999. Contraband cigarettes, too, were a huge problem. Imperial Tobacco estimated in 2000 that one in three cigarettes smoked in the UK were non-duty paid, amounting to a yearly loss to the Exchequer from smuggling of around £4 billion. The following year, one Brighton newsagent claimed losses of £400 a week.

SQUATTING

The Brighton Vigilantes

Harry Cowley (1891–1971) was a Brighton chimney sweep who battled for the homeless and unemployed, for market traders and for old age pensioners.

Immediately after the First World War, there was an acute housing shortage in Brighton, a situation which repeated itself after the Second. Cowley's response on both occasions was to get ex-servicemen into houses that lay empty through his 'Vigilantes'. Their methods were simple: a house was chosen and – often under cover of darkness – a family was moved in. The group provided the family with food and heating and contacted the owner so that rent could be agreed. But there was opposition from the courts and from the police, who, unable to move a family once it was installed, tried to catch the Vigilantes in the act. Sometimes, however, they would turn a blind eye. Cowley waged a successful and popular local and national campaign for housing reform, canvassing Brighton Council and even writing to Winston Churchill. After Parliament passed a Bill in 1945 enabling local councils to requisition houses which had been empty for 18 months, the Vigilantes went into decline. Cowley did try to revive the movement a couple of times in the 1950s and 1960s but it did not have the same impetus as in the 1940s.

Harry Cowley's name and spirit live on at the *Cowley Club*, 12 London Road, Brighton. Set up to promote solidarity and mutual aid, it is run entirely by volunteers. The centre facilities include a café, a bookshop, an infopoint and meeting space for local groups and campaigns. It also offers confidential advice and help with welfare issues and is able to host talks, meetings, film shows and events.

The Brighton Rents Project

The Brighton Rents Project was a broad-based campaign for better housing which started occupying empty property in 1969 and received widespread support, including that of the Labour MP for Kemp Town, Dennis Hobden. Squatting was seen as a last resort in the face of an intransigent Conservative Council. Promptly announcing that the squatters would be struck off the housing waiting list, it immediately began court proceedings for eviction. With no concern for the homeless, it proceeded to sell No. 70 Church Street, a house in the town centre which it had kept empty for 20 years. Despite numerous arrests of supporters on minor charges, the campaign continued to grow. Towards the end of July 1969, houses in Queen Square and Wykeham Terrace were squatted. The army, which owned the properties, had been intending to sell them with vacant possession, but the presence of squatters meant that this had to be postponed. The squatters dug in to fight and called for support. The Assize judge later described these Territorial Army married quarters at Brighton as having been turned into 'something like a fortress'. In the months up to the eviction (on 28 November) the local press pilloried the Rents Project and its helpers, warning of 'private armies' and 'terrible weapons' waiting at Wykeham Terrace. Three people from the squat were, indeed, arrested for firebombing a local army recruitment office using petrol bombs made at the squat. Several of the occupants were later sent to prison and one to borstal. Of the five who appeared in court, three came from Manchester, one from London and one from Abingdon. These events were widely publicised with disastrous consequences. Torn apart by external hostility and internal divisions, the Brighton Rents Project disintegrated.

Big Bruno

Bruno Crosby, the 'King of the Squatters' left half his house, worth about £40,000, to Brighton Housing Trust when he died in 2002 at the age of 51. He co-ordinated squatting activities in Brighton during the 1970s when the movement was at its height.

177

At one stage, hundreds of squatters were housed across the town in squats he had organised. He had had a drink problem as a young man, which he blamed on the boredom of working in a seafront hotel. He started wandering the streets and taking drugs, but he turned his life around, kicking heroin and starting social work to help people. He began the Bit by Bit helpline service and started the vegetarian *Open Café* in Victoria Road, which became a meeting-place for all kinds of unconventional organisations, from the Claimants' Union to the alternative newspaper *Brighton Voice*. Profits from the café went to Bit by Bit. Crosby also started the Brighton and Hove Squatters' Union, which occupied scores of empty houses in the town. He renamed it the Sussex Housing Movement. Bruno's house was a squat in Argyle Road which had been empty for five years and was completely renovated by Crosby and his fellow-squatters. It eventually became the oldest squat in Brighton. When he ultimately won over the Tory-led council and landlords, council leader, Bob Cristofoli, actually went to Argyle Road for tea. Crosby moved onto the board of Brighton Housing Trust. In 1979, he negotiated between the Trust, the Council and squatters who had taken over derelict buildings in Springfield Road, Brighton. Later it was arranged the Trust should take over the buildings from the Council and help many of the squatters to be housed.

Eventually, Crosby tired of his work and moved to Cornwall, where he died.

Eviction in West Hill Road

We will gladly vacate the premises if we are assured that the family at the top of the housing list is given the house to live in.
>   (Steve Bassam, unemployed graduate, now Lord Bassam of Brighton)

A member of the Brighton and Hove Squatters' Union, Bassam made periodic speeches to the officials carrying out the eviction of squatters from a Council-owned two-storey terraced house in West Hill Road, Brighton, on 21 January 1976. Some 15 members of the Union had occupied the house in protest against the Council's decision to sell the property – valued at about £8,500 – on the open market instead of using it to provide for a family on the 1,600-long waiting list. Leaflets were handed round outside the house. Some people took them, others waved the squatters away. There was no violence and no arrests as 20 bailiffs, council officials and workmen took over the premises. Out-manoeuvring the occupants, the men avoided the ground-floor front door (to which squatter Ernest James had chained himself) and instead broke down the locked basement door to gain access.

The Justice? collective

'Justice?' was a collective formed in April 1994 to oppose the Criminal Justice and Public Order Bill, introduced just before the previous Christmas. They canvassed pubs, clubs and other venues to warn that the rights of vulnerable categories of people were endangered by the Bill. The group was famous for squatting a number of buildings in the town – notably the former Courthouse in Prince's Street – to highlight the scandal of empty buildings not being used to house homeless people or for socially beneficial community functions.

In November 1994, the pilot issue of the group's extraordinarily successful newsletter, *SchNEWS*, was published. It was meant not only to be read but read out loud to listeners as a satire on conventional news broadcasts. A popular early venue for this was the *New*

Solidarity outside the former Courthouse, Princes Street, in 1994. SchNews at Ten, Brighton, 2004

Kensington pub in the North Laine area. Other pubs followed suit. Activist Gibby Zobel began the live news-reading and, along with David Berry, started the newsletter. The first ever copy included a report that eviction from the Courthouse had taken place the previous Thursday, i.e. 10 November, and that Holy Trinity Church on Ship Street had been taken over temporarily.

The collective then moved to CJ's on Western Road and from there to housing association premises on Grand Parade. Justice? received mainstream attention – including coverage on the BBC *Newsnight* programme – when it launched its 'Squatters' Estate Agents' in squatted retail premises. Its slogan was 'Deeds not words'. In 1996 came the 'Anarchist Teapot', the name given to a series of squatted cafés that popped up around Brighton.

As for the newsletter, production could probably not have continued had it not been for an office made available in the early days by the Brighton rock group, the Levellers. Warren Carter, who had been in the Courthouse squat, was involved with the publication from the second or third issue and went on to edit and shape *SchNEWS* for over a decade. There were, however, many hands at the wheel and this has remained the case to the present day.

Much jostling as police and bailiffs try to evict a family of six from a Council-owned property in Terminus Road, near the Station, in 1974. Flour, sand, coffee and water were used by the resolute squatters against officials. Chris Horlock collection

STURT, WILLIAM

Mary Ann Day died in 1863 after eating a penny mince pie given to her the day before (Valentine's Day) by her husband-to-be, a 46-year-old house painter named William Sturt, at her home at 14 Rock Street, Kemp Town. George Gere, the surgeon called on the day she died, said he suspected the presence of an irritant poison. An inquest did in fact reveal large quantities of white arsenic in her stomach and liver. At the preliminary hearings before Brighton magistrates, the owner of the pie shop was anxious to point out there had been no complaints about the pies he had on sale.

The Coroner's Court investigating the death returned a verdict of murder, adding that they did not believe the poison was in the pie when it was bought. Sturt was duly committed for trial.

The unfortunate woman had been living in great distress and poverty, the family having insufficient food. The eldest daughter, Charlotte, 25, said her mother (like the rest of the family) had eaten stale bread before going out and had drunk a glass of gin. There were, she said, seven in the family, all living in one room in Rock Street. Another daughter, Sophia, said her mother had complained later that the mince pie given her by Mr Sturt had made her sick and burned her throat, so she had to drink water continually.

William Sturt had been infatuated with Mrs Day and had promised to marry her and to help her family. He had never gone empty-handed to 14 Rock Street on his frequent

14 Rock Street may appear spacious today but the Day family lived virtually destitute in a rented portion of it. The author

visits there. Mary Barnett, who lodged with the Days, said the deceased had always appeared friendly with Mr Sturt. The view of the public, however, was that William Sturt had killed Mrs Day to escape marrying her. Sturt had once told Charles Jutten, landlord of the *Windsor Castle* beerhouse in Montague Place, that Mrs Day was a bad character. She had deceived him about her age, told him she had three children instead of eight and on one occasion there had been a row when she stayed late with a friend in Over Street.

Sturt stood trial at Lewes Assizes on 23 March on a charge of wilful murder. Although quiet and unemotional, he had cried at the inquest, was greatly distressed by the tragedy and had, said Jutten, kissed Mrs Day's body in his presence.

David Black, the Brighton coroner, read a statement made by Sturt at the inquest, in which he admitted he had exchanged words with Mrs Day about 'a young man she formerly kept company with'. She had not complained about the pie but said it was very nice.

The defence told the jury that the prisoner was a highly respected man. There was no doubt about the arsenic's presence but how had it arrived in the dead woman's stomach? There was no evidence and the case against Sturt was weak, feeble, inconsistent and partly impossible. The prosecution had failed to find a motive or to prove that the mince pie had ever been poisoned. The jury, without leaving the box, took only eight minutes to announce they found William Sturt not guilty of murder. The trial had lasted nine hours, during which Sturt had appeared quietly indifferent – his profound deafness had prevented him from reacting to most of the proceedings.

SUICIDE – see also WARDER, Dr ALFRED and the Clifford Case, 1914 (in HOTELS AND BOARDING HOUSES)
Until the Suicide Act of 1961, suicide used to be a criminal offence. Even today, British Coroners' Courts determine a suicide verdict strictly (i.e. is the person guilty of committing suicide?) in the same way as criminal courts do, although Coroners may record an open verdict or death from an undetermined cause.

In 1995, the Mental Health Line scheme, part of the Rethink charity, was set up in Brighton and Hove, where the suicide rate is above the national average. It is a helpline which counsels 2,000 people a year through depression, offering help to those feeling lonely, depressed and suicidal.

Broken crockery the last straw, 1866
Before the Brighton Borough Bench on 12 July 1866 was respectably-dressed Frances Patching, 19, charged with attempting to commit suicide. The previous evening, between eight and nine o'clock, Superintendent Crowhurst had been called to 166 North Street, where Patching was in the service of a Mrs Edwards. There was much agitation at the property. He was told the woman had taken poison and had locked herself in the water closet and could not be induced to leave it. He called at the door several times but, receiving no answer, burst the door open and found Patching behind it. He asked her if she had taken poison and she replied that she had, from a small bottle of liquid. This he afterwards found in her box. When she was taken to the Town Hall, she was given an emetic. Asked why she had done what she did, she said that she had broken several plates and dishes, and this had annoyed her so much that she had taken the poison.

In court, Mrs Edwards testified that Patching was of a most excitable disposition, which might account for her action. She was quite willing to take her back again if she would conduct herself properly. The Bench then discharged the prisoner with an admonition.

Two attempted drownings
In the summer of 1881, Ada Rachel Williams was charged with attempting suicide. She had, she said, been enticed down from London by some people and they had treated her badly. At about 9.10 on the evening of 2 August, the steward of the Brighton Cyclists' Club saw her go past the Club's arch towards the sea. She did not return and about five

minutes later he went after her. He heard a groan and saw her lying on her back in about two feet of water. He dragged her out and she appeared to be unconscious. He obtained help and she was taken to the bowling saloon. PC Fellingham was sent for and applied artificial respiration, and Williams recovered. She was taken to the police station and then to Sussex County Hospital. She was remanded for enquiries to be made.

Twenty years later, Elizabeth May was charged with attempting to commit suicide and was remanded for a week from 21 June 1901. She had been found by a fisherman and another man lying in the sea unconscious. On recovering, she asked to be taken to the Town Hall, where she told police she was sorry she had not succeeded in drowning herself, and while in the cell attempted to commit suicide by strangulation.

Hard on the heels of that case came that of 19-year-old Rose Gibson, who at the beginning of July 1901 stood in the dock charged with attempted suicide. When on the seafront one previous evening with two other girls and a sailor, a quarrel had broken out and Gibson had been left alone. At about 10.30 she had come up to the others on a seat and said: 'Good-bye. I'm going away.' She had then walked down to the sea and into the water. The sailor had run after her and pulled her out of a depth of about five feet of water. She had been rapidly revived with the help of Sergeant Snuggs – who had then arrested her. Like Ada Williams, she was remanded for enquiries to be made.

The 'Death Compact' case, 1922

> *If two persons agree to commit suicide together and only one dies, then the survivor is guilty of murder.* (JE Bush, Coroner, Brighton, 12 May 1922)

No. 71a Queen's Road, a stone's throw from Brighton Station, was the scene of a bizarre tragedy on 10 May 1922. The case had features eerily reminiscent of a murder which had taken place eight years earlier in a boarding house several hundred yards away (see HOTELS/BOARDING HOUSES – CLIFFORD). In both instances, the woman involved was called Maud, the surviving party was taken to the Royal Sussex County Hospital to recover and the drama took place in temporary accommodation. Whereas Percy Clifford shot his wife then unsuccessfully tried to kill himself, however, George William Hibbert took his own life but failed to take his (willing but unaware) partner with him to the hereafter.

Their relationship had developed against a complicated family background. Among the brothers of George Hibbert, 38, a father of six, was a younger sibling, Frederick Arthur Hibbert. His 25-year-old wife was called Maud and they had one child. She and George became intimate and Frederick commenced divorce proceedings against his wife on learning of their relationship. George's own wife, also a Maud Hibbert, left him when she found out about her husband's affair with her sister-in-law. The lovers cared only for each other, and did not even spare a thought for their respective children (one of George's was only three months old at the time of the tragedy).

A letter from the 'new' Maud to George prior to their running away together refers to their forthcoming stay in London before going to Brighton and contains a request for money – to buy 'a pretty nightie for our last week together'. Suicide was the only way forward, for their relationship was doomed. She wrote, among other relevant statements, 'I am sorry for those we leave behind.' The pair arrived in Brighton on 3 May and leased a flat as man and wife in the Morley Benjamin Apartments. These would have stood north of today's *Queen's Head* and have long since vanished. It is now the scene of very busy traffic, with many buses passing in front of Brighton Station.

The couple enjoyed what George described in another letter, sent from Brighton to a brother, John Brown Hibbert, as a 'glorious week together' and were supremely happy. He added:

... we have just lived this time for one another, knowing full well the final consequence, which we are both prepared [for] and willing to take. [...] I admire M.E.'s [Maud's] pluck. She is meeting this with more fortitude than I yet she does not know the form it is to take. [...] Was there ever such a woman?

The form it took was gas poisoning. George persuaded Maud to sleep with him at the opposite end of the bed to usual, which was nearer the centre of the room. He ran a length of flexible tubing from the gas chandelier above them to between the pillows and under their sheet. She complied, despite having been told nothing of his precise plan. She trusted him. He had first made her drowsy by urging her to drink a large glass of port, whereupon she slept. She was sick later but could not get out of bed. Other than that, she knew nothing more until she was found. The gas was on all night.

The next morning, George was discovered stone dead by the landlady, who entered after repeatedly having no response from the room to her knocking. Maud was barely alive, and just looked at her. She refused an emetic which a policeman tried to administer to her, and, on seeing George's body, sobbed 'Oh! Don't take me away from him!'

The inquest was held two days later but had to be adjourned since Maud was still too unwell to attend. Much information was elicited, however, including the fact that the various Hibbert family members were based in Kettering, that George and his wife had been married no less than 20 years, and that Maud the lover had followed George to Scotland, where he had been employed as the manager of a boot and shoe company. He had latterly been employed in a similar capacity in Leeds, where his wife had seen him for the last time a month before the tragedy. The 'new' Maud had been living with her own mother in Kettering for some time before coming to Brighton.

Maud Hibbert, the contrite and devastated lover, cut a sorry figure the following week when she appeared at the resumed inquest and then before the magistrates. In tears and in a half-fainting condition, she was partly shielded from general view by a police matron who stood protectively in front of her. The coroner's verdict was that the deceased feloniously killed himself by wilfully inhaling coal gas and that before he had done so, Maud Hibbert feloniously incited, aided and encouraged him so to kill himself. Immediately after the inquest, she was formally charged in the Police Court with wilful murder.

At the Sussex Assizes on 8 July 1922, Maud Hibbert pleaded not guilty to the charge of the murder of her lover or of being an accessory before the fact, but she did admit attempting to commit suicide. Mr Justice Horridge decided not to put her on trial but directed the jury to find her not guilty of the murder charge. He did, however, have harsh words for her and declined her sister's mediating offer to take charge of her:

You, a married woman of 25, with a child of your own, violated your duty as wife and mother and went off to gratify your own lust with this brother-in-law of yours and wickedly agreed that both you and he would commit suicide. I must pass on you a substantial sentence. It is that you be imprisoned and kept to such hard labour as you are fitted to do for nine calendar months.

Maud Hibbert burst into tears and was led sobbing bitterly to the cells.

Suicide of a rapist, 2001

On 19 January 2001, a suspected rapist committed suicide in a hospital wing of Lewes Prison. Unemployed Rashid Kausmally, former nurse, of Bear Road, Brighton, had been charged several days earlier with raping a 26-year-old Australian visitor while holding a knife to her throat. The attack had taken place in Queensbury Mews, Brighton, on 20 December 2000, as the woman walked into the *Cecil House Hotel* in King's Road, Brighton. The rape was one of a series of frightening attacks against no fewer than ten people on the streets of Brighton and Hove between October and December that year. The youngest victim had been a 16-year-old girl, who was told: 'I'm going to kill you.' In the other assaults, eight women were either robbed or abducted, many at knifepoint and once with a threat of being injected with the Aids virus; in one case a 66-year-old man was stabbed in the back and slashed across the face.

Mauritius-born Kausmally suffered from Parkinson's disease and it was through a drug which he took for his illness that he had been finally traced; the product was made by only one pharmaceutical company in the UK, which alerted detectives when the man submitted a prescription at a chemist's in Wood Green, North London.

T

TAYLOR, WEAVER AND DONOVAN

I did 13 years on the Moor and in Parkhurst for something I never did. . . . I've got nothing on my conscience, but people still point me out in the street. (James Weaver, 1955)

Friend Ernest Smith, 68, a retired wholesale druggist, returned to his Brighton home at 10.15 on the night of 14 April 1928 so badly beaten up that his wife was terrified by what she saw. At first she shut the door against him, but recognised him by his voice. He had been stunned by a man who had spoken to him on Brighton seafront and had afterwards been taken by car up onto the Downs, where he was assaulted and robbed. He died on 18 May in a Hove nursing home as an indirect result of his wounds, since they turned septic and pleurisy and pneumonia developed.

At the end of that month, Percival Leonard Taylor, 24, a painter, James Weaver, 23, a hawker, and George Thomas Donovan, 32, a motor mechanic, were remanded in Brighton until 7 June charged with the murder. Taylor and Weaver both protested at being remanded for an incident they knew 'nothing at all about'. A barmaid in a hotel in St James's Street, however, said she saw the three men with an elderly man resembling the victim. Also, pieces of white, green and brown fluff found on the victim's clothing matched material found on the cushions and floor mats in the car. All three accused were found guilty at Sussex Assizes in Lewes and sentenced to death. Almost at the last hour, however, the death sentences were commuted to long terms of imprisonment. Donovan and Taylor eventually served 11 and 12 years respectively after having their sentences reduced for good conduct. Weaver was released after 13 years.

Yet question marks still hang over the case. These are set out in a local publication on the people's champion Harry Cowley (see SQUATTERS). Overhearing Weaver say to Taylor at the Police Court 'I want to go home. We know nothing about this', Cowley spent 11 years researching the case, convinced the men were innocent. So much information reached him that, pretending to be drunk, he actually accused one man of being the murderer:

> *He is the member of a gang which beats up and robs people. No, he didn't deny the accusation I'd made. He didn't even reply. He just edged out of the place.*

Cowley took dozens of statements and, armed with new evidence, petitioned his local MP, Sir Cooper Rawson, who sent a full written report to the Home Office. The last-minute reprieve was granted even though the men's innocence had still not been established. Locally, it was believed Cowley was behind it. In his campaign, he wrote to both the national press and the King (it is claimed the King queried the men's guilt). He also held meetings in Brighton to continue the fight.

Yet two undated and unattributed newspaper cuttings reproduced in the biographical book *Who was Harry Cowley?* are contradictory. They both appeared a week or so after Friend Smith's 86-year-old widow died, 27 years after her loss. In one, James Weaver, long since released, is described as working late at a Brighton market bric-a-brac stall to earn money (in the event, 10s) to buy daffodils to place on Mrs Smith's grave. He reportedly said: 'I know the agony of mind Mrs Smith must have suffered. I, *her husband's murderer*, have suffered too.' (author's italics). In the other cutting, Smith's tribute card reportedly read 'God Rest Your Soul. He Knows I Am Innocent'. We then read that Weaver had always protested his innocence. He then claimed that only one person – a woman – could clear his name and hoped 'to God' that she would come forward soon, not for his sake but for his wife and three children. He had just been to see William Teeling, MP for Brighton Pavilion, who had promised to investigate the facts of the case with a view to raising the matter in the House of Commons.

It should, finally, be noted that from first to last, Friend Ernest Smith declined to give the police a detailed description of what had happened. This severely hampered the investigations in the early days.

THEFT – see also ROBBERY, SHOPLIFTING, TRANSPORTATION

A separate volume could be written about two centuries of theft in Brighton. This crime is one for which punishment has varied most in severity during the period. In the early 1800s, many miscreants stole simply to live, or live better (three men who broke into a house to steal wine and food were found guilty at the 1830 Sussex Assizes and sentenced to death). Today the motivation is in many cases more likely to arise from an addiction to DRUGS (see '*Mark Kenyon says sorry*') than acquisitiveness.

Men committed a wider range of crimes than women and the range of merchandise they stole was generally varied. Watches were often targeted (as at the RACECOURSE) and culprits caught could expect imprisonment from 21 days to 6 months for watches valued at about £4. More severe penalties were applied to the theft of other goods of similar value.

Sentences were almost always harsh in the early days, although an occasional instance of leniency surfaced. Richard Gillam, discharged in 1816 by Magistrate Bates for lodging in the outhouse of a brewhouse, was imprisoned for a fortnight by John Cripps four years later for stealing a sack, and was again discharged by Bates in the same year for refusing to pay a fine and illegally playing a game.

Brighton's Chapman, Bishop and Gillam families were frequently in trouble, paying regular visits to the Courts.

An Old Bailey case, 1802

Few local cases made it to the Central Criminal Court but the following one did. It fell into the official category of 'Theft from a Specified Place' and concerned 18-year-old Eliza Jones, who was indicted on 28 April 1802 of stealing a considerable number of items, mainly from the Brighton dwelling house of one Thomas Sowerby, a milliner and 'fancy-dress maker'. She and others lodged with him to improve their knowledge of those trades and she had boarded from the end of December 1801 until 10 April 1802. The catalogue of articles stolen from Sowerby was a long one and included 58 pairs of stockings, lace (the highest value item at £25), muslin, sarcenet (a fine soft silk cloth), cambric and two silver tablespoons; from Thomas Lockwood, a silver tablespoon, value 10s; and from Susan Lockwood, a silver cream ewer (a decorative pitcher), value £1.5s. Jones was found part-guilty, that is to say guilty of stealing the goods, but not in the specified place of the dwelling house. She was sentenced to seven years' transportation.

Light-fingered juveniles, 1837

In January 1837, two boys named Coates and Philcox were charged with stealing some fruit from the shop of Madame App, in Middle Street. The two boys had apparently absconded with clothes belonging to the workhouse in company with another named Parsons, who was still at large. They were remanded until the following day when the Governor of the institution was ordered to be present.

In November, a lad named John Johnson, who reportedly appeared at the bar almost as frequently as the magistrates did on the Bench, was charged with stealing a whip from a milkman's wagon while it was being unloaded. He was remanded and committed for trial.

Mercer records the following early cases heard at the Epiphany Quarter Sessions in Lewes:

William Gates (14) Francis Watts (14) and James Reed (11) pleaded guilty to stealing a pair of galoshes from the shop of Mr Lulham, of Brighton. Gates and Watts, were each sentenced to three months hard labour, excluding the last fortnight in solitary; Reed, to one month's hard labour, and the last week in solitary.

John Ireland, fisherman, aged 15, for stealing 11 feet of copper pipe, the property of William Hope and others. Three months' imprisonment with hard labour, excluding the last fortnight in solitary.

A year later, Alfred Burnt, aged 13, received a three-month sentence for stealing lead and Charles Carpenter, aged 10, a month in the HOUSE OF CORRECTION plus a whipping for stealing money.

Severe penalties

Harsh sentences were handed out at the 1830 Assizes, when George Meason got a 6-month prison sentence with hard labour for stealing a pencil box. This was nothing compared with the case of three men who conspired to steal books in Lewes. Mercer relates they were caught on the Brighton Road and each received the death sentence.

Even as late as 1853, excessive punishments were being handed down. A magistrate named Carpenter sentenced 18-year-old Charles Tester to six months' hard labour for stealing one pot of marmalade.

Two female cases a century apart

Jane Archer, a single woman, aged 18, pleaded guilty at the 1837 Epiphany Quarter Sessions in Lewes to stealing, at Brighton, three glasses and other articles, the property of Edward Conford, her master. She was sentenced to three months' imprisonment with hard labour. Elizabeth Williams was charged at the same sessions with stealing, at Brighton, one pair of half boots, the property of William Tozer, and was given six months' imprisonment with hard labour.

A strange coincidence linked to a Brighton theft occurred at Southsea in 1937. Petulengro's band was playing on the pier when a spectator noticed that a pretty blonde violinist was wearing a bracelet similar to one missed by a friend of hers from a Brighton boarding house five months earlier. The musician, 23-year-old Ethel Jowsey, admitted stealing the bracelet when she appeared before Brighton magistrates. The bandmaster's wife pleaded for lenient treatment on her behalf. It transpired that during March and April, the band was playing on the West Pier. Jowsey was at that time lodging in Montpelier Place. When she left, her landlady, Mrs Dorothy Tindall, missed the bracelet. Questioned by police, Jowsey said it had been given to her six years earlier by an Indian student but later confessed she had taken it. 'I cannot think why I took it,' she told magistrates, 'it was a momentary weakness for which I am terribly sorry.' In view of the support from Mrs Petulengro, Jowsey was bound over on payment of 20s costs.

TOWN HALL – see also POLICE, BLACK HOLE

First impressions

The first stone of Brighton's present-day Town Hall was laid by TE Kemp in 1830.

JD Parry, visiting the new building three years later, describes in his *Guide* the lower storey of the edifice, containing its various offices for the MAGISTRATES and the 'handsomely fitted up' smaller rooms for their private sittings on the second floor, on which were also 'very capacious rooms for the Petty Sessions'.

The east elevation of the Town Hall c.1844. The artist, Brighton-born Frederick W Woledge, had three albums of his Brighton views published in the early 1840s. From 'Brighton revealed through artists' eyes', c.1960

An 1860s' snapshot
Erredge records the Town Hall being used for town meetings, public assemblies, the Council meetings, and the general purposes of the Borough. In it were offices for the Town Clerk and his staff, for the Collectors of the municipal and parish rates and for the Borough Surveyor and his staff. The MAGISTRATES occupied the southern basement and this was likewise used for the Borough Quarter Sessions.

The POLICE force, Erredge tells us, was originally established in the spring of 1830 under Chief-Officer Pilbeam, the Police Station then being in Steine Lane. The Superintendents were Owen Crowhurst and Isaiah Barnden. Officially, however, the year 1838 is taken as marking the start of the Constabulary (a centenary dinner was held in the Royal Pavilion on 18 May 1938). On its removal to the Town Hall, the force consisted of 80 men – inspectors, sergeants, and privates – who occupied the south-west portion of the basement, immediately adjacent to the Magistrates' Court. The dungeons for – perhaps innocent – detainees were in the most remote portion of the underground vaults at the north-east end of the building (see BLACK HOLE).

A portion of the principal room in the basement, to form the COUNTY COURT, was temporarily taken off by means of a partition, in two sections, which swung back on hinges to the side walls. The Court was held every alternate Friday, William Furner being the Judge (see SHERWOOD, CAROLINE). The only residents of the building were Friend Paine – the Hall-Keeper – and his wife.

TRADERS
Licensing and hawking
On 28 June 1800, George Jaques, a travelling hawker, was convicted by the Magistrates of trading without a licence in Brighton and was fined £10.

A curious case before the magistrates on 26 October 1837 was the charge brought under the Chimney Sweepers' Act against a little boy named Layton, employed by a sweep named Bolter, for hawking the streets in his trade. The penalty for the offence was 40s, or £2. A fellow-sweep by the name of Hill stated he had seen the boy hawking at two gentlemen's houses in Norfolk Square. This, he claimed, was prohibited by Act of Parliament. There was a distinction between *calling* in the street and *hawking* at the doors. A further opinion was sought in the court, which elicited that the definition of the verb 'to hawk' was 'to sell by proclaiming in the street'. As the charge against the lad was for 'hawking the streets', the Bench did not think this was what he had done and he was discharged. Hill, served with a demand for payment of the costs, commented: 'Then this Act of Parliament is no good to us at all.'

George Harris was placed in the dock on 8 June 1878 on a charge of hawking without a licence. Detective Roser said he saw him in North Street annoying passers-by and asked him if he had a licence. Harris produced two pieces of card but they were not a licence and he was taken into custody. He was fined 5s and costs or seven days' imprisonment.

TRADING STANDARDS
In April 1800, the Constables of Brighton found a quantity of new butter displayed for sale which was deficient in weight. They seized it and distributed it among the poor whom they deemed the most deserving.

A reference is made in the *Brighton Guardian* for 8 April 1835 to the cases of William Hellyer and Isaac Bass, on whom was imposed the standard £10 fine for defective weights.

James Barnes was summoned by the Town Clerk on 26 June 1878 for selling milk adulterated up to 10% with water. He pleaded guilty and was fined 20s and costs, or, in default, seven days' imprisonment. On the same occasion, Ann Baker was also charged with selling adulterated milk on 28 May. The product was 30% deficient of butterfat. She was given the same penalty as Barnes.

A serious charge of supplying diseased meat to the soldiers at Preston Barracks was brought in a summons in early December 1901 against John Henry Eckworth Trott of Camden Town, London. His agent, Joseph Jennings, of 11 Ephraim Villas, Bear Road, Brighton was summoned for aiding and abetting in the offence. When the slaughterhouse at 57 Oxford Court was visited on 6 November, the right and left hindquarter of an aged cow, with other portions of the carcase, were found. The carcase was emaciated and the cow had, during life, suffered from general tuberculosis. It was contended that the slaughterman could easily have seen that the meat was diseased. Even if the TB germs were killed by thorough cooking, the meat would have been unwholesome from the poison caused by the germs. The inflammation alone made the flesh unfit for food.

Trott, 77, thought the animal, purchased with others, had been sound enough. He had instructed Jennings to report to the Sanitary Inspector any problems he identified with meat. The charge against the agent was serious, for by stripping the diaphragm (which was not usually done) he revealed he had discovered the disease when dressing the carcase. The Bench fined Trott £5 on each of the two pieces of meat seized, while Jennings, who pleaded guilty to aiding and abetting, had to pay £2 10s on each piece plus costs.

TRAIN ROBBERIES

Although no mailbag heist can compare with the Great Train Robbery from the Glasgow-London express in August 1963 when the fabulous haul exceeded £2,500,000, there were local precedents – a number of raids had been made on the Brighton line in the previous three years.

On 18 August 1960, railway guard Reginald Scammel was overpowered on an afternoon express between Brighton and London by four men with flour bags over their heads. They escaped with £8,000 worth of registered packages – ripped out of a dozen mailbags – by walking away at Victoria with the loot in suitcases. Just over a month later, there was another, even more daring, robbery. Using a false key, three masked men in plastic raincoats entered the guard's van of the semi-fast 9.28 pm Victoria-Brighton train. As it approached Patcham, they overpowered the guard, Leonard Hooper, trussed him up and sorted through the mailbags. Hooper remembered the leader was brandishing a cosh and wore a red mask. The other two wore black masks. The men clearly knew exactly what they were looking for, since they quickly selected six mailbags containing registered packages. Near Patcham tunnel, an accomplice on the line switched a signal from green to red. As soon as the train stopped, the three robbers threw the bags onto the track, jumped down, and scrambled unseen over the embankment to a waiting car. The stolen mailbags, filled with unopened letters and soaked by rain, were later found by a postman in a ditch near Lewes. All the registered packets – including £9,000 worth of new pound notes expected by Brighton banks – had been removed. Following nationwide police investigations, three men and a girl were charged in January 1961 with receiving stolen property found in a Chingford house. The prosecution claimed that 176 travellers' cheques found there were part of the proceeds of the September robbery.

Tampering with signals would, of course, also be a feature of the Great Train Robbery.

By December 1960, railway guards were refusing to work on the Brighton line without adequate protection, so British Rail agreed to fit bolts and chains to the mail vans.

For well over a year, there were no more incidents. But on 11 April 1962, five men posing as railwaymen made a daring midnight mail snatch at Brighton Station. At 11.40 pm they casually picked out a buff-labelled white bag containing registered mail from a stack of postbags lying on the platform. The bags had been unloaded from the 10.28 train from Victoria. Although the thieves, wearing peaked caps and dark uniforms, were challenged by a postman, one of them said: 'It's all right, mate. We will look after this one. It's ours.' It certainly was. In the bag there were 222 registered items, mostly banknotes, worth about £15,000. Picking it up, they strolled to the end of Platform 5, dropped down onto the lines, and disappeared into the mist towards New England Road. The operation took seven minutes from start to finish.

Only four months later, in August, bandits struck again. This time a new method was used – fire. The men set light to an empty compartment of the 10.28 Wednesday night train from Victoria to Brighton. The blaze was seen when the train pulled into Preston Park. Passengers were ordered out and the electric current was switched off. Directly the guard left the van to help extinguish the flames, the rest of the gang stole two mailbags and walked unchallenged to a getaway car.

When police reconstructed the crime it became clear that one of the men had left a delayed-action firebomb in the train when he got out at Haywards Heath. The following April the mailbags were recovered from bushes near Devil's Dyke.

There was then a considerable lull, loudly punctuated by the mother of all train robberies in August that year.

But on the night of 23 November 1967, three bogus postmen bluffed railway staff at Hassocks station into handing over 13 mailbags. They strolled onto the platform as the London-Brighton train drew in and their leader calmly told the guard: 'We have come

The 3.47 Victoria-Brighton train at Gatwick Airport on 30 August 1958. There would be a number of robberies from mail vans on such units during the next decade. Jim Aston

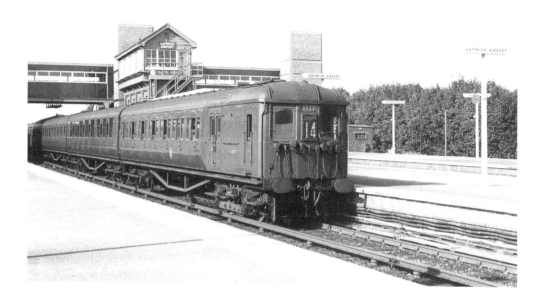

for the mail. There's a bit of congestion at Brighton tonight.' The loot was bundled into a red van, but despite the alarm being raised by a porter-signalman who realised it was the wrong time for collecting mail, the police road blocks failed to prevent the van's escape. Home-made postmen's uniforms were found the next day near Albourne and Balcombe.

In April 1970, two raiders halted a train outside Brighton's London Road station by pulling the communication cord. As soon as the guard had gone to investigate, a man ran into the van, grabbed a mailbag – containing 30 registered packets valued at about £3,000 – threw it over a fence to a waiting green van and was driven away. This time, finally, a culprit was caught. James Harris, 46, of East Dulwich, was charged and sent to prison for 18 months – a light sentence for someone with 10 previous convictions.

TRANSPORTATION

Transportation, i.e. the deporting of convicted criminals to a penal colony, punished both major and petty crimes in Britain from the seventeenth century until well into the nineteenth. It was seen at the time as a more humane alternative to execution. A sentence of transportation could apply for life or for a specified period. Returning from transportation was at one time a hanging offence.

Insights from Quarter Sessions rolls

Valuable insights into transportation sentences imposed on Brighton miscreants, *inter alia*, can be gained from the Quarter Sessions rolls of the first half of the nineteenth century for the Eastern Division of Sussex (i.e. the three eastern rapes of the County, including places now in West Sussex). A 1988 study by the Friends of East Sussex Record Office showed that of around 11,000 cases on index slips for the years 1810–1854, some 790 resulted in sentences of transportation overseas.

The listing prepared by the Friends contains only the names of those sentenced at Quarter Sessions. Since more serious cases were dealt with by the Assizes (whose records are in London), the number of potential transportees should probably at least be doubled. Also, sentences did not by any means equate to actual transportations, particularly in the earlier years.

Age, sex and occupation of transportees

The number of women sentenced throughout the period was low (7.9%), although this proportion rose slightly in the later period 1831–1854. The youth of those sentenced was striking, with nearly two-thirds aged 25 or under, and 8% aged 15 or under. It is worth remembering that women prisoners often saw transportation as a chance of a new future and many either admitted their guilt or grossly misbehaved in prison in the hope of transportation.

A Brighton boy (Edwin Robinson), at 9 years of age, was the youngest transportee. Twenty-five children (all boys) were sentenced who were aged 13 or under. Most were second offenders. Australian statistics, however, suggest that only 1% of those actually transported were under 15. They also show that the average age of criminals actually transported was 26, and that about 75% were single.

With Hastings virtually excluded from these lists, it is Brighton, with nearly one-third of all the East Sussex entries (268 out of 827), which overwhelmingly predominates in any 'league table' of transportation sentences.

In the great majority of cases, 'labourer' is the occupation recorded. 'Chimney sweep' was a common specific occupation and others included cordwainer, shoemaker, baker, bricklayer and carpenter.

Offences and sentencing patterns

Larceny – often of quite minor items – was the offence recorded in 96.5% of cases (the growth of Brighton as a town provided opportunities for urban crimes, such as theft from shops and businesses and picking pockets). Receiving accounted for a further 1% and fraud, embezzlement and false pretences for a further 1.3%. Australian figures suggest that between half and two-thirds of all those actually transported probably had previous convictions.

There were no records at all of transportation sentences in 1800, 1804–6 and 1810–11.

The fact that there were only three sentences in the timespan 1800–04 was probably due, in part at least, to the practical difficulties of sea transport in the period of the Napoleonic Wars. In 1831, 31 Sussex transportees were sent to Australia, eight of whom had been sentenced at Quarter Sessions. The late 1830s and early 1840s saw the highest rate of transportation sentencing. Nearly two-thirds of all transportation sentences (62.5%) were for seven years.

Interim accommodation and destinations

From 1790 to 1835, transportees from the County's Eastern Division were usually housed in Horsham Gaol until they could be forwarded to hulks or prisons in the Portsmouth Harbour area for onward dispatch. Later in this period the Thames began to be used more and more as an alternative destination.

A Thames hulk. Author's collection

Hulks were not used after 1843, when London's Millbank Prison became the sole destination. Horsham Gaol was superseded from 1835 by Lewes House of Correction as the local holding premises.

TREADMILL

Treadmills appeared in English gaols following the Penitentiary Act of 1779, under which prisoners should be given '. . . labour of the hardest and most servile kind in which drudgery is chiefly required and where the work is little liable to be spoiled by ignorance, neglect, or obstinacy . . .'

Sir William Cubitt, the noted nineteenth century civil engineer, designed a treadmill for English prisons whose aim was to generate power for mills. The contraption looked like a very wide paddle wheel. Workers held onto a bar and climbed the paddle blades in shifts that typically lasted eight hours. As many as ten prisoners worked the mill, being on the wheel for fifteen minutes and then resting for three.

Brighton had a treadmill and, of the four Sussex PRISONS in 1833 – Horsham (221 prisoners), Petworth (318), Lewes (1,085) and the smaller prison at Battle (44) – only Petworth and Lewes had treadmills.

John Davis and John Davey, 'two of the returned British Legion from Spain', charged with being drunk and begging in North Street in 1837, were discharged when asked whether they wanted 'to go to the treadmill or leave town'. They opted to leave town.

In 1838, vertical separators were placed between prisoners, each of whom laboured in isolation, repenting his crimes.

Treadmills were used right up to the end of the nineteenth century – Oscar Wilde, sent to prison for gross indecency in 1895, worked on one.

The Treadmill, House of Correction, Brighton. The illustration was submitted by a reader to Sussex County Magazine *in May 1932. His/her query as to the precise location of the (original) House remained – and remains, to this author's knowledge – unanswered.* Sussex County Magazine

TRUNK CRIME No. 1 – see also MANCINI, TONI

This was the name given by the police in the summer of 1934 to the murder of an unknown woman whose torso was discovered in a trunk deposited at Brighton railway station. Trunk Crime No. 2 was the murder of Violette Kaye, perpetrated earlier by TONI MANCINI but discovered later.

By an extraordinary coincidence, the discovery of the grisly contents of the trunk at the station happened at a time when Mancini was harbouring his partner's body in a trunk in Kemp Street, just a few hundred yards away.

Hardly anything is known about the left-luggage crime – who was killed, where the killing took place, or why. Mancini had nothing to do with it but his own crime was indirectly uncovered as a result of the investigation.

The drama began on the evening of Sunday 17 June 1934, when a brown trunk in the station luggage room was forced open. One of the staff, William Vinnicombe, had complained to the police about its offensive smell.

When Det Sgt Percy Scales (the brother of William – see RACECOURSE/RACES) opened the trunk, he found the naked torso of a woman. The body had been placed between two pieces of plywood and the trunk was stuffed with cotton wool to prevent any blood seeping through. The new canvas trunk, of a kind sold and bought every day, had been taken to the station and deposited on Derby Day. The remains were tied up with window cord and wrapped in brown paper. On the edge of the paper, written in blue pencil, was the word 'ford', which could have been part of a person's name or the final part of any number of place-names.

Chief Det Insp Robert Donaldson and Det Sgt Sergeant Sewell arrived in Brighton from Scotland Yard to assist Brighton's Chief Constable, Captain WJ Hutchinson, and a nationwide search was at once started.

There was a startling development on the evening of the day following the discovery. Acting on information from Brighton Police, Scotland Yard detectives visited London's King's Cross station and in the left-luggage department found a suitcase containing the body's legs. The case had been deposited on 7 June, the day after Derby Day, and in this instance too a railway attendant had noticed a peculiar smell. The legs were wrapped in newspaper and had been dissected through the knees.

Sir Bernard Spilsbury travelled to Brighton two days after the torso was found. His three-hour examination led him to call in Dr Roche Lynch, another pathologist, who made further examinations. Next day, Sir Bernard returned to London and examined the legs found at the LNER terminus. He confirmed they came from the Brighton body but although police searched everywhere for the killer, no progress was made. Spilsbury reported she was in her twenties, and certainly under 30. She was found to be pregnant and was about five foot three inches tall; she had brown hair and well-kept and trim toenails and had been healthy and well-nourished but not fat. Her arms had probably been severed and destroyed in case she was identified from her fingerprints.

Brighton journalist Leonard Knowles disclosed in March 1961, in an *Evening Argus* series 'Death in my Notebook', that the head had probably been found a week before the murder hunt without the police being aware of it. A young man, Frederick Claridge, and his fiancée, who lived in Blaker Street, said that while walking under the cliffs at Black Rock they had looked in one of the chalky rock pools of sea water and had seen a bloodstained newspaper and what they were sure was a woman's head. The girl had wanted to pull it from the water but the young man would not let her and they had left it. A report of this incident ultimately drifted through to the police, who raced to interview the couple, together and separately, and searched the foreshore area in question, with, as might be expected, no success.

Eight months after the discovery of the trunk at Brighton station, the investigation into the cause of death was officially closed at an inquest held on 20 February 1935. The Borough Coroner, Mr Charles Webb, sitting with a jury of seven men, announced that the case remained in the hands of the police, as the cause of death was deemed unascertainable.

TRUNK CRIME No. 2 – see MANCINI, TONI

U

UNREST, CIVIL – see also MODS AND ROCKERS

Fireworks in every sense, 1817

On Tuesday, 4 November 1817, the town Principal, James Day, and the High Constable, John Williams, resurrected an act originally introduced in Tudor times when many of Brighton's houses had thatched roofs. It banned the uncontrolled use of fire within the town and prohibited celebrations to commemorate the gunpowder plot which involved letting off fireworks and parading a blazing tar barrel through the streets.

Despite the prohibition, a number of people – chiefly boys – gathered at the Old Steine at twilight on the following evening and let off squibs, crackers and other fireworks. A 16-strong civil force of headboroughs and police, headed by Williams, immediately intervened and apprehended the offenders. This clash continued until nine o'clock, when a lighted tar-barrel made its appearance. The authorities captured and extinguished it, despite stout resistance by the populace, who directed their displeasure at the High Constable. They attacked his house, *The Baths*, in Castle Square and also turned on James White, the local rate collector and Williams' near neighbour, who had played a very prominent part in the affair. Stones were thrown with great violence and the windows of their houses were soon shattered. Greatly alarmed, Williams sent a message to Serjeant Runnington, Chairman of the Brighton Bench of Magistrates, and also to the guard-house at the Infantry barracks in nearby Church Street demanding help from the military. Several companies of the 21st Fusiliers, who had only arrived in Brighton that day, marched with fixed bayonets to the Steine, the avenues to which they quickly occupied.

The Riot Act was read by Runnington but several squibs were let off near the MILITIA so an attempt was made to capture the offenders. Egged on by the rate collector, the furious Principal repeatedly ordered the Fusiliers to advance into the crowd, which they reluctantly did. In the ensuing clashes one woman was shot in the head and two Fusiliers, Slaughter and Burt, were also wounded so badly by the stones thrown by the mob that they had to be carried to their quarters, where they remained for some time in a critical condition. John Rowles, 40, a local headborough, was bayoneted just above the hip by a soldier – so vigorously that three inches of blade emerged on the other side of his body. He lingered in the utmost agony until, at half-past seven the following evening, he died, leaving behind a pregnant wife and three infant children.

His passing is recorded in the severe lampoon by local poet Thomas Herbert (*War at Brighton, or The Battle of the Tar Tub, a short November Tale*) against the key players in this disturbance:

The word is pass'd, the soldiers prompt obey,
And to the Steine that instant march away.
[. . .]
The charge is made, alas poor luckless Rowles,
Thy life is gone, through these ambitious fools.

The affray went on for hours and it was not until two or three o'clock the next morning that the military returned to their barracks. On the following morning, the rioters were brought before the sitting magistrates – Serjeant Runnington and one Hopkins – at the Town Hall. The civil power was blamed for calling in the military. The coroner's inquest on Rowles returned a verdict, after eight days, of 'Wilful Murder' against James Day, the Principal, John Williams, the High Constable, and James White, stationer and general collector of rates, as accessories before the act.

Day, Williams and White surrendered to their bail at Horsham Assizes on 25 March 1818, where they were found not guilty. The judge expressed the strong view in regard to Williams and White that, far from any blame being attached to them, they had acted throughout with the greatest prudence, coolness and discretion.

An anti-profiteering protest, 1918
Munitions profiteers from the First World War, with their fat cigars and gold watch chains, were pilloried in *Punch* and doubtless fuelled the indignation of the poorer inhabitants of Brighton. Their wartime deprivations led to them making a protest march in 1918 to the offices of the Brighton Food Committee, carrying banners proclaiming: 'The Wives and Children of our Fighters shall not want for Food.'

Community charge demo, 1990
A rally was held on the Level in April 1990 to protest against the hated Community Charge, or 'poll tax', which had been brought in to replace the rating system. A 'Socialist Worker' banner in a photograph of the event proclaims 'STUFF THE POLL TAX'. Many of the demonstrators had burnt the bills they had received, as they had no intention of paying them.

'Reclaim the Streets', 1996
The only conclusion I can draw from Saturday is that the police don't get much opportunity down here to beat people up. (Teresa Blades, solicitor)

The aim of the RTS group in their beach party and demonstration of 24 August 1996 was not to close any roads but to open them for a few hours *'to give a vision of a car-free Brighton where we are not excluded from our streets through fear of death or injury, and where the streets are for people, not cars'.*

The event turned out to be anything but peaceful. Riot vans were stationed on many streets in the town. Some were parked across the bottom of West Street and riot police advanced from them. People were dragged from the marching crowd and bundled into the waiting vehicles. One woman was separated from her 10-month-old baby and put into the back of a van. The police used their vehicles to pursue the 500-strong spontaneous street march, which snaked through blocked roads for much of the afternoon. By 2 pm, they had seized a sound system, a bouncy castle and 100 bags of sand and collared two legal observers – all this before the event had started. In the mêlée, a woman on crutches was floored.

Green Party Councillor Pete West, who was asked to liaise with police on the day, was threatened with arrest when he tried to talk to Chief Inspector Mark Streater. He complained: 'The police absolutely lost control and self discipline.' He said that what had started off as a peaceful demonstration with dozens of small children and babies amongst the partygoers had ended with the police terrorising people with riot gear and fierce dogs.

The police described their operation, which cost £100,000, as successful. By the end of it all, 80 people had been arrested and 49 charged with various public order offences.

UNREST, INDUSTRIAL – see also POLICE

What has become known as the 'Battle of Lewes Road' occurred during the 1926 General Strike. It was preceded by about 6,000 trade unionists stopping work in Brighton in a show of their solidarity with their striking colleagues across the country – especially the miners, who were threatened with longer hours for lower pay. Many people in the town, which was brought to a halt more completely than any other in southern England, were, however, disgusted by the strike action of their fellow townspeople.

Days before the clash, about 2,000 strikers marched to the Town Hall in a bid to persuade the Transport Committee, then meeting, that trams should not be run by volunteers. But they were prevented from making their case by a large contingent of police in front of the building who diverted them away.

A week later, on that fateful Tuesday, 11 May, there were rumours that 13 volunteers had in fact entered the depot on Lewes Road and were going to take trams out to get public transport moving. Actually, what was being attempted was the introduction of volunteer drivers and conductors into the depot so that they could be trained in their duties. No fewer than 4,000 people – strikers, their families and onlookers – gathered outside the depot. Facing them were 200 policemen on foot, reinforced by 50 on horseback. These were hastily-recruited special constables (dubbed the 'Black and Tans' by the strikers after the brutal paramilitary force in Ireland), drawn from local farmers, sportsmen and other members of the middle classes. Each was armed with two batons. The combined force advanced on the crowd to clear the road, led by Chief Constable Griffin on foot.

The *Brighton and Hove Herald* of 15 May reported the incident as follows:

> *Outside the tram depot in Lewes Road, police and strikers came into violent collision. A great crowd, mostly of well-intentioned people, but with an infusion of dangerous and despicable roughs, found itself in conflict with the forces of law and order [. . .] It was a deplorable sight, such as has not been equalled in the memory of the oldest inhabitant. It was also an unforgettable sight to see the steady advance of the police, in a wedge formation that widened out until it filled the roadway. At the head walked the Chief Constable, Mr Charles Griffin. He was heard calling out to the strikers to disperse and not to use violence. His attitude was firm, and conciliatory. He seemed quite indifferent to his personal danger.*

Griffin later said he gave four warnings before ordering the specials to charge. Although struck with batons as the horses charged into them, the strikers hit back, using stones, bottles and pieces of wooden fence. Many among the crowd were injured, as were several police officers – one seriously. The demonstrators were finally forced back until they reached the Saunders Recreation Ground.

The foot police made 22 arrests among the scattering crowd. Following the arrival of police reinforcements and a cordon being thrown around the depot, the area was quiet again by 2 pm.

Ready for any eventuality. Brighton's mounted police in Brighton Place, probably between the wars.
Chris Horlock collection

Handcuffed and paraded through the town to the cells, the arrested men appeared the next day before the magistrates, chaired by John Lord Thompson, Mayor of Brighton.

The rebels were severely punished, some receiving up to six months' hard labour. Relatives and friends watched them being transported from the Town Hall to Portsmouth Gaol in a fleet of cars. An even more bitter blow for Brighton's unionists came that day with the TUC calling off the General Strike.

The forces of order were rewarded by certificates from the council and each serving officer was given three days' leave. In a resolution passed by the Watch Committee, the men were praised for their 'splendid services'. The mounted specials held a victory parade near the Town Hall and many of them attended a celebration dinner. A large number of bystanders who had seen them in action, however, would be deeply resentful and distrustful of them and the regular police for a very long time. The managers of the transport company were also resented for never taking back many of the strikers.

UNREST, STUDENT

One of the most infamous protest incidents of the 1960s took place at the University of Sussex in February 1968. Red paint (it was originally intended to have been pig's blood) was thrown over an American attaché, Robert M Beers, who gave a talk, 'Vietnam in Depth', at Falmer House. A major rumpus was caused by the burning of the US flag. Sean Lineham, who had thrown the paint, was suspended. This led to a student strike, with picket lines and placards. Only with the personal intervention of the Vice-Chancellor, Professor Asa Briggs, was the matter resolved. He said the student's suspension was only temporary. There were subsequently accusations that plain-clothes policemen were operating at the University looking out for who might cause further trouble.

UPTON, THOMAS

There are still unanswered questions about the shooting of attractive 20-year-old Nellie Vivian, or Peacock, at 6 Clifton Street, Brighton, on 26 November 1901, at the hands of Thomas Alfred Upton, 29, her lover – a lover who then blew his brains out. The case is riddled with lies, half-truths and enigma. The motive behind the killing can only be conjectured.

The property stood not far west of Brighton Station and the drama unfolded in the first-floor front room, used as a bedsit by Mrs Vivian. The couple had separate accommodation in the house, since Upton, who lodged in the top back bedroom, was an occasional visitor from his home town of Aldershot. Mrs Bate, the landlady was oblivious to – or more likely connived at – the time he spent in the woman's accommodation. Upton, with a wife and five children back home (the youngest just a month old) had only been seeing Nellie Vivian for a month before the tragedy. He had been coming to Brighton to (also) visit his brother, William, who lived at 6 Islingword Street.

At lunchtime on the fatal day, Mrs Bate called her lodger down for her meal and was assured she would be straight down. She failed to appear, and the landlady heard her scream: 'Don't, Tom!' Almost immediately afterwards, a shot rang out, followed by a second when she reached the landing to investigate. The couple were on the floor of Nellie's room. Upton had his arm around his mistress and blood was pouring from their heads. Mrs Bate ran terrified into the street to raise the alarm. Upton died as soon as the doctor entered the room and the girl, although only unconscious, died later at the County Hospital, her face and head terribly shattered by the bullet. She lingered until within an hour or so of the opening of the inquest on the body of her lover, on Wednesday afternoon, but never recovered sufficiently to be able to give any statement.

At the inquest, some truths began to emerge. Thomas Upton had purportedly been a gymnastics instructor in the army stationed at Aldershot but his wife revealed he had been a lithographer and had never been in the Army. He had been giving her £2 a week, but not recently. The weapon he used was an out-of-date service revolver. Medical evidence showed he had probably put his arm around his lover to hold her still while he shot her, then had put the gun into his own mouth and fired.

One week before the tragedy, Mrs Vivian had told Mrs Bate of a death threat from Upton. Following a quarrel on the eve of the shooting, she told the same thing to Ada Bowler, the landlady's domestic assistant/companion – and relative. Yet neither of the women had asked the reason for it.

Several letters to his lover, some with army addresses, were read. They were affectionate but all mentioned suicide. In one he wrote that he was trying to give up heavy drinking, in another he declared: '... I hope you will believe me when I say I care for you more than anything else' and in a third – ominously – 'you will be in my last thoughts.' Suicide had also figured in Nellie's thoughts. In an undated note in pencil found in her room, she had written: 'Everything that I leave behind, please send to Mrs Peacock, Church Farm, north Lancing. Tell her my husband is dead.' On the envelope she had written: 'To be opened when I am dead.'

In fact, Elizabeth Anne Peacock, a farm labourer's wife, did not believe her daughter had ever married a man by the name of Herbert Vivian since Nellie would never bring him home to meet her. Although she had seen her the previous month, she had never heard her speak of Upton. She understood the girl had been in service as a parlourmaid, first in Brighton then in Ventnor Villas, Hove.

Ada Bowler said Nellie had always paid her 25s a week promptly. She thought the girl had an allowance and believed her work had been at a confectioner's. She reluctantly

No. 6 Clifton Street, is behind the tree. Was it also a house of ill-repute? A previous suicide there was mentioned at the Coroner's inquest. The author

admitted, when pressed, that men had called at the house in connection with that employment. This, combined with the landlady's shiftiness and lack of cooperation, put a different slant on life at 6 Clifton Street. The coroner expressed what was obviously in people's minds when he said: 'It has been hinted that this [house] has been used for improper purposes.' Mrs Bate also came into direct confrontation with Tom Upton's widow. Suspecting what her husband was up to, Mrs Upton had written to her from Aldershot under the false name of Manthorpe asking for apartments, having found an advertisement card for the address in Clifton Street in her husband's clothes. She had thought of going to Brighton to find out who he was seeing in the town. Mrs Bate strongly denied receiving any such letter and claimed never to have replied to anyone in Aldershot in her life. Yet Mrs Upton was emphatic that she had had the letter, signed 'K. Bate', in which the landlady had written that her husband had just died and she had no room. She had shown it to several people.

After 10 minutes' absence, the jury returned a verdict of wilful murder against Thomas Upton for the death, by shooting, of Nellie Vivian. They also found that he had committed *felo de se*.

Mrs Bate and Ada Bowler were judged to have been such unsatisfactory witnesses that their attendance expenses were withheld. By contrast, a subscription was opened by the coroner for the penniless Mrs Upton and her young family (in a strange parallel with the Hibbert case, which had unfolded a few hundred yards away, she attended the inquest with her baby in her arms). The sum raised at the court was £5 16s, boosted later by readers of the *Gazette* and *Herald* when they learned of the unusual and deserving appeal.

USURY

Erredge recorded that discounters and usurious money-lenders abounded in the town in his day. Their main business was conducted amongst those whose bills and promissory notes were not recognised by the regular bankers, who refrained from any transactions which could lead to proceedings in the County Court. Thus exorbitant bonuses and interest were exacted, the levels exceeding what fair trading could meet. Non-fulfilment of payment became, then as now, the precursor of ruin.

V

VAGRANCY

The 1824 Vagrancy Act was introduced in the depression after the Napoleonic Wars to get destitute soldiers off the streets. Both begging and 'wandering abroad and lodging in the open air' were made an offence. The police thus had powers to arrest a wide variety of undesirables found loitering in the streets, including Poor Law offenders, various prostitutes, beggars and tramps, fortune-tellers, unlicensed pedlars, sellers of obscene literature and persons suspected of intending to commit more serious crimes.

By and large, the police found enforcing the Vagrancy Act tedious, at best. The distinction between drunks and vagrants was in practice often arbitrary and both groups clogged up the legal system with men (and sometimes women) who were more of a danger to themselves than to the public at large. In the later decades of the nineteenth century, vagrancy was seen as almost as great an evil as drunkenness, and in some ways a more complex one.

Under English law today, it is not only tramps who do not make use of available shelter who are classified as vagrants but also prostitutes behaving indecently in public, pedlars trading without a licence, persons collecting for charity under FALSE PRETENCES and those armed with offensive weapons.

Pre-Victorian vagrancy cases

By order of Brighton's Vestry in 1796, all vagrants and beggars were to be apprehended by the Crier, who was to receive a shilling a head for their capture. JG Bishop comments, in *A Peep into the Past*, that this was a 'substantial addition to his salary, possibly; and, as beggar-hunting was profitable, doubtless the town enjoyed considerable immunity from vagrants'.

Early female vagrants in Brighton included 15-year-old Jane Hughes, who in 1814 was committed to hard labour for seven days for vagrancy. Because Elizabeth Connary had three children she was dismissed in 1817 on a similar charge of vagrancy and begging. A woman seen begging in Bread Street in the same year was committed for one month.

The Petty Sessions Minute Books covering the period 1816–30 record that a large number of vagrants, drawn by the prospect of work and cheap lodging houses, found themselves before the Bench, to be returned to their own parish or thrown out. Some were put to work on bridges or roads. Those with no work, lodgings, money or food were mainly discharged providing they left town. Loitering charges became more common as the number of watchmen was increased.

One Randle was seen begging on 11 April 1816 and asked to stop; later in the day, he was seen begging in Ship Street and again he promised to stop. Later still he was 'knocking at Mrs Bryan's house'. Despite offending three times, he was discharged and promised to leave town. Yet in the same year, a man called Penfold was given his longest sentence for begging: 3 months. In 1829, it was noted that beggars became insulting if refused money at the door.

In that year, the magistrate Samuel Milford had 15-year-old William Cox imprisoned with hard labour and whipped twice privately for 'wandering unlawfully and being a rogue and a vagabond'. Three years later Milford had the same youth imprisoned for 12 months and whipped again privately, his crime being that he was a rogue, vagabond and beggar.

Alexander Cole had the misfortune to fall into the authorities' hands. He was committed to the House of Correction at Lewes for three months, as a 'Vagrant for telling fortunes'. He had lived in Brighton since September 1832 with wife Elizabeth and their six children and traded as, in his own words, a 'dealer in feathers and hare and rabbit skins'. In May of the following year, two officers came to his house and took away his wife on a charge of telling fortunes. He followed to the Town Hall with the rest of his family to hear the charge against her. In fact, he and his whole family were sent to Lewes House of Correction for three months, Cole himself being kept to hard labour. Worse was to come. While the family were at Lewes their household furniture and effects were sold. Cole was especially concerned about the loss of £40, in a feather bolster, that he 'had particularly put by for the purpose of setting his two boys one 14 the other 10 years old to some business,' together with the £7 that was in a stocking, of which only £5-11-6 was accounted for.

At the end of January 1837, John Corney, a lad who was an itinerant singer and dancer at public houses, was charged with being found, two days earlier, in the churchyard at night going to sleep. He said he was from Liverpool, but that he had been travelling round Chatham, London, etc. and that it was too late to get a lodging after he had done his amusements on Saturday evening. He was committed for one month and warned by the harsh magistrate Sir David Scott that he would go for three if he came before the Bench again. Corney laughingly thanked him. Scott's response: 'You are very welcome', provoked laughter in the Court.

In the same year, three men were discovered 'sleeping in flys in West Street' and a vagrant was committed for six weeks.

No laughing matter, 1866
John Barber, 25, of respectable demeanour, was charged on 5 July 1866 with begging in Glo'ster [sic] Place the previous day. He had been in Brighton for quite some time and had recently fixed upon that locality as a suitable spot, taking up his position on the edge of the kerb, with a child in his arms. The scantily-clad child, lacking protection from occasional downpours of rain, had died. Barber claimed he had no other means of getting a livelihood, as his health did not permit him to work. The Clerk to the Magistrates, Mr Verrall, said he would not have interested himself so much in the case had the prisoner not treated the matter with such levity and shown such a disinclination to give any explanation of his circumstances. The Bench committed Barber to the HOUSE OF CORRECTION for seven days with hard labour.

A week later, William Fox was likewise committed to the House with the same sentence for begging in Camelford Street.

Twentieth Century developments
At the beginning of the twentieth century, 30% of all males in English prisons were without fixed abode and with no regular means of subsistence; while approximately half were birds of passage charged specifically under the Vagrancy Act. Available figures suggest that each year up to 1914 between 5,000 and 12,000 tramps were prosecuted for sleeping rough; about twice as many beggars were prosecuted.

On 20 June 1901, for example, Catherine McCarthy, 36, was charged with begging in Western Road the previous afternoon. She was convicted and committed to seven days' hard labour.

A reform of the Vagrancy Act in 1935 confined the law to those persistently refusing the offer of a bed or directly causing a nuisance. Mere sleeping-out ceased to be a crime, while prosecutions for begging remained well below the figures from the beginning of the century. The campaigns in the 1960s demonstrated, however, that homelessness and destitution had by no means been abolished but largely transferred to the responsibility of the welfare system instead of the police.

Although repealed in Scotland, the 1824 Vagrancy Act was increasingly used against the homeless in England in the 1980s and 1990s. In 1989 in London there were 1,386 convictions for vagrancy.

VEHICLE CRIME

Briggs *et al* record that in 1900, six years after the first vehicle appeared on the roads, transgressions of the law constituted just four cases in a thousand found guilty in magistrates' courts. By 1930, with a little over two million vehicles on the road, they accounted for 43% of all non-indictable offences and had passed 60% by the time war broke out.

The speed limit was raised from 4 to 12 miles per hour in 1898 and to 20 in 1904, where it remained until it was abolished in 1930; it was reimposed in 1935 at 30 miles per hour in built-up areas.

Early fines

Dangerous driving, albeit a rare offence two centuries ago, might now and then come up at the Petty Sessions. For driving a carriage in a furious manner on Marine Parade in 1816, a driver was fined 10s plus costs of 12s 6d. A similar fine was imposed in 1825 on a driver caught driving a horse-drawn wagon on the pavement.

One of the very first parking fines was handed out to one Henry Boxall, 'a sort of ruler of the market', for leaving his horse and cart for one and a half hours whilst unloading.

Incidents in 1901

In November and December of this year, a number of cases came before magistrates which reveal an extraordinary (to our eyes) perception of speed.

Max Lawrence of Birmingham was summoned by the Chief Constable for having driven at an excessive rate of speed along Gloucester Place and St George's Place. The defendant admitted he was 'travelling at a fair pace'. A witness being driven in a cab northwards along Gloucester Road testified to being passed by a motor car at about 20 miles an hour. The maximum speed anywhere was 12 miles an hour and even that would be too great having regard to the traffic. The cabman said the car 'went by like a flash of lightning'. The magistrate imposed a penalty of £5 and costs, which, he pointed out, 'was by no means the limit to the fines which could be imposed for a similar offence'.

Also before the Bench was Rowland Brown of Clarendon Terrace, Kemp Town, and Branham Gardens, Earl's Court. He had been driving his car at too great a speed on Marine Parade, namely 16–18 miles per hour. A witnessing cabman agreed with the

A 1903 Lanchester 12 hp 4-litre motor car (Dr FW Lanchester (1868–1946) designed and built the first practical British 4-wheeled petrol vehicle in 1895). Author's collection

estimated speed but grudgingly admitted that the driver did seem to have proper control of his machine. The defendant argued he was going at less than even the statutory maximum of 12 mph. But this case was the last straw: he had endured so much police persecution that he had sent his machine back to London. In this case, also, a penalty of £5 and costs was imposed.

By contrast, Ambrose Gander was fined 10s and costs at the same session for driving a horse and cart at too great a pace in North Street.

North Street was also the thoroughfare along which a cyclist rode furiously ('at quite twelve miles an hour'), according to PC Sicklemore. Henry Gates, of Ranelagh Villas, Hove, and a witness on his behalf, did not think he had been going above eight miles an hour. The policeman pointed out that the defendant not only had to duck under the head of horse pulling a van from out of Ship Street but, as a result, collided with a sandwichman. Both men were thrown to the ground. Fine: 2s 6d. Another cyclist, George Hogarth, had gone even faster than Gates in Ditchling Road on the same day, for which he was fined 5s and costs.

The following month, Cope Cornford of 54 Eaton Place was fined as much for insolence as the offence of riding his bicycle without lights in the town after dark. In the first case of such a nature to come up for a long time, the defendant was ordered to pay £1 and costs. He would probably not even have been summoned had he not been excessively rude to the policeman who stopped him. He insulted the officer and swore at him, and finally jumped on his machine and rode away. Rudeness does not pay.

Encouraging figures

It was reported in August 2000 that car crimes had been slashed in Brighton after a new crackdown (see BURGLARY). Thefts of and from vehicles had been cut by more than a quarter – from 101 cases a week to 78 – since June, figures that bucked national trends. But a car crime still occurred every two hours.

In 2006, vehicle crime was at its lowest for a decade.

VICTIM CONTACT SCHEME

This offshoot of the Probation Service was set up in Sussex in 1995 through a Government directive whereby victims of crime and their families should be offered support after conviction. Prior to that date, the victims of violent sexual offences were often left in the dark about what had become of their assailant or when – if ever – the person was likely to be released.

The Scheme's role was to get in touch with victims of serious crime (murder, manslaughter, death by dangerous driving, all sex offences, actual bodily harm (ABH), grievous bodily harm (GBH) and robbery).

When it started in 1995 the victim would only be contacted if their attacker had received more than four years in custody. This, however, changed in 2001 when it was realised there were many people needing help who did not fit the Scheme's criteria – namely that the offender had to have received a custodial sentence of 12 months or more, that there had to be a sexual or violent element to the crime, and that there had to be an identifiable victim.

Support workers, of whom there are three in Brighton and Hove, East Sussex and West Sussex, take on an average of nearly one new case every day and will stay in touch with the victim while their attacker is in prison or out on licence. The Scheme has reportedly encouraged more people to come forward and report crimes because they know there is a network in place to support them throughout the process and afterwards.

In contrast to the Probation Service, which works only with offenders, the team will only work with victims who are contacted only if something significant happens, such as the offender appealing against his/her consideration for parole or any form of temporary release, or if he/she is moved from a high-category prison to an open one. Victims of lifers who were imprisoned before the Scheme started have also been contacted and given the chance to opt in, as have, in discretionary cases, elderly or vulnerable people in fear of violence.

WARDER, Dr ALFRED

Dr Alfred Warder was a lecturer on poisons at the Grosvenor Place School of Medicine in London. On 23 May 1866, he and his 36-year-old wife, Ellen (who had married the doctor only five months earlier – without the knowledge of any of her family), took furnished rooms at 36 Bedford Square, Brighton. Ellen's brother, Richard Branwell, was a well-known local surgeon and lived in nearby Cambridge Road, Hove.

She soon became unwell, having hysterical attacks, constantly having to pass water and suffering severe bladder pains. She was initially treated by her husband but her condition deteriorated. Her brother anxiously called in the widely-respected Dr RPB Taaffe, (who would two years later found the Brighton Hospital for Sick Children at 178 Western Road). Yet the medicine he prescribed (Fleming's Tincture of Aconite) failed to restore the patient, although it did allay the pain. He changed the remedies but Dr Warder told him after some days that his wife had tired of them and could not keep them down.

Despite a further change in medicines, Ellen Warder's condition worsened, with continuing vomiting and pains. Fresh symptoms appeared, including a swelling and whitening of the tongue. All these were explained away by her husband.

On Sunday, 1 July, an anxious Mr Branwell called at the house at 5.30 am and found his sister dead. He was puzzled by the death and could not understand the cause. When Dr Taaffe examined her later, he was not satisfied that her death was natural. The post mortem did not reveal the cause of death, so he refused to sign the death certificate. This meant an inquest had to be held. It took place some days later at the *Olive Branch Inn* (later the *Rockingham Inn* and now *Whelan's Lion and Lobster*) in nearby Silwood Street, but was adjourned for six days to allow another doctor to make a detailed analysis of the contents of the dead woman's stomach. The widower was served with a notice to attend the adjourned inquest a week later.

Warder had, however, made up his mind to kill himself directly his wife's death began to be investigated. He wrote to a friend, making arrangements for the disposal of his personal property 'in the event of anything happening' to him. On 9 July he went to London, returning in the evening to his lodgings in Bedford Square. After asking his landlady for his bill, which was sent up by a servant the next morning, he booked in at the nearby *Bedford Hotel*.

When he did not appear downstairs next morning, his hotel room was entered and his lifeless, undressed body was found on the bed. A bottle and a nearby glass on a bedside table were found to contain prussic acid. A note he had delivered by hand to his landlady began: 'You have already suffered enough through me and mine and another death in your house would, of course, be worse.'

Dr Alfred Warder was buried at 10.30 on the night of his death, with no ceremony and in considerable haste, for in those days SUICIDE was regarded as a civil crime as well as a religious sin. The hearse was accompanied to the parish cemetery by a few policemen holding lanterns and followed by an understandably curious crowd. The whole ritual, from the arrival of the hearse at the gates to the completion of the interment, took about four minutes.

The final inquest on Ellen Warder was held at the *Olive Branch* on 16 July, following an adjournment three days earlier. Two toxicologists from Guy's Hospital reported that, while no poisons had been found in the body, this was quite consistent with poisoning by aconite (also known as wolf's bane). If small doses had been given within two or three hours of death, no trace would be found in the stomach. No other man knew better than Dr Warder, of course, how to administer the substance. The jury almost immediately returned a verdict that Mrs Ellen Vivian Warder had died from the effects of aconite administered wilfully and of malice aforethought by her late husband, Alfred William Warder, who had since killed himself.

The *Brighton Herald* suggested that Mrs Warder was not his first victim, but his third, for the doctor had been married three times. Each wife had died in suspicious circumstances and each time the evil doctor's motive had been greed for what he could inherit.

WELSHING – see also RACECOURSE

Welshing is swindling a person by not paying a debt or wager, or failing to fulfil an obligation.

In *The Brighton Races*, Jim Beavis describes the growing prevalence of this form of dishonesty. 'Welshers', whose numbers increased as more and more bookmakers appeared during the nineteenth century, would vanish without paying winning punters. To lure bets, they offered slightly better odds on some horses, although if the wrong horse looked like winning, they would make their escape while the race was in progress. Others stood their ground and resorted to violence: bookmaker Dyke Wilkinson wrote of being beaten up in the ring at Brighton in the 1870s after becoming involved in a dispute with some of the most notorious welshers. These more aggressive types of welshing bookmakers faced up to some punters when they came to collect and simply refused to pay. The punter had made a mistake, they would say, or was trying to pull a fast one. Beavis remarks:

> *With some burly accomplices on hand to look threatening, and ready to resort to violence, the betting ring could indeed be a jungle, especially when members of the local constabulary could be bribed to turn a blind eye. Many were based in London, which was particularly fertile territory for them given the number of race meetings held in its suburbs at that time.*

WHITTAKER, MARK

Mark Whittaker was arrested on 16 November 1998 in St James's Street, Brighton, during an on-the-spot drug search. He was remanded in custody at Lewes Prison as it was found that he was wanted for an offence in Seaford in which he had burgled the local library. Just over a fortnight later, he was overheard by a warden talking on the telephone to his brother, saying: 'What happened was manslaughter on the grounds of diminished responsibility.' When questioned about this, he responded: 'I do not remember a thing about it. I panicked.'

The event he was referring to was the murder, in a frenzied axe attack in the early hours of 14 November, of Michael Furnival, 34, known as 'the cowboy man' because of the distinctive hat and boots he always wore. The victim lay undiscovered in his flat in Queensway, in Brighton's Craven Vale area, for more than two weeks until concerned neighbours told police they had not seen him around. Whittaker, who admitted murder, had been close friends with Furnival but a row over drugs soured their friendship.

When police broke into the locked flat they found the victim lying face-down on a mattress covered with a duvet. Forensic experts discovered there had been a fight in the living room. The weapon was found lying on a coffee table. A pathologist discovered 27 separate injuries to his head, at least 20 of which had been caused by heavy blows from the axe. What was worse, Whittaker had, soon after the attack, cashed the social security benefits book belonging to Furnival and another man living in the flat. He told the postmaster that 'the cowboy man' was unable to collect his benefit because he had drunk too much.

Both the victim and his killer had a drink and drug problem. Nick Price, defending Whittaker, said the prisoner remembered hitting Mr Furnival in the face but was 'astonished and horrified' to discover that he had hit him so many times with the axe. He claimed on his client's behalf that there could be 'no better example of a genuine, heartfelt sense of remorse than this case'. Judge Richard Brown, however, jailing Whittaker for life, described the murder as a 'horrendous and wicked attack'.

Less than 48 hours after Furnival's body was found battered to death, a second murder inquiry was launched in Brighton – see NIGEL NOLAN.

WIFE-SELLING

At Brighton in February 1799 a Mr Staines sold his wife to a Mr James Marten for 5s and eight pots of beer.

In May 1826 a wife was sold at Brighton market for a sovereign and four half crowns. She had two children; the elder was retained by the husband while the baby was 'thrown in' as part of the deal. The sale was entered in the Brighton market register, and the purchaser paid a shilling to the auctioneer, and a shilling for the halter. It was reported that the woman seemed perfectly happy and went off with her new master with her infant in her arms.

WILTON, WILLIAM

For 15-year-old George Hollingdale, the nightmare began at his home, 10 Cavendish Street, Brighton, early on the morning of Saturday, 9 July 1887. He lived there with his mother, Sarah Wilton, and stepfather, William Wilton, a wheelwright. The property had been rented since March and was so small that they all shared a bedroom. The relationship between husband and wife, both drinkers, was a troubled one.

The lad left for work at 5.10 am and returned at 7.55 am. The front door was locked, so he got in through the window. Then he saw blood dripping from the side of the bed onto the floor. Pulling the bed covering down, he saw his mother with her throat cut. On the washstand he saw a knife covered with blood. He screamed for help and rushed for assistance from his next door neighbour.

Wilton's working clothes were found in the room so he must have put on his best clothes before leaving the house. Young George gave the police the names of the public houses frequented by his stepfather. It was only a matter of hours before the murderer was apprehended at the *Windmill Inn*, Dyke Road (now the *Dyke Road Tavern*) on the strength of that information alone. Wilton knew he would be tracked down. Apprehending him, PC Standing told him he would be charged with murdering his wife that morning by cutting her throat with a knife. He replied: 'Yes, I done it; she deserved it a long time ago.' When charged at the Town Hall, he responded: 'Yes, I did it.'

The examination of the case by magistrates at Brighton Town Hall was held very promptly on the morning of Monday, 11 July. Among the exhibits shown were the ordinary dinner table-knife, similar to a cheese knife, used to cut the victim's throat, and the other weapon used, a heavy carpenter's hammer, with which Sarah Wilton's skull was smashed. Both these murderous implements had been left quite openly in the family bedroom with no attempt at concealment. Disturbing medical evidence was heard by the court. None of the wounds could have been self-inflicted. The fracture of the skull with the hammer would by itself have caused death – mercifully before the cutting of the throat. During the 5-hour-long proceedings at Lewes Assizes in August, the defence valiantly tried to show, by citing the behaviour of relatives and of Wilton himself, that the man was insane due to a hereditary taint. As for the attack, it was theorised that Wilton had a struggle with his wife and in a moment of passion threw her back against the bedpost. The wound to her temple killed her.

This argument was speedily demolished by the prosecution. Mr Justice Hawkins, addressing Wilton, told him that even if his poor wife had given some offence in pawning some of his property, it was a cruel, wicked, merciless revenge he had inflicted on her without one moment's warning. It took the jury less than quarter of an hour to bring in a verdict of Guilty.

Wilton heard the sentence unmoved. Until the week before his execution, on Monday 29 August 1887, he showed no remorse or contrition. The scaffold was the one which had been used for LEFROY six years earlier. The hangman, Berry, who during his four years' experience had despatched no fewer than 106 persons, said that Wilton was the strongest-nerved man he had ever executed.

WOOD, GEORGE

On the afternoon of Friday, 11 December 1891, the mutilated body of 5-year-old Edith Jeal from Bedford Buildings was found by a Corporation workman. It lay in a large shed in a playing field bounded to the north by Eastern Road, Kemp Town and to the south by Chesham Road. She had been strangled and sexually assaulted, her private parts being severely lacerated.

The previous evening, Edith had been sent on some errands, in company with her 9-year-old brother, Bertram. When he went into Trengrove's, at the corner of Manchester Row, off Upper Bedford Street, he left his sister standing outside. It was there that she met the stranger who violently murdered her. Bertram, on emerging from the shop, thought she might have run home. Neighbours whom the little girl might have gone to were visited and Edith's father went out searching for her all night, to no avail.

The perpetrator was, however, quickly traced. George Henry Wood, 29, a delivery man at Brighton Station, lived a couple of hundred yards away from the crime scene, at 11 Rock Street. On the night of the murder, he had left his work at the station at about 6 pm and, still in railway uniform, had gone out drinking locally. The police were able to trace his movements without difficulty. After visiting a number of pubs in Trafalgar Street, he was seen around 45 minutes later in Sydney Street carrying a small child in his arms. When he fell over in the roadway, she ran off. Several people noticed him staggering about on his route eastwards to Edward Street, where he found another tavern. At about 8 pm, he was met in Lavender Street by a policeman who had known him for 10 years. PC Tuppen advised him to go home but he went off unsteadily round the corner.

Wood actually fell up against one witness, Rose Leggatt, at the corner of Montague Street and Upper Bedford Street. She saw him putting his hand towards a little child outside Trengrove's and saw her follow him to the middle of Somerset Street. There he was sighted by Mrs Alice Guy, who saw him pass her house at 8.20. She was standing by her front door and watched him walking unsteadily carrying a little girl, who was crying. She called out: 'Don't hurt that poor little thing.' The man turned round under the lamplight and she saw his face distinctly. She was sure it was Wood. Harry Spicer, a printer, saw a man carrying a child pass him in Eastern Road at about ten to nine. His face was hidden in the child's clothes.

Blood was found on the murderer's clothes when he was arrested on the afternoon the body was found. He had, in addition, apparently talked about the murder before it had been announced. His response throughout subsequent proceedings, and in personal letters, was that he had been drunk and could not now believe he had committed such a terrible act, of which he had no recollection.

Wood (who had, incidentally, been engaged to be married) was brought to trial for Edith's murder at Lewes on 6 April 1892 before Mr Justice Mathew. Defending counsel, Mr CF Gill – a noted Sussex barrister who was MARSHALL HALL's senior partner – told the jury that the prisoner had been suffering from epileptic insanity. The crime was so horrible that it must have been performed by an insane man. He said Wood was a confirmed epileptic and when drunk had no idea what he was doing. Dr CE Saunders, Medical Superintendent of the Sussex County Lunatic Asylum, said he had made a special study of insanity and epilepsy. He had examined the prisoner twice and he seemed perfectly rational. There were no indications of epileptic mania. Dr Sheppard, another specialist, gave evidence that he had found Wood depressed but quite collected. He was not insane by any means.

The judge had no time for the epilepsy/insanity speculations. If Wood had no recollection of what had happened on the fateful evening, why had he claimed that he had been at the circus? Was he unconscious when carrying the child through the street? The jury, too, were quite clear in their view. After only eight minutes, they returned a verdict that Wood was guilty of wilful murder and sentence of death was duly passed.

The Home Secretary rejected a petition started in Brighton for Wood to be sent to a criminal lunatic asylum. He saw no reason to interfere with the law and child-killer George Henry Wood was executed at Lewes Prison on 26 April 1892.

Bibliography

Books

Baines, Gerald W — *History of the Brighton Police, 1838–1967*, c.1967, Brighton, Borough Police Watch Committee.

Bardens, Dennis — *Famous Cases of Norman Birkett K.C.*, London, Robert Hale Ltd, 1963.

Beavis, Jim — *The Brighton Races*, Brighton, Jim Beavis, 2003.

Berry, Sue — *Georgian Brighton*, Chichester, Phillimore & Co Ltd, 2005.

Berry-Dee, Christopher, with Odell, Robin — *A Question of Evidence – Who killed the Babes in the Wood?*, WH Allen, 1991.

Bishop, John G — *Brighton in the Olden Time*, Brighton, JG Bishop, 'Herald' Office, 1892 (People's Edition).

Briffett, David — *Sussex Murders*, Southampton, Ensign Publications, 1990.

Briggs, J, Harrison, C, McInnes, A & Vincent, D — *Crime and Punishment in England – An Introductory History*, London, UCL Press Ltd, 1996.

Carder, Timothy — *The Encyclopaedia of Brighton*, East Sussex County Libraries, 1990.

Chibnall, Steve — *Brighton Rock*, a Turner Classic Movie British Film Guide, London, I B Taurus, 2005.

Collis, Rose — *Brighton Boozers – A History of the City's Pub Culture*, Royal Pavilion, Libraries and Museums, Brighton and Hove City Council, 2005.

d'Enno, Douglas — *Foul Deeds and Suspicious Deaths around Brighton*, Barnsley, Wharncliffe, 2004.

Dale, Antony — *Brighton Town and Brighton People*, Chichester, Phillimore & Co Ltd, 1976.

Davey, Roger — *East Sussex Quarter Sessions 1810–1854* Eastbourne, PBN Publications, 2000.

David, Saul — *Prince of Pleasure*, London, Little, Brown and Company, 1998.

Eddleston, John J — *Murderous Sussex – The executed of the Twentieth Century*, Derby, The Breedon Books Publishing Company Limited, 1997.

Erredge, John Ackerson — *History of Brighthelmston or Brighton as I View it and others knew it, with a Chronological Table of Local Events*, Brighton, Printed by E Lewis, 'Observer' Office, 52a, North Street, 1862. Reprinted: Forest Row, Brambletye Books 2005.

Friends of the East Sussex Record Office — *East Sussex Sentences of Transportation at Quarter Sessions, 1790–1854*, 1988.

Goodman, Jonathan (Ed.) — *The Seaside Murders – Thirteen classic true crime stories*, London, Sphere Books Ltd, 1987 (first published by Allison & Busby, London, 1985).

'Graduate' ('a Graduate of the University of London') — *Brighton As It Is: Its Pleasures Practices and Pastimes – with a Short Account of the Social and Inner Life of its Inhabitants, being a Complete Guide Book for Residents and Visitors*. Published in 1860.

Grant, RC — *The Brighton Garrison, 1793–1900*, A Layman's Publication, Brighton (41 Osborne Road, Preston Park Road BN1 6LR), nd.

Harrison, Frederick & North, James Sharp — *Old Brighton, Old Hove, Old Preston*, Hassocks, Flare Books, 1937, reprinted 1974.

Hill, Rocky	*Underdog Brighton: A Rather Different History of the Town*, Brighton, Iconoclast Press, 1991.
Hollingdale, Eileen	*Old Brighton*, Norwich, George Nobbs Publishing Ltd, 1979.
Horlock, Christopher	*Brighton: The Sixties*, Seaford, S.B. Publications, 2006
Horlock, Christopher	*Brighton & Hove Then and Now – Volume II,* Seaford, S.B. Publications, 2003.
Hufton, Geoffrey & Baird, Elaine	*The Scarecrow's Legion – Smuggling in Kent and Sussex*, Sittingbourne, Kent, Rochester Press Ltd, 1983.
Johnson, WH	*Brighton's First Trunk Murderer, 1831*, Eastbourne, Downsway Books, Eastbourne, 1995.
Johnson, WH	*Previous Offences – Sussex crimes and punishments in the past*, Seaford, S.B. Publications, 1997.
Johnson, WH	*Sussex Tales of Mystery and Murder,* Newbury, Countryside Books, 2002.
Johnson, WH	*Sussex Villains,* Newbury, Countryside Books, 2003.
Knowles, Leonard	*Court of Drama – Famous Trials at Lewes Assizes*, London, John Long Ltd, 1966.
Linnane, Fergus	*The Encyclopaedia of London Crime & Vice,* Stroud, Sutton Publishing Ltd, 2003.
Low, Donald A	*Thieves' Kitchen – The Regency Underworld*, London, JM Dent & Sons Ltd, 1982.
Mayhew, Henry	*London's Underworld,* Ed. Quennell, Peter, Feltham, Hamlyn Publishing Group, 1950.
Meyrick, Kate	*Secrets of the 43 Club*, Dublin, Parkgate Publications Ltd, 1994 (republication of 1933 original edition).
Middleton, Judy	*The Brighton Metropole*, self-published, 1992.
Middleton, Judy	*Encyclopaedia of Hove and Portslade*, Portslade, 2001–2003.
Montford, S, Pollard, J & Sanderson, R	*The Vanishing Villas of Preston & Withdean*, Brighton, Brighton Books Publishing, 1996.
Musgrave, Clifford	*Life in Brighton*, Rochester, Rochester Press, 1981.
Parry JD, Dr	*An Historical and Descriptive Account of the Coast of Sussex* Brighton, 1833; facsimile edition produced by E & W Books (Publishers) Ltd, 1970, & distributed by Robert Hale & Co, London.
Patcham U3A	*Brighton 1837*, 2004 (An 82-page A4 typescript).
Rackham, John	*Brighton Ghosts, Hove Hauntings*, Brighton, Latimer Publications, 2001.
Richardson, Dick	*Hanged for a Sheep*, Bakewell, Country Books, 2003.
Rowland, David	*On the Brighton Beat – Memoirs of an old-time copper*, Telscombe Cliffs, Finsbury Publishing, 2006.
Royal Pavilion, Libraries and Museums, Brighton/Hove	*Kiss and Kill* – Film Visions of Brighton [published to coincide with exhibition of the same name held at Brighton Museum and Art Gallery, 4 May–1 September 2002].
Rutherford, Jessica	*A Prince's Passion – The Life of the Royal Pavilion*, Brighton/Hove, Royal Pavilion, Libraries and Museums, (Brighton and Hove City Council), 2003.
Sellwood, Arthur and Mary	*The Victorian Railway Murders*, Newton Abbot, David & Charles, 1979.
Stern, Chester	*Dr Iain West's Casebook*, London, Little, Brown and Company, 1996.
Taylor, Rupert	*Sussex Scandals*, Newbury, Berks., Countryside Books, 1987.
Taylor, Rupert	*Murders of Old Sussex*, Newbury, Berks., Countryside Books, 1991.
Taylor, Rupert	*Sussex Murder Casebook,* Newbury, Berks., Countryside Books, 1994.

BIBLIOGRAPHY

Tullett, Tom	*Clues to Murder*, London, The Bodley Head, 1986.
Underwood, Eric	*Brighton*, London, Batsford, 1978.
Various contributors	*Who was Harry Cowley?* Brighton, QueenSpark Books [No. 13], nd [ca. 1984].
Various contributors	*Backyard Brighton – Photographs and Memories of Brighton in the thirties*, Brighton QueenSpark Books [No. 20], 1988.
Various contributors	*Infamous Crimes that shocked the World*, London, Macdonald & Co (Publishers) Ltd, 1989, reprinted 1990 under the Black Cat imprint.
Various contributors	*Daring Hearts: Lesbian and Gay lives of 50s and 60s Brighton*, Brighton Ourstory Project, 1992.
Various contributors	*Back Street Brighton – Photographs and Memories*, Brighton QueenSpark Books [No. 22] and Lewis Cohen Urban Studies Centre, Brighton Polytechnic, nd [ca. 1993].
Various contributors	*Rose Hill to Roundhill: a Brighton Community*, Brighton, Brighton Books Publishing, 2004.
Various contributors	*SchNews at Ten*, Brighton, SchNews, 2004.
Wagner, Anthony & Dale, Antony	*The Wagners of Brighton*, Chichester, Phillimore & Co, 1983.
Walker, John (ed.)	*Halliwell's Film, Video and DVD Guide 2006*, 20th Edn, London, HarperCollins Entertainment, 2005.
Waugh, Mary	*Smuggling in Kent and Sussex 1700–1840*, Newbury, Berks., Countryside Books, 1985.
Williams, Montagu	*Leaves of a Life*, being the reminiscences of Mr Montagu Williams QC, Vol. II, Macmillan, London & New York, 1890 (pp. 246–251 cover the Brighton Bigamy Case).
Wojtczak, Helen	*Women of Victorian Sussex*, Hastings, The Hastings Press, 2003.
Wright, Charles	*The Brighton Ambulator*, Print of Donaldson's Library, 1818 (Hine's Office, 52 East Street, St Jas's St, 'the Bond Street of Brighton').

Newspapers, periodicals and other documents

Annual Register, The	'The Brighton Poisoning Case', *Remarkable Trials* Series, pp. 189–201, Rivingtons, 1873.
Argus/Evening Argus	Various dates & Centenary Supplement, 31.3.1980. Murders Supplement, various dates 1998. Series of supplements celebrating 125 years of publication (various dates in 2005).
Brighton Gazette	Various dates. Formerly the *Brighton Daily Gazette and Sussex Telegraph*.
Brighton Guardian	Various dates.
Brighton Herald	Various dates.
Mapleton, Percy Lefroy	Unpublished MS., PRO HO 144/83 A6404.
Mercer, Peter R	'Brighton: Crime in a Fashionable Town c.1800–1850'. Dissertation for MA in English Local and Regional History, 26 August 2001.
Real-Life Crimes (partwork)	*The Brighton Trunk Murders*, Vol. 3, Part 39, London, Eaglemoss Publications Ltd, 1993.
Royal Pavilion Review	'More images of Brighton' by Henry Smith, issue of July 2004.
Sussex County Magazine	'The Newtimber Murder Mystery', Ackerman, Lewis T, Vol. 26 (8), August 1952, 387–388.
Sussex County Magazine	'A Downland Mystery', Beckett, Arthur, Vol. 6 (4), April 1932.
Sussex County Magazine	'The Sussex County Gaol at Horsham', Albery, William, Vol. 6 (12), December 1932, p. 810.
Sussex Daily News	Various dates.
Sussex Express	Various dates.
Sussex Weekly Advertiser	Various dates.